D0538609

THE WAR CORRESPONDENTS

THE
BOER WAR

Looking into the Orange Free State over 12th Brigade camp and Signal Hill, Slingersfontein

THE WAR CORRESPONDENTS

THE
BOER WAR

RAYMOND SIBBALD

Bramley Books

First published in 1993 by
Alan Sutton Publishing Limited, an imprint of Sutton Publishing Limited

This edition published in 1997 by Bramley Books, an imprint of Quadrillion Publishing

Copyright © Raymond Sibbald, 1993

All rights reserved. No part of this publication may be reproduced, stored in a retrieval
system, or transmitted, in any form, or by any means, electronic, mechanical,
photocopying, recording or otherwise, without the prior permission of the publishers
and copyright holders.

British Library Cataloguing in Publication Data

Sibbald, Raymond
The War Correspondents: The Boer War
I. Title
968.04

ISBN 1-85833-733-X

This book was designed and produced by
Sutton Publishing Limited · Phoenix Mill · Thrupp · Stroud · Gloucestershire

Typeset in 10/12 Times.
Typesetting and origination by
Sutton Publishing Limited.
Printed in Great Britain by
WBC Limited, Bridgend.

CONTENTS

LIST OF ILLUSTRATIONS

ACKNOWLEDGEMENTS

Photographs and illustrations are reproduced by courtesy of the following:

Regiments of Gloucestershire Museum (pages ii, 8, 10, 21, 40, 42, 51, 57, 74, 84, 86, 106, 118, 127, 128, 152, 157, 159, 164, 171, 174, 175, 176, 190, 201, 213); Imperial War Museum, London (pages 17, 32, 90, 145, 166, 207, 215).

INTRODUCTION

WAR CORRESPONDENTS AND *THE TIMES*

'. . . those newly invented curse to armies who eat the rations of the fighting man and do no work at all' (Sir Garnet Wolsey writing about war correspondents, in *The Soldier's Pocketbook*, 1869).

Whether his opinion was correct or not, Sir Garnet was incorrect in assuming the war correspondents were a 'newly invented curse'. Reports of wars are an ancient and honourable form of literature; Xenophon's *Anabasis* immediately springs to mind as a good example of this genre. In this work Xenophon describes his experiences as a mercenary general in the service of Persia, *circa* 401 BC. The *Anabasis* serves two purposes: a memoir of Xenophon's exploits and a treatise on leadership in war. It is from these ancient and distinguished roots that modern war journalism has sprung. Given humanity's insatiable curiosity about all things martial, it is not surprising that descriptions of battles and wars, especially eye-witness accounts, should prove such popular reading material.

Jean de Waurin, a French knight present at the Battle of Agincourt in 1415, provides a graphic account of the French defeat and why it happened. 'The Constable, the Marshal, the admirals and the other princes earnestly exhorted their men to fight the English well and bravely; and when it came to the approach the trumpets and clarions resounded everywhere; but the French began to hold down their heads, especially those who had no bucklers, for the impetuosity of the English arrows, which fell so heavily that no one durst uncover or look up. Thus they went forward a little, then made a little retreat, but before they could come to close quarters, many of the French were disabled and wounded by the arrows; and when they came quite up to the English, they were, as has been said, so closely pressed one against another that none of them could lift their arms to strike their enemies, except some that were in front.'[1] These eye-witness accounts serve today's historians as source material, but they also served as the basis for the songs and epic poems that formed the repertoire of the wandering minstrels, the news services of their day.

Of course, minstrels following the conventions of their time tended to emphasize the heroic and glorious aspects of war; little consideration was given to the horror and carnage. As the nature of war changed so did its depiction in memoirs and eye-witness reports, but the essential idea of war's 'nobility' remained, despite realistic portrayals of such horrors as the destructive nature of artillery. However, some reports concentrated on the true cost of war, and did not shy away from describing the frequently squalid and repulsive nature of warfare. One such report came from the pen of George Gascoigne, an English writer present at the sack of Antwerp by the Spanish in 1576. 'And surely as their valiance was to be much commended; so yet I can much discommend their barbarous cruelty in many respects. . . . when the blood is cold and the fury over, methinks that a true Christian heart should stand content with victory; and refrain to provoke God's wrath by shedding of innocent blood. . . . For Age and Sex, Young and Old; they slew great numbers of young children; but many more women more than four score years of age. . . . neither can I refrain to tell their shameful rapes and outrageous forces presented unto sundry honest dames and virgins.'[2] This represents a much clearer and honest picture of the realities of war, than the *chansons* of the minstrels, but while it depicts war as something brutal and ignoble it recognizes that war has a place in the society of the time. Writers such as John Donne and John Milton echo this sentiment in their work. Philosopher Emmanuel Kant was very much a lonely voice when he called for the abolition of war.

While war continued there was always a ready demand for tales from the battlefield. When newspapers began to appear in England in the early seventeenth century[3] it was only natural that they should seek to provide their readers with descriptions of the latest conflicts. Indeed the first boom in newspaper circulation in this country can be traced to the public's desire for news during the Civil War; by 1645 fourteen newspapers were available in London. Newspapers from the very outset sought to cover the whole gamut of human existence: gossip, crime, politics, human interest stories and, of course, war reports.

For many years the most up to date reports of battles were provided by officers actually involved in the fighting. These officers would send letters describing the events of a battle and perhaps more importantly their part in those events. The following account of the Battle of Schellenberg (1704) illustrates one of the main problems associated with this type of report. 'I made a point of impressing upon my men the necessity of attention to orders, and of prompt obedience in carrying out any manoeuvres during the action with courage and in good order. I assured them that herein lay our safety and, perhaps, victory. I had scarcely finished speaking when the enemy's battery opened fire upon us, and raked us through and through. They concentrated their fire upon us, and in their first discharge carried off Count de la Bastide, the lieutenant of my own company with whom at the moment I was speaking, and twelve grenadiers, who fell side by side in the ranks, so that my coat was covered with brains and blood. So accurate was the fire that each discharge of the cannon stretched some of my men on the ground. I suffered agonies at seeing these brave fellows perish without a chance of defending themselves, but it was absolutely necessary that they should not move from their posts.'[4] Vivid though M. de la Colonie's description is, it only tells the reader about the part of the battle that this French officer witnessed. So while the reader is presented with a glimpse of the battle endured by M. de la Colonie and his men, the wider picture of what actually occurred across the whole battlefield is lost. The inability of human beings to occupy more than one place at a time is understandable and easily forgiven. However, this type of report too often fell prey to another easily understood human frailty, the desire of people to exaggerate their own importance. Officers' letters purporting to provide a true and accurate picture of events instead concentrated on describing the courage and spectacular acts of the letter writer. Anyone familiar with Conan-Doyle's Brigadier Gerard would immediately recognize a kindred spirit in this type of report.

Although this kind of reporting presented a distorted picture of events, it did at least provide the public with a steady diet of dramatic events, and these of course sold newspapers. Far more serious from the point of view of distortion was the fact that officers, being part of an institution, were expected to follow the line laid down by that institution. This was not a great problem when armies were fairly loosely organized agglomerations, made up in large part by mercenary contingents. But as armies began to take on more formal structures, and became national institutions as opposed to purely commercial enterprises, so the pressure grew for officers to fall in with the official view of the institution.

Newspaper editors wishing to present their readers with an accurate and impartial picture of the events of war were therefore placed in a difficult position; officers being present on the battlefield obviously possessed a distinct advantage, but the problems outlined above tended to nullify this advantage. What could the newspapermen do? The solution was fairly simple: instead of relying upon the reports of soldiers, newspapers could employ men to accompany the soldiers to war and report on their actions. Thus the modern war correspondent was born. The man with the strongest claim to be the first war correspondent, or 'special', is Henry Crabb Robinson. Robinson, a barrister by profession, was sent by the owner of *The Times*, John Walter, to cover Napoleon's campaign in Germany in 1807. Robinson proved a poor reporter: his report of the Battle of Friedland was a compilation of the experiences of people who had actually seen the battle, while he himself had stayed a safe distance from the battlefield, preferring the comforts of civilized living to the rigours and dangers of war. In 1808 Robinson was once more sent to Europe, this time to Spain to cover the actions of Sir John Moore's troops. Robinson again culled his reports from sources other than his own experiences, this time using a synthesis of pieces that appeared in local newspapers. In his reports Robinson managed to report the climax of this campaign without mentioning either the death of Sir John Moore or the fact that Britain had won a famous victory.[5]

Needless to say Robinson's career as a war correspondent was short lived; after the Corunna débâcle his association with *The Times* was terminated. Other reporters tried to establish the credibility of the 'special' by providing comprehensive and timely reports of the events that they were sent to cover. Charles Lewis Guneison was such a correspondent. So accurate were Guneison's despatches during the Spanish Civil War of 1834–9 that he was arrested by the conservative forces of Don Carlos (the Carlists), pretender to the throne of Spain, and tried as a spy; only the intervention of the British government saved his life.

At the time of his arrest Guneison was working for the *Morning Post*, one of *The Times*' rivals. Once *The Times* had experimented with the idea of sending civilian writers to cover battles, other newspapers followed suit, creating a press corps almost overnight. The creation of this body of war reporters and the arrest of Guneison illustrates one of the central dilemmas of the war correspondent's existence. To perform as a conscientious reporter the war correspondent must report events at the very front line of combat, but this often brings the war reporter into conflict with the military, who believe that reports of this nature put their operations in jeopardy. This conflict of interest has remained central to the life of the war correspondent ever since; indeed, as technology has advanced and communication become instantaneous, this problem has become ever more acute. One only has to recall the acrimonious debate over the BBC's coverage of certain aspects of the 1982 Falklands War, or the rumours about American reporters impersonating servicemen during the 1991 Gulf War to realize that this is a problem that will not go away.

The technological advances of the nineteenth century, primitive as they might seem today, caused a revolution in how wars were covered in newspapers. In particular the development of the telegraph in the 1840s galvanized war reporting; no longer did reporters have to rely upon the vagaries of the postal system. A report that might have taken weeks to arrive at the home office of the reporter would in future take only hours or days depending on circumstances. The first major war that was affected by this change in communications technology was the Crimean War of 1854–6: for the first time the public could read about events almost as they happened, and in Britain the public was agog with excitement about the war. *The Times*, the biggest selling newspaper of the day, was determined to provide the reading public with what it wanted. Mowbray Morris the manager of *The Times* wrote, 'The public expects that we shall have our own agents. . . . And as it has long been accustomed to look to *The Times* . . . for the truth in all things, we disappoint a reasonable expectation when we offer nothing better than reports from other journals, however authentic.'[6]

These sentiments led to *The Times* sending William Howard Russell to the Crimea to act as their correspondent. Russell has justly been described as the greatest war reporter of his generation. Russell had been born in Ireland on 28 March 1820 or 1821. Initially he was intent upon joining the medical profession, but in 1841 a cousin of his was sent by *The Times* to cover the Irish elections of that year. Russell's cousin experienced great difficulty in trying to penetrate the labyrinthine toils of Irish politics, so he enlisted the aid of his young cousin. Russell, well used to the political shenanigans of Dublin, soon proved himself to be a useful addition to the staff of *The Times*, but it was as a war reporter that he was to win lasting fame. Russell covered the Schleswig-Holstein–Denmark-Prussia war of 1864, the Crimean War 1854–6, the Indian Mutiny 1857–8, the American Civil War 1861–5, the Austro-Prussian War of 1866, the Franco-Prussian War 1870–1, the Paris Commune and finally the Zulu War of 1879. But of all these campaigns it was the Crimean War that earned Russell his place in history.

Russell was a keen observer and produced some of the most vivid battle reports ever written. One of the most famous of these is his despatch covering the Charge of the Light Brigade on 25 October 1854: 'Lord Lucan, with reluctance, gave the order to Lord Cardigan to advance upon the guns, conceiving that his orders compelled him to do so. The noble Earl though he did not shrink, also saw the fearful odds against him. . . . The whole brigade scarcely made one effective regiment, according to the numbers of continental armies. . . . As they passed towards the front, the Russians opened on them from the guns in the redoubt on the right, with volleys of musketry and rifles. They swept proudly past, glittering in the morning sun in all the pride and splendour of war. We could scarcely believe the evidence of our senses! Surely that handful of men are not going to charge an army in position? Alas! it was too true – their desperate valour knew no bounds, and far indeed was it removed from its so-called better part- discretion. They advanced in two lines, quickening their pace as they closed towards the enemy. . . . At the distance of 1,200 yards the whole line of the enemy belched forth, from 30 iron mouths, a flood of smoke and flame, through which hissed the deadly balls. Their flight was marked by instant gaps in our ranks, by dead men and horses, by steeds flying wounded or riderless across the plain. The first line is broken, it is joined by the second, they never halt or check their speed an instant; with diminished ranks, thinned by those 30 guns, which the Russians had laid with the most deadly accuracy, with a halo of flashing steel above their heads, and with a cheer which was many a noble fellows death-cry, they flew into the smoke of the batteries. . . . We saw them riding through the guns. . . . To our delight we saw them returning. . . . When the flank fire of the battery on the hill swept them down, scattered and broken as they were. Wounded men and dismounted troopers flying towards us told us a sad tale – demi-gods could not have done what we had failed to do. . . . At 11.35 not a British soldier except the dead and dying, was left in front of those bloody Muscovite guns.'[7] Russell provided a picture that his fellow Victorians could identify with: the nobility of death for Queen and country, the self-sacrifice and gallantry of the soldiers. All this is summed up in his description of another event that took place during the same battle as the Charge of the Light Brigade, the Battle of Balaclava. During the early stages of the Battle of Balaclava a great mass of Russian cavalry swept toward the British naval base in Balaclava harbour. All that stood between the Russians and the British supplies was the 93rd regiment of foot, commanded by a redoubtable veteran of the Peninsula War, Sir Colin Campbell. Russell described what happened when the 'irresistible force', the Russian cavalry, met the 'immovable object', the Scottish infantry, drawn up in two lines to meet the onslaught. 'The silence is oppressive; between the cannon bursts one can hear the champing of bits and the clink of sabres in the valley below. The Russians on their left drew breath for a moment, and then in one grand line dashed at the Highlanders. The ground flies beneath their horses' feet; gathering speed at every stride, they dash on toward that thin red streak topped with a line of steel. . . . With breathless suspense everyone awaits the bursting of the wave upon the line of Gaelic rock: but ere they come within 150 yards another deadly volley flashes from the levelled rifles and carries death and terror into the Russians. They wheel about, open files right and left and fly back faster than they came. "Bravo Highlanders! Well done!" shout the excited spectators.'[8]

These reports outline Russell's mastery of the traditional subject matter of the war writer: heroic deeds and the glory of warfare. But it was in a much more radical vein of war reporting that he had his greatest impact. From the very outset of the Crimean campaign, Russell realized that the British Army had many serious problems. It had not fought a major war against a European opponent since the end of the Napoleonic Wars in 1815, and very little had changed in its administration since that date. Although the soldiers and some of the commanders were of the highest calibre, the organizational structure of the Army was in poor shape; in particular the logistical apparatus was dreadfully out of date and inefficient. The ramshackle state of affairs is best illustrated by referring to one of Russell's earliest reports of the war. 'With the augmentation of the Allied forces, the privations to which the men were at first exposed became greater, the inefficiency of our arrangements more evident. . . . Amid the multitude of complaints which met the ear from every side, the most prominent were charges against the commissariat. . . . Early and late these officers might be seen toiling amid a set of apathetic Turks and stupid araba drivers, trying in vain to make bargains and give orders in the language of signs.'[9] In another report Russell is even more scathing in his description of the conditions faced by the British troops. 'The men suffered exceedingly from the cold, some of them, officers and privates, had no beds to lie upon. None of the soldiers had more than their single regulation blanket. They therefore reversed the order of things and dressed up to go to bed, putting on all their spare clothing before they tried to go to sleep. The worst thing was the continued want of the comforts for the sick. Many of the men were labouring under diseases contracted in Malta were obliged to stay in camp in the cold, with only one blanket under them, as there was no provision for them at the temporary hospital.'[10] Clearly all was not well with the supply system adopted by the British Army, and the effect that this inefficiency had upon the well-being of the troops was devastating. 'This army has melted away almost to a drop of miserable, washed-out, worn-out spiritless wretches, who muster out of 55,000 just 11,000 now fit to shoulder a musket, but certainly not fit to do duty against the enemy. Let no one at home attempt to throw dust in your eyes. This army is to all intents and purposes, with the exception of a very few regiments used up, destroyed and ruined.'[11] This drastic opinion of the state of the British Army was contained in a letter written by Russell to the editor of *The Times* in January 1855. Russell was not alone in condemning the poor state of the Army's organization: in particular the provision of care for the sick and wounded came in for heavy criticism from a number of correspondents. Thomas Chenery, the Constantinople correspondent of *The Times*, was a fierce critic of the Army's medical provisions, 'it is with feelings of surprise and anger that the public will learn that no sufficient medical preparations have been made for the proper care of the wounded. Not only are there not sufficient surgeons . . . that it might be urged, was unavoidable . . . not only are there no dressers and nurses . . . that might be a defect of system for which no one is to blame . . . but what will be said when it is known that there is not even linen to make bandages for the wounded? The greatest commiseration prevails for the suffering of the unhappy inmates of Scutari, and every family is giving sheets and garments to supply their want. But, why could not this clearly foreseen event have been supplied? . . . It rests with the Government to make enquiries into the conduct of those who must have so greatly neglected their duty.'[12] But the Government was slow to respond to the criticisms voiced by *The Times*, and faced by the intransigence of the authorities and the worsening situation in the Crimea, Russell and other correspondents saw it as their clear duty to attempt to present a clear picture of what was happening to their army to the British public.

This despatch from Russell paints a vivid picture of the suffering endured by the soldiers and the sick and injured. 'Hundreds of men had to go into the trenches at night with no covering but their greatcoats, and no protection for their feet but their regimental shoes. The trenches were two and three feet deep with mud, snow and half-frozen slush. . . . As to the town itself (Balaclava), words could not describe its filth, its horrors, its burials, its dead and dying Turks, its crowded lanes, its noisome sheds, its beastly purlieus, or its decay. The dead, laid out as they died, were lying side by side with the living, and the latter presented a spectacle beyond all imagination. The commonest accessories of a hospital were wanting; there was not the least attention paid to decency or cleanliness – the stench was appalling – the foetid air could barely struggle out to taint the atmosphere, save through the chinks in the walls and roofs, and for all I could observe, these men died without the least effort to save them. They were laid just as they were let gently down upon the ground by the poor fellows their comrades, who brought them on their backs from the camp with the greatest tenderness, but who were not allowed to remain with them. The sick appeared to be tended by the sick, and the dying by the dying.'[13] Finally frustrated by the Government's inaction, *The Times* launched an appeal for funds and volunteers to provide a medical service for the troops in the Crimea. The creation of *The Times*' fund was instrumental in the arrival of Florence Nightingale in the Crimea, and for the duration of her stay in the theatre of operations it continued to supply money for medical necessities. All of this took place in the face of determined opposition from the Government and the military establishment.

Russell was continually accused of misleading the public and distorting the truth. In general the Army's commanders regarded him as a gossiping busybody. Sir George Brown, commander of the Light Division wrote, 'During the few days I remained at Scutari, instead of having leisure to look about me or time to attend to necessary business, I was most unprofitably occupied in entering into explanations as regards to charges of neglect preferred in Mr Russell's gossiping letters from Gallipoli, which the Duke of Newcastle had considered of sufficient importance to cause to be cut from *The Times* newspaper, and referred to Lord Raglan.'[14] But both at home and in the Army itself Russell's despatches were believed, and his description of the conditions endured by the troops and the overall conduct of the war began to place the Government under greater and greater pressure. The Government retaliated by accusing *The Times* and Russell in particular of compromising the security of Allied operations in the Crimea. On this point the Government did have some grounds for criticism. It became known after the war that the Russian commander of Sebastopol, Prince Gortschakoff, was an avid reader of *The Times*; he had had copies of the newspaper forwarded to him from Warsaw throughout the siege of Sebastopol. Although Gortschakoff stated that he had learnt nothing of value militarily from his reading of *The Times*, it is very doubtful that this was the whole truth given the comprehensive nature of some of the correspondents' reports.

However, *The Times* was able to defuse this potentially disastrous situation by revealing that Russell and the other correspondents had offered to allow their reports to be read and censored by the authorities before publication. This of course turned the tables on the Government, reinforcing in the public's mind the picture of a government mired in incompetence. The result of all this was a vote of no confidence in the Government on 29 January 1855. The Government lost the vote by a majority of 157 and had to resign. *The Times* and its correspondent Russell had scored a massive victory against an incompetent and complacent administration. By reporting the news from the front, Russell had brought home to the British people for the first time the true horror of war and the hideous suffering endured by those who fought wars in the name of Britain. In doing this Russell had widened the parameters of war reporting, so that by the end of the Crimean War in 1856, war in all its aspects, not just the tales of heroism previously thought of as fit matter for publication, was within the purlieu of the war correspondent. This war also ushered in a new era of power for newspapers and *The Times* in particular: from this time onward *The Times* was to hold a place of particular influence and esteem in the minds of the British people. *The Times* had

Interviewing a Boer farmer at his home near Brandfort during Lord Roberts' great march

established a reputation for itself as a fearless reporter of the truth that could not be held back even by Government from its task of informing the public.

The success of *The Times* was at this time and for many years to come associated with the concept of war reporting. Whenever and wherever wars occurred, the British public turned to *The Times* as a trusted voice to explain the rights and wrongs of the situation to them. This remained essentially true throughout the nineteenth century, despite the rise of other newspapers such as *The Daily Telegraph* (founded 1855) and the *Daily News*, which was founded in 1846 with Charles Dickens as its first editor. Even the enmity of a good proportion of the British establishment, aroused by *The Times*' reporting of the failures of the Army and the Government during the Crimean War, failed to dent the paper's reputation. This reputation was confirmed and enhanced by such journalistic scoops as obtaining and publishing a copy of the treaty to be signed at the Congress of Berlin in 1878, before the actual treaty was signed by the participating countries. This feat helped to establish a European reputation for *The Times* where previously the paper's fame had largely been confined to its native country. After the Congress of Berlin, *The Times* was able to take a place at the forefront of European journalism.

Although *The Times* was able to maintain its pre-eminent position in British journalism with relative ease, it is interesting to note that its commercial success was not so easily continued. Competition from the newly established 'quality' papers, then the advent of cheaper down-market rivals, ate into the circulation level of *The Times*, and this of course had an effect on both advertising revenue and profitability. This problem grew until *The Times* became a newspaper whose circulation was largely confined to London and the Home Counties.

However, this had little effect on the prestige of the paper, as this extract from a letter written by Frank Power (*The Times*' correspondent in Egypt and the Sudan) in 1884 confirms, 'You would be surprised how much influence being British Consul and *Times* correspondent gives me here. The people here have a very high opinion of the power of *The Times*. They say "that it was not Europe but *The Times* deposed Ismail Pacha" (and in this they are au fond right), and say "if this paper can change one Khedive, why not another".'[15] Power was to go on to enhance the prestige of the paper he represented by providing *The Times* with the only correspondent's reports of the siege of Khartoum, a siege that was to cost both General Gordon and Frank Power their lives.

The death of General Gordon at Khartoum was one of the seminal events of Victorian Britain. Gordon was a hero cast in the true Victorian mould: a devout Christian, he had made his reputation as the leader of the 'Ever Victorious Army' a mercenary force fighting for the Chinese Government during the Taiping Rebellion (1850–64). Yet again it was *The Times* that captured the news for the public.

By the time of the Second Boer War, *The Times* was firmly established at the heart of both the British newspaper industry and, belying its earlier troubles, the British establishment.

BACKGROUND TO THE WAR

'Englishmen will find it difficult to reconcile themselves to the forcible occupation of a country whose people declare that they never have been and do not wish to be Her Majesty's subjects' (*The Times*, June 1880).

When the Second Boer War began in October 1899 Britain was at the height of its imperial power. Not only was the British Empire the greatest imperial entity that the world had ever seen, but Britain also represented the very cutting edge of progress in almost every field of human activity. Britain had led the world into the industrial revolution and was now reaping the benefits of this vast leap forward in human achievement. Britain's railway system was the envy of the world: it was possible for example to reach the incredible speed of seventy-four mph on some of the express services. Not content with building railways that covered the face of the land, the Victorians delved deep into the earth beneath London to open the world's first underground railway system in 1889. Britain's great battle fleets communicated using wireless, and the use of the telegraph had made possible relatively rapid communication with even the most far-flung outpost of the empire. In other fields also Britain led the way. The publication of Charles Darwin's *The Origin of Species* in 1859 promised that the deepest mysteries of Man's very existence would eventually be unravelled. The industries of Britain provided the engine that powered the greatest trade machine that had ever existed and Britain's wealth seemed to grow with every year that passed.

Imperial Britain seemed destined to remain the greatest power in the world for the foreseeable future. True, the USA and Germany were growing in power and importance, but the British were confident that their grip on the levers of progress

Correspondents' carts
awaiting Lord
Roberts' entry to
Kroonstad

would enable them to remain ahead of their rivals. Authors such as Kipling and
politicians such as Joseph Chamberlain and Cecil Rhodes expressed the view that it
was Britain's destiny to bring civilization and the benefits of progress to the four
corners of the world. Victorian Britain as a whole heartily concurred with this opinion.
Some people did disagree, mainly with the idea that the British Empire should continue
to expand, but these people expressed a minority opinion. The majority of Britain's
population were fervent supporters of empire and imperial expansion.

As the nineteenth century drew to a close the main theatre for Britain's imperial
expansion was Africa. During these years Britain was engaged in a race for territory
with European rivals such as France and Germany. This race was not a straightforward
drive for territorial acquisition; it was a complex blend of exploration, search for trade
opportunities as well as the aforementioned desire for more land. What has since been
termed 'the race for Africa' was the product of a number of often contradictory factors:
for example, the desire to bring Christianity to African natives (that drove men such as
David Livingstone to risk their lives in the heart of the 'Dark Continent') clashed
constantly with the desire for material gain and power that drove men such as Cecil
Rhodes.[16]

The expansion of Britain's empire in the nineteenth century was not only a source of
pride to the average Briton, it also accustomed him (or her) to the idea that war was a
necessary evil, and in some cases it was regarded not as an act of evil, but as the
supreme act of virtue. This was almost always the case when Britain was fighting to
subdue a native people in order to bring the benefits of civilization to those poor
misguided 'savages'. War came to be regarded by the average Victorian, to paraphrase

Clausewitz, as merely an extension of policy. The supreme example of this can be seen in the phrase coined to describe Britain's preferred *modus operandi* when dealing with recalcitrant states or peoples. 'Gunboat diplomacy', by providing a link between warfare and policy, made the transition from 'jaw jaw' to war war' an obvious and painless choice for most nineteenth-century British governments.

The Boer War of 1899–1902 was the result of a long-term process that went back as far as the arrival of British troops in 1795. Britain took over Cape Colony from the Dutch as part of her war against republican France. In 1802 Cape Colony was transferred to the newly created Batavian Republic as part of the terms of the Peace of Amiens that briefly halted hostilities between France and Britain. But in 1806 the British returned. At first the Dutch settlers largely ignored their erstwhile British governors, adopting the simple expedient of moving as far away from the British administrative centres as possible. These hardy people, known to themselves as Boers (farmers), were fiercely independent, acknowledging no authority other than the elders of their rigidly Calvinist church. But British authority had a habit of following the mobile Boers and initial Boer hostility to British government was intensified by the introduction of laws such as the adoption of English as the official language in 1828, and the 1833 emancipation of slaves within the British Empire.

The latter law struck at two fundamental pillars of Boer life: freeing the slaves undermined the economic viability of large numbers of Boer farms, free labour being essential to the profitability of most Boer enterprises. But perhaps more importantly, the emancipation of the slaves struck at the root of Boer religious thought. The Boers regarded themselves as the 'chosen people of God' (this is a sentiment still expressed by some of the extreme right-wing *Afrikaners* in South Africa today), and as such it was their God-given right to use the 'inferior' indigenous population of Africa in any way that they saw fit.

The emancipation of the slaves, coupled with the activities of British Protestant missionaries who preached that all men, black and white, were equal in the eyes of God, infuriated the Boers. The result was the event that came to be known in Boer legend as 'The Great Trek'. Boers had embarked upon treks before (the trek was a mass emigration of whole communities, with all their worldly goods packed aboard covered wagons, reminiscent of the American West). The 'Great Trek' that started in 1834 was, however, different in a number of ways from the treks that had occurred in the past. Within a couple of years, over half of the non-British white population of Cape Colony had left their homes on the coast and were moving into the interior of South Africa. Also unlike the treks of the past the 'Great Trek' was well organized and it had recognized leaders. The hardships faced by the Boers turned what had originally been a loose grouping of dissenters into a 'nation' on the move. This reinforced the Boers' biblical view of themselves as the 'chosen people'; they saw the 'Great Trek' as their search for a 'promised land'. The Boers failed to see that most of the hardships endured by them as they travelled to the 'promised land' were caused by their destructive intrusion into the territory of other people.

Perhaps the best example of this tendency on the part of the Boers to see themselves in the role of a people suffering biblical persecution is the Battle of Blood River. After moving into Zululand the Boers began to demand that the Zulu king Dingane should cede territory to them so that they could establish farms. The Zulus, a warrior people, reacted violently to the prospect of allowing the land-hungry Boers to settle in their midst. Piet Retief, head of the Boer negotiating party, was murdered by Dingane, but the Zulus were subsequently defeated on 16 December 1838 at Blood River. A neutral observer of these events might conclude that the Zulus were guilty of bad faith in murdering envoys, but that the Boers were the real villains of the peace, having moved on to other people's land. In Boer mythology, however, the Battle of Blood River is held up as a shining example of how the Boers coped with adversity.

As a direct result of the 'Great Trek' three Boer republics were established. The first of these, Natal, was rather short lived. After defeating Dingane, Retief's trek established the Republic of Natal in 1842. With its capital the port of Durban, Natal was regarded by the British as far too valuable in strategic terms (as a maritime empire Britain always regarded deep-water ports as valuable assets to be controlled at all times) to remain under the control of the recalcitrant Boers. After barely three years of independent existence Natal was annexed by Britain and became a province of Cape Colony in 1845.

Large numbers of Boers unhappy at the prospect of restrictive British rule moved out of Natal and travelled to join other groups of trekkers who were settling in the land between the Orange and Vaal Rivers. In 1848 the British Governor of Cape Colony, Sir Harry Smith, moved to forestall the establishment of another Boer republic by annexing to Cape Colony all the country within the boundaries formed by the Orange and Vaal Rivers and the Drakensberg Mountains. Once this was done, however, the British began to realize that governing and defending such a vast area of land was going to be a very expensive business indeed. Accordingly a convention was held at Sand River in 1852, where it was agreed that the Boers living north of the Vaal River would be free to govern themselves. Thus the Boer republic of Transvaal (South African Republic) came into being. Typically it took the quarrelsome Boers six years to elect the first President of their new state; Marthinus Pretorius Wessels taking office in 1858.

Two years after the Sand River Convention another convention held in Bloemfontein created a third Boer republic. This time Britain granted self-government to the people of the Orange River Territory, and the Orange Free State came into existence.

However, once the common enemy (Britain) had been removed and the common aim (independence) achieved, the Boers' quarrelsome nature reasserted itself. By 1857 disruptive elements within the two Boer republics had brought about the formation of three breakaway republics Lydenburg, Utrecht and Zoutpansberg. Apart from bickering among themselves, the Boers also continued their policy of aggressive expansion at the expense of their native neighbours. The constant fighting that this expansionist policy entailed, coupled with the Boers' seeming inability to govern themselves, led the British to consider taking over the Transvaal as the instability of the Boer republic was affecting conditions in Britain's South African possessions.

Relations between the Boers and the British were not helped by the discovery of diamonds in 1867 on land that was clearly an integral part of the Orange Free State. Using the somewhat flimsy pretext that it was protecting the rights of the native owner of the land, Britain declared the land surrounding the diamond mines British territory in 1871. In 1877 Britain followed this up by annexing the Transvaal. Although it was clear to many of the inhabitants of the Transvaal that their country was in a parlous state, both financially and militarily (in 1876 the Transvaalers had been defeated by a native chief called Pedi), the annexation was seen as a grievous insult to Boer nationalism.

It was almost inevitable that the Boers would respond to the annexation of the Transvaal by rebelling against British rule. On 16 December 1880 the Boers raised the flag of the Transvaal over the town of Heidelberg in a symbolic act of rebellion. In the fighting that followed, British troops were defeated at the decisive battle of Majuba Hill. However, it must be stated that the Transvaal regained its independence more as a result of a change in British government (Gladstone's Liberals replaced Disraeli's Conservatives in April 1880, the Liberals favouring a policy of non-involvement in the affairs of the Boer republics) rather than as the result of their military prowess. The First Boer War dragged on in a desultory manner after the battle of Majuba Hill, with little fighting actually taking place, until the Pretoria Convention of August 1881 brought hostilities to an end. As a result of the Pretoria Convention the Transvaal was granted self-governing status in all internal matters and the boundaries of the state were laid down and formally recognized by Britain. However, the Transvaal remained a colony of Britain and was thus not really an independent state. This fact rankled with the Boers and was to remain a constant obstacle to good Anglo-Boer relations. On the other side, British pride had been stung by the defeat of Majuba Hill and the desire for revenge was to provide a strong sub-theme to the worsening Anglo-Boer relations that eventually led to war in the last year of the century.

The complex situation in Southern Africa was made worse when in 1883 the newly united Germany (1871) began to establish trading posts in what is present day Namibia. It is not necessary to give a detailed picture of Anglo-German rivalry in this period; it is sufficient to state that Britain was suspicious of German ambitions in the fields of trade, military strength and colonial expansion. The German move into Southern Africa touched upon all of these areas of British unease. In 1884 Germany formally annexed all of the territory between the Orange River and the Portuguese colony of Angola (except Walvis Bay). In the same year Namibia was taken under German protection. As a reaction to this German encroachment, Britain annexed the southern part of Bechuanaland to the Cape Colony and in the same year, 1885, the remaining part of Bechuanaland was made a protectorate of the British Crown.

The tripartite territorial rivalry between Britain, Germany and the Boers was made worse by what might be termed 'Nature's double-edged blessing'. We have already seen how the discovery of diamonds at Kimberley in 1869 led to an increase in Anglo-Boer hostility that culminated in the First Boer War. In 1884 massive gold deposits were found beneath the Witwatersrand in the Transvaal. Almost inevitably this led to a vast influx of miners, somewhat reminiscent of the 'gold-rushes' in the USA. The miners soon threatened to outnumber the local Boer population and this led to serious political complications. Before 1882 a new resident in the Transvaal had only to wait one year to gain the vote. In 1882 this waiting period was increased to five years and in 1890, in direct response to Boer fears of being swamped by the so-called *Uitlanders* (outlanders), the waiting period was further increased to fourteen years by President Kruger's Transvaal government. That the majoirty of the *Uitlanders* were British nationals merely served to exacerbate Boer unease.

In the Transvaal these franchise protection measures predictably led to intense unrest in the foreign mining community. This unrest was further increased by the interference of men such as Cecil Rhodes (of whom we will hear more later), Chairman of the De Beers mining group and Prime Minister of the Cape Colony. Rhodes was active in organizing dissent among the *Uitlander* community in the Transvaal. Rhodes' aim was to secure the incorporation of the Boer republics and Britain's possessions in South Africa, to form one South African state under British rule. His motives for wishing to achieve this goal were twofold: first, he was an inordinately greedy man and he saw the formation of a united South Africa as the way to make more money and gain more power for both himself and his company; second, he undoubtedly believed in the expansion of Britain's Empire for what might be called 'ideological' reasons. Put simply, Rhodes firmly believed that it was Britain's destiny to rule large parts of the world, and that this was as much to the benefit of the people that were placed under British rule as it was to Britain herself.

Rhodes was not alone in these beliefs: many people in Britain including the Colonial Secretary Joseph Chamberlain were firm advocates of British imperial expansion. Chamberlain and Rhodes seized on the *Uitlander* franchise controversy as a means to bring the Transvaal firmly under British rule. If *Uitlanders* were granted the vote it was probable that the first act of a *Uitlander* dominated Transvaal parliament would be to vote for total incorporation within the British Empire. In London *The Times* was an outspoken advocate for *Uitlander* enfranchisement.

T he extraordinary state of things in the Transvaal, as described in the article on the Colonies which we publish to-day, deserves the attention of all who take an interest in South African affairs. Those who are unacquainted with the details of South African politics, but who regard that region as one of the most go-ahead parts of the world, will be surprised to learn that in the midst of it there is an islet of blind, uncompromising conservatism of the medieval type, with which even the most retrograde of our old Tories would feel ashamed to sympathize. The autocrat of this islet is PRESIDENT KRUGER, who is, doubtless, a very worthy man according to his lights, but who was unfortunately born at least a hundred years too late. Regardless of all warnings and protests, he imagines that the Transvaal of to-day, containing an energetic industrial community which outnumbers by more than three to one the original population of the State, can be ruled in the same way as the old-fashioned, sleepy, pastoral Transvaal was governed half a century ago; and that the ever-increasing crowd of new settlers can be compelled for an indefinite period to pay nine-tenths of the revenue without receiving in return even the elementary municipal rights to which they are fairly entitled. Their modest demands for an efficient police, for competent mining inspectors, and for primary schools to which they might send their children are peremptorily rejected, and they are not even allowed to supply these deficiencies by private initiative and voluntary association. Fortunately for the peace of the country these settlers are on the whole an orderly, industrious set of people, who evidently wish to avoid violent methods of action; but it seems to us that PRESIDENT KRUGER is putting their patience to a severe test, and that he would do well not to turn a deaf ear any longer to their grievances. They have transformed the Transvaal from a practically bankrupt State into a thriving, wealthy community, and this fact ought to be frankly recognized by the Boer Government. The time is past, even in South Africa, when a Helot system of administration, organized for the exclusive advantage of a privileged minority, can long resist the force of enlightened public opinion. If PRESIDENT KRUGER really possesses any of those statesmanlike qualities which are sometimes ascribed to him, he will hasten to accept the loyal co-operation of those *uitlanders* who have already done so much, and who are anxious to do more, for the prosperity and progress of the South African Republic.

But, to be fair to *The Times*, it would appear that the Boer treatment of the natives under their rule was also of great concern to the 'Thunderer'.

THE ALLEGED ATROCITIES IN THE TRANSVAAL

Some few weeks ago we published a letter from Mr. H. Hess giving the contents of a cable received by him from his Johannesburg office to the effect that the necessary proofs for establishing a *prima facie* case against the Transvaal Government on this question were being forwarded to him for the perusal of Mr. Chamberlain. Mr. Hess has now received the documents, and has given notice to the Secretary of State for the Colonies that they are at his disposal.

In the *African Critic* of to-day Mr. Hess says:–

I print a detailed summary of the case against the Boers in regard to their treatment of natives within the Transvaal. It has been supplied by the editor-in-charge of my Johannesburg paper, Mr. Gustave Hallé, son of the late Sir Charles Hallé. For the information of my readers in Europe it is necessary to state that Mr. Gustave Hallé is a gentleman in whose honour and probity I have entire confidence, of which the fact that I delegated to him the responsible editorship of the *Johannesburg Critic* during my absence in England is the best proof. Mr. Hallé's record in South Africa has been one of which any man might be proud, and his career has been, and promises to be in the future, a brilliant one. In short, Mr. Gustave Hallé is a worthy son of a worthy father. The evidence in support of the allegations contained in Mr. Hallé's report is now in my possession, and will be laid before the Right Hon. Joseph Chamberlain, in his official capacity as the Secretary of State for the Colonies, without delay.

In the course of his report Mr. Hallé says:–

I maintain that the facts hereinafter laid down prove that the habitual attitude of the Transvaal Boers towards the three-quarters of a million of natives handed over to them by her Majesty's Government in 1884 is that of a master-race to a set of beings entirely dependent (without appeal) on their decision as to what is justifiable in their treatment of them, and that, owing to the fact that the Boers of the Transvaal have been for 200 years at constant warfare with the natives of South Africa, and have during that period opposed, and still do steadily oppose, the advance of European civilization, their idea of what is justifiable towards the natives of this country is at one with that entertained by Europeans in the old slave-trading days, but is not compatible with the idea of civilization of the present day, and is not to be endured.

I maintain that the following proofs as to their habitual conduct towards the natives of the Transvaal in peace and at war prove this contention, and prove also that it is the solemn duty of the British Government to intervene on behalf of those three-quarters of a million of natives whom they – under assurance that their rights would be secured – handed over to the Transvaal Government. The Boer of the Transvaal does not understand that the native has rights in the sense intended in the convention, and it is for the British Government now to define those rights and to make the necessary provision that they be observed.

I maintain, and will adduce proof:–

I. That the late native wars have been caused by deliberate oppression of the natives, designed either to enrich individual officials, obtain the land on which they were dwelling, or to provide labour for the Boer farmers of the country.

II. (a) That the manner of conducting the said wars was stained by brutal and inhuman cruelty and treachery, both to their native foes and allies and to those newcomers of other European origin who were assisting the Boer commandos. That abuse of the flag of truce and the shooting down of native women were habitual, and were marked by the vilest outrages.

(b) That after the wars were concluded not only the conquered tribes, but even those that had served as allies and others that were neutral, were seized and divided up among the Boer farmers of the Transvaal into practical slavery, and that the method of conveying bodies of thousands of these people, whether foes or friends, distances before distribution was such as to cause death by starvation and distress to large numbers. The lands and cattle of foes and friendlies were alike seized, sold, or stolen.

III. That this habitual contempt for the claim of the native to have a right to security of life and property is proved to obtain also in peace by a whole host of instances of cruelty, oppression, and depredation by Transvaal officials on individual natives and on tribes, of which I quote particulars.

Mr. Hallé then adduces his proofs and authorities for his contentions. Amongst his numerous other points he states that "the habit of shooting under flags of truce and firing on and killing native women had grown so general during the Maláboch campaign that Commandant-General Joubert was compelled to issue a general order sternly prohibiting either practice, and decreeing penalties"; and that "the capture of Magoeba was attended by the most ferocious incidents of decapitation and mutilation of male and female natives taken prisoner by the native allies of the Boers, and that these atrocious incidents were permitted by the Boer commandos."

As to corroboration of statements in the *Johannesburg Critic*, Mr Hallé says:–

Not only will Mr. Henry Hess be able to supply the Secretary of State for the Colonies with ample authority for the statements appearing in the *Critic*, prior to his departure for England, on this subject, but I have been able to forward him the names and addresses of no fewer than 18 gentlemen, resident and well known in this country, on whose authority statements published by me since Mr. Hess's departure have been made. These gentlemen are all prepared to appear before a British or a mixed British and Transvaal commission of Inquiry and repeat their statements upon oath. They decline to do so before a Transvaal commission, as they are convinced of the uselessness of so doing.

President Kruger in Pretoria

In conclusion Mr. Hess expresses a fervent hope that Mr. Chamberlain will devote his attention to the matter.

However, even if one takes into account *The Times*' laudable concern for the victims of Boer intolerance (although it must be said that in the case of the *Uitlanders* one can at least understand the Boer reluctance to surrender their independence), the extent to which *The Times* became involved in the actual political manoeuvring that surrounded the *Uitlander* question is surprising to say the least, given the newspaper's reputation for impartiality. The best example of this political meddling came in the buildup to the Jameson Raid (December 1895).

In 1893 Kruger was elected to a second term of office as President of the Transvaal. This put paid to any hopes that the *Uitlanders* might have had that reform was in the offing. Faced with the prospect of legal reform being blocked indefinitely by the intransigence of Kruger, the *Uitlanders* began to plot rebellion. Rhodes was the central figure in this plot: he worked ceaselessly to encourage unrest among the *Uitlanders*. At the same time he sought to enrol the support of the British Government for a popular uprising in the Transvaal. Rhodes' plan called for a force of mounted irregulars led by his friend and confidant, Dr Leander Starr Jameson to invade the Transvaal. This invasion was to take place in response to an appeal for help that was to come from the *Uitlanders*.

When this appeal was not forthcoming, *The Times*' correspondent, Captain Francis Younghusband, finally convinced Rhodes that there would be no uprising in Johannesburg. Rhodes was so dismayed by this news that he was driven to ask Younghusband to act as a leader for the proposed uprising. Younghusband declined this decidedly dangerous offer.[17] Rhodes then tried to cancel Jameson's invasion, but he was too late. The evening before the raid started, Jameson dealt out copious bottles of champagne to his followers as a sort of sending-off present. Fairly predictably this had a seriously detrimental effect on the military capabilities of the raiding party. The following day a desperately hung-over group of raiders was instructed to cut the telegraph lines to the Transvaal. They managed instead to mistake a farmer's wire fence for the telegraph line, and thus ensured that the Boers would be waiting for them. Jameson and his men were captured by the first Boer commando that they ran into: the Boers inflicted forty casualties (16 killed) on Jameson's group for the cost of 11 casualties to themselves.

In the ensuing fall-out from the raid and the subsequent enquiry to determine who was responsible for planning Jameson's abortive invasion, it quickly became apparent that *The Times* had played a much more significant role than that of impartial observer. The enquiry held into the Jameson raid largely exonerated Chamberlain of actively encouraging and actual participation in the organizing of the raid, but it was established that one of *The Times*' senior correspondents, Flora Shaw, was deeply implicated along with the newspaper itself in Rhodes' plot. 'Flora and Bell [Moberley Bell, editor of *The Times*] were acting of course in the interests of the paper; they wanted to be sure of getting the news. But they were also ideologically committed to the expansion of the British Empire. From time to time they crossed the line between the strict duties of a journalist and the temptation to take a direct hand in events.'[18] *The Times* had clearly taken sides against the Boers, and this was to remain true throughout the Second Boer War.

The result of the Jameson fiasco was twofold: first, Rhodes was largely discredited; he had to resign his position as Premier of Cape Colony and relinquish his control over the Chartered Company. Second, Kruger's position in the Transvaal was immeasurably strengthened and his status as a leader was given international recognition. However, the seeds of Kruger's eventual downfall were sown at the same time as his success. Kruger's strength at home led him to discount the possibility of any reform of the Transvaal political system, which led to continued unrest in the foreign community in the Transvaal. The foreign acclaim for Kruger was led by Germany. The Kaiser unwisely sent the Transvaal President a telegram congratulating him on the success of his army, while at the same time the Germans offered to protect the Boers in the event of any other attack. To prove the worth of their offer, the Germans tried to land troops at Louden Marques, but the Portuguese authorities refused them transit rights.

Both of these factors led to a hardening of British public opinion against the Boers and President Kruger in particular. In 1898 Kruger was re-elected for his fourth term of office. In the same year Sir Alfred Milner took over as British representative at the Cape. Milner was a strong believer in Britain's imperial mission in South Africa and a fierce opponent of what he termed 'Krugerism'. Milner's opportunity to test the resolve of Kruger and his government came with the shooting of a British subject, a miner called Tom Eggars, by a Boer policeman. Although Eggars had been unarmed except for a stick at the time of the shooting, a Boer jury found the policeman innocent of manslaughter. This decision created uproar in the foreign community in Johannesburg, and led to a petition signed by over 21,000 British subjects resident in the Transvaal.[19]

The petition was addressed to Queen Victoria, and it asked in clear and sober words whether it was reasonable that a group that made up the majority of a country's population, and provided five-sixths of its tax revenues, should be deprived of political rights.[20]

Milner and Kruger met at Bloemfontein in May 1899 to try to resolve the knotty problem of *Uitlander* representation in the Transvaal. Milner was from the very outset of the conference determined to push Kruger into a corner. When the conference broke up Milner blamed Kruger, saying that the Transvaal President had never intended to negotiate. Worried by the ominous turn of events, Boer moderates in the Transvaal pressured Kruger into making concessions: foreigners resident in the Transvaal were offered the franchise after nine years residence in the state. But Milner was determined to push Kruger to the limit, and he declared that he could not negotiate until all the *Uitlander* demands had been met in full. In response to the heightened tension both sides began to mobilize their armed forces. Britain in particular was alarmed at the weakness of its troop levels in South Africa. The subsequent move made by Britain to reinforce its garrison in the country led to an ultimatum being delivered by the Boers calling on the British to immediately cease all troop movements into the region. When Britain refused to comply with the terms of the ultimatum all hope of a peaceful solution disappeared and the grievances of both countries were submitted to the 'court of Mars'.

THE TWO ARMIES

In 1899 the British Army was generally thought to be at the peak of military preparedness. Since the Crimean War it had emerged the victor from numerous 'native' wars all over the empire. But these very victories concealed a serious weakness in the British military. Having fought in minor wars for over forty years, the Army was only prepared to fight minor wars, and it was thinly spread around the world in small penny-packet garrisons. Ironically, South Africa was regarded as an area unlikely to cause the Empire trouble, so that the garrison in the country was tiny even by British standards: only some 14,500 men. But the British Government thought that they would be able to reinforce the colony within a few weeks of the outbreak of war and thus frustrate any Boer invasion.

The British Army was, for once, well equipped. The Lee-Enfield MK II and the Lee-Metford rifles, although not as good as the Boer Mausers, were still very good infantry weapons. The artillery was in very good condition, having been tested in arduous conditions all over the globe. Field guns and howitzers were therefore mobile and accurate. Most units had the Maxim gun, an early, but effective, machine-gun. The larger British guns fired Lyddite shells: an explosive said to be capable of killing everything within fifty yards of its detonation point, and over a much wider area by the poison fumes given off by the explosion. (The Boers proved during the course of the war that well-dug trenches provided a more than adequate defence against Lyddite shells.)

The biggest problem for the British Army lay with its infantrymen. Conditions in the infantry were very poor: the regular army was badly paid, food was generally awful and clothing little better, promotion was very hard to come by, and it was very rare for a man to rise from the ranks and become an officer. As a result of this the men that the Army recruited tended to be uneducated, unhealthy and, by and large, lacking in ambition. Once in the Army these men were largely regarded as 'machines of war', their officers were encouraged to treat them harshly, and their training was rudimentary to say the least. Very little attention was paid to marksmanship as the troops were still taught to fire in volleys. Initiative on the part of the troops was forbidden as it went against the rigid discipline favoured by the Army.

The forces in South Africa and those initially earmarked for its reinforcement were primarily infantry and artillery. The Government went as far as refusing the offers of contingents of mounted infantry that it received from the colonies, an error that was to cause it much embarrassment.

After the initial stages of the war were over, and Britain had suffered a number of reverses, a great deal of criticism was levelled at the army intelligence service for its failure to provide an accurate picture of the Boer army and its capabilities. The following extract from *The Times* tends to disprove the theory that the Army was let down by its intelligence service.

THE INTELLIGENCE DIVISION AND THE SOUTH AFRICAN WAR

In the earlier stages of the war, more especially during the period immediately succeeding the series of reverses which marked the second week of December, 1899, it was a very common thing for the critics to lay the chief blame on the Intelligence Division of the War Office. That department was accused of having failed to provide those reponsible for the conduct of the war with a proper knowledge of the strength of the Boer forces, of their military equipment, more especially of their artillery, or with proper maps of the regions which were destined to become the scene of military operations. But as the war progressed the critics gradually came to realize that the fault lay not so much with the Intelligence department for failing to supply information as with the heads of the military hierarchy for failing to make use of the information supplied. Soon opinion swung round to the other extreme, and it was freely bruited about that the Intelligence Division at Queen Anne's-gate had long before the war compiled the fullest and most accurate information about every detail of the armaments and forces of the Boer Republics, information which had been promptly pigeon-holed and done away with when it reached Pall Mall or left lying in stacks on the quays at Cape Town. An examination of the little volume of 120 pages issued by Sir John Ardagh's department in a revised form in June, 1899, and entitled "Military Notes on the Dutch Republics of South Africa," will help to show how far these different views are justified. These notes do not represent by any means the whole of the work done by the Intelligence Division during the three years before the war. The preface to them mentions that they are intended to supplement the following series of reports:– Reconnaissance of the bridges over the Vaal and Orange Rivers, 1897;

Lancashire Fusiliers on the
Roslin Castle bound for Natal

reconnaissance reports on the lines of advance through the Orange Free State (in three parts), 1897–98; report on the Natal Government Railways, 1897; report on the communications in Natal, north of Ladysmith, 1897; road and railway reports of the South African Republic, revised up to 1899; two *précis* of information on Swaziland and Basutoland, 1898; and notes on the lines of communications in Cape Colony, 1899. Besides these reports a certain amount of useful cartographical work was done, as far as the very limited means put at the disposal of the department allowed, surveys of the advance into the Orange Free State, a careful survey of Natal north of the latitude of Ladysmith, &c. Still the "Military Notes" represent the results of the labours of the Intelligence Division in their most complete form, and it is by them that those labours will generally be estimated.

The book is divided into 12 chapters, to which are subjoined four appendices, and, enclosed in a pocket, a general map of South Africa, a rough sketch of Pretoria with its forts, and a plan of the Johannesburg fort. The first two chapters deal with the physical features of the two Republics very much in the style of the ordinary geographies. The Transvaal is divided into four regions, the High Veld, the Bush Veld (we may note that the Intelligence Division gives the correct Dutch spelling of the word), the mountain ranges, and the low country on the Portuguese border. The Free State belongs almost entirely to the first category, that of High Veld. The centre and western districts of the Free State are described as "one of the finest terrains for cavalry in the world," the only obstacles being occasional dongas and wire fences, which could be allowed for by a careful use of ground scouts. There are also some useful remarks about the general character of the rivers and drifts. The third chapter, which is the most important, deals with the military forces, armament, and forts of the Transvaal. The constitutional aspect of the Transvaal forces, the powers of the President and Commandant-General, the absence of a general staff, and the character of general military councils composed of all the commandants and field-cornets present are first touched on. Of these last the report remarks:–

It is obvious that this system of leaving not only administrative details, but even strategical and tactical questions to the decision of a large body of officers, elected by the votes of the burghers they command, must inevitably involve inefficiency, and renders it improbable that a burgher force under such conditions will ever carry through any great enterprise requiring steadfastness of purpose, or that in case of defeat it would be in a position to continue any prolonged resistance.

The former of these conclusions has been justified by events, the latter not. It is true that on more than one occasion, as after Lord Roberts's march to Bloemfontein, and again on his entry into Pretoria, resistance collapsed almost entirely, but only to spring up again on the rumours of Boer successes. Nor has a complete defeat of the bulk of the Boer forces in the field, such as the above remarks evidently conceive, ever been inflicted by us in this war. Of the Transvaal supply services the report thinks but little, basing its judgment on the results of the Mpefu campaign of 1898. It remarks that, in spite of the large sums spent for military purposes, little progress has been made by the Boers towards the improvement of their primitive military organization, and hints that General Joubert, whom it describes as "a man of vacillating purpose, easily influenced by those near him," has not made much use of his opportunities in that respect. There is a good deal of truth in this estimate both of General Joubert and of the Boer organization. But hardly enough allowance is made for the difference between the way in which a people like the Boers would conduct what they considered a petty expedition, which was only the Government's concern, or a war for their national independence, which concerned every single burgher. As a matter of fact, by taking over the Netherlands Railway, by organizing large wagon convoys, and by private supplies brought to the individual burghers by their wives or their Kaffir servants, the supply question was solved quite sufficiently for the needs of the commandos at the front. There is a distinct shade of wistfulness in the references to the sums at the disposal of the Transvaal Intelligence Department, sums almost beyond the dreams of the Intelligence Division of a penny-wise empire. In 1896 the Transvaal spent £191,000, in 1897 £53,000, and in 1898 £42,000 on intelligence alone. In 1898 the department was spending, monthly, £850 in Johannesburg £1,500 in Cape Colony and Natal, and £900 to agents in England, some of whom had, it is suggested, even attempted to test the loyalty of the Irish among her Majesty's troops. These agents received almost *carte blanche* as to expenses. The report then goes on to deal with the burgher forces of the Transvaal. The total number of burghers liable to service – *i.e.*, between 16 and 60 years of age – is given from the State Almanac for 1899 as 29,279. The number of modern military rifles in the country, exclusive of Westley-Richards and other sporting rifles, with which the Boers were mainly armed in 1881, and of some 2,000 carbines, is estimated at 62,900, of which 34,000 were Martini-Henry and 24,000 Mausers. The rather curious statement is made in this connexion that the Boers were mainly armed with the Martini, as they distrusted the Mausers, and had returned them to store. It is true that many of the conservative Boers at first looked a little askance at the new rifle, but the statement in the report seems exaggerated. At any rate, by the time the war broke out all the Mausers were in the hands of the burghers, who were very proud of the new weapon and anxious to use it. The Transvaal had thus a reserve of more than 30,000 rifles with which to arm the disloyal in Cape Colony and Natal. The report next passes on to the permanent forces of the Transvaal. These consisted, first, of the State Artillery, which, including some 70 men belonging to telegraph, signalling, band, and departmental sections, amounted to 543 officers and men, with a reserve of some 200 or 300. A detailed account of the composition, pay, &c., of the corps is given. The account of the guns possessed by the Transvaal artillery is perhaps the passage which interests the general public most. The following is the list arrived at by the report:–

(1) Six q.f. 75mm. Creuzot field guns imported in 1896, which are fully described and are summed up as being too heavy to be very mobile, and rather delicate in the breech mechanism; (2) three 75mm. Vickers-Maxim mountain guns; (3) four 4.7in. howitzers; (4) 22 37mm. Vickers-Maxim automatic guns or "Pom-Poms"; (5) some 18 older guns, 6.5 and 8.5 Krupps, muzzle-loading mountain guns, 5-pounder Armstrongs, an old 64-pounder howitzer, &c. These are classed as field guns. The fortress armament is given as 16 6in. Creuzot guns ("Long Toms") carrying a 94lb. shell, and six $1\frac{1}{2}$-pounder Hotchkiss guns. Of the "Long Toms" the report says that they might possibly be used as guns of position, though their mobility is slight, and that the narrowness of their wheels, which are entirely of metal, makes them "quite unsuitable for travelling over roads." Besides the fortress and field artillery the report mentions 31 Maxims. It is perfectly clear from the above that the Intelligence Division had a very fair idea of the armaments of the Transvaal. There are, of course, inaccuracies of detail. The field artillery was somewhat under-estimated; the Nordenfelts taken from the raiders and recaptured at Elandslaagte are omitted; possibly, too, additional guns came in at the last moment – the report refers to a rumour of the purchase of eight new 8.5 Creuzots. On the other hand, there is a curious overestimate of the number of "Long Toms". Of these guns, at the outbreak of war, two were dragged on to the top of Mount Pogwani to command Langs Nek, one was taken down with the army of invasion in Natal and shelled General Yule out of Dundee, and a fourth was used against Mafeking. There were never more than three of these guns round Ladysmith. When we blew up one of them in December, it was replaced by the Mafeking one, while the damaged one was taken to Pretoria, and after being repaired was sent on to Kimberley. It is hardly conceivable that if the Boers had had twelve of these guns to spare they would not have brought down several more to Ladysmith. The only other regular forces of the Transvaal besides the artillery mentioned are the Transvaal police, some 1,500 strong in all, and some 300 to 400 Swaziland police. Some general notes appended to this summary of the Transvaal forces estimate the supply of ammunition in the Republic as sufficient for a

protracted campaign. Twenty-three million rounds of small arms ammunition are mentioned as stored in the Pretoria magazine alone, apart from the other magazines all over the country, of which a list is given. There are notes on the supply of transport of animals and of provisions in the country, and a fairly full account of the Pretoria and Johannesburg forts. Of these forts the report has no very high opinion, believing them to have been built largely by speculators to quiet Mr. Kruger's fears of a sudden attack from Johannesburg, and it expresses a shrewd doubt as to whether the Boers would make any very determined effort to hold them.

The Free State forces are similarly discussed in chapter 4. The total number of burghers liable to service is estimated at somewhat over 20,000, armed mainly with Martini-Henrys. Their artillery is given as 14 75mm. Krupps, five 9-pounder Armstrongs, six smaller muzzle-loading and mountain guns, and three Maxims, besides three quick-firing guns and three more Maxims ordered in June, 1899. The fifth chapter gives some account of the distribution and characteristics of the native population, the general gist of which is that, though it would not do to enlist natives to fight against the Boers, the fear of trouble with them would compel the Boers to keep a proportion of their forces watching the Swazi and Basuto borders, as well as the northern and eastern frontiers of the Transvaal. In the sixth chapter the distribution of the total Boer forces in the field is discussed. Touching on the question of disloyalty in the colonies, the report finds little reason to fear that any large number of men with a stake in the country will rise, provided that the penalties of rebellion are made quite clear, but expects a considerable number of landless poor whites, at the most 4,000 for the two colonies, to join the Boers. The actual number of those who went into rebellion during the course of the war must have been nearer 10,000, and might have been two or three times that number if the Boers had invaded Cape Colony in force at the beginning, or if Ladysmith had fallen. But on the assumption, which underlies the whole of the present work, that a war between the Republics and the British forces would be carried on in Republican territory, the estimate is quite a liberal one. The possibility of any large number of foreigners, whether Uitlanders or sympathizers from Europe, joining the Boers does not seem to have been contemplated by the Intelligence Division. It has sometimes been said that the War Office never seriously contemplated the possibility that the Free State might take a part in a war against Great Britain. There is no encouragement for this view in the present report, which says that the Free State "will undoubtedly throw in her lot with the sister Republic," as bound by the treaties which are quoted among the appendices. Taking the total Boer forces, including colonial rebels, as some 55,000, the report then proceeds to make certain deductions from them, to arrive at an estimate of the force that could be put in the field on the southern frontiers of the two Republics. The chief deduction from the Transvaal forces is one for the purpose of watching the Uitlander population. The report considers any real help from Johannesburg as out of the question, though it admits that certain Uitlanders had attempted to provide arms for the eventuality of war and had even talked of seizing the fort. The report, it must be remembered, was revived just after the arrest of Nicholls and the other "conspirators," and assumes that there was something in that conspiracy. Subsequent revelations, which figure in the Blue-books, showed clearly that the whole conspiracy was a farce organized by the police. In any case the report assumes that Johannesburg will be useful in containing some 5,000 burghers. The Boers solved that problem much more simply. They expelled practically the whole Uitlander population, "commandeering" nearly all their personal property, and working their mines, and, so far from finding Johannesburg a thorn in their side, made the very largest use of its remaining population and its resources.

Ten per cent., or 2,930 are deducted for sick and caretakers of farms, 1,200 for police duties, 1,000 for the Swazi border, 2,500 to watch Rhodesia and the Zoutpansberg. These deductions were somewhat too large. The sick and caretakers of farms probably covered the police duties as well; the Swazi border was guarded by about 500 men at first, and later on by about 50 bicyclists; Rhodesia and the north took some 1,500 to 2,000, but only for the earlier part of the war. On the other hand, the report allows only 500 men to watch Mafeking. There were over 6,000 round Mafeking for some weeks, and never less than 1,500 to 2,000 afterwards. For the Free State 10 per cent. are similarly deducted for caretakers, 3,000 to watch Basutoland, 1,000 to watch Kimberley, and 500 as garrison for Bloemfontein. Basutoland certainly contained a very large proportion of the Free State forces for the first few weeks, while it was uncertain what the Basutos would do, but later on the border was practically left undefended. Kimberley, on the other hand, absorbed at least 3,000 from the first. The total effective field force of the Republics is estimated in the report as 33,500. This figure, owing to the fact that the errors made in the deductions more or less neutralize each other, represents fairly accurately the actual total of the Boer forces on the southern borders of the Republics. The total Boer forces actually in the field at the outbreak of war were about 42,000, and may have been a little higher in December, 1899, though the total number of those who at one time or another took up arms, including rebels and foreigners, must have been nearly 60,000.

The seventh chapter treats Boer tactics and field organization. It attributes the Boer successes in 1881 to straighter shooting, greater mobility, and better tactical use of ground. The report considers, and on the whole rightly, that the difference in shooting is no longer as great as it was. An excellent description is given of the general character of Boer tactics:–

The tactics employed by the Boers were, in fact, such as they had learnt by hunting experiences on the veld. Alike in attack and defence, they acted on the same principle, containing the enemy's front with a thin but well-posted body of skirmishers; they utilized every fold of ground to gallop unseen round his flanks, and then, leaving their horses, which are trained to stand without holders, under cover, gradually concentrated a ring of overwhelming fire on their objective. . . . A remarkable feature of these enveloping tactics is the care taken by the Boers to avoid exposure . . . this dislike to risk death diminishes their military value in offensive operations or in any position the flanks of which can be turned.

It does not appear that the military authorities in Pall-mall drew any special conclusion from this excellent analysis of Boer methods, any more than they did from the statement, "South Africa is of all countries perhaps the most dangerous in the world for infantry to operate in without a screen of mounted troops in their front and on their flanks." A few weeks after this was written the War Office advised Mr. Chamberlain, to reply to offers of colonial assistance that unmounted men would be preferred. The chapter goes on to point out that the Boers, though possessing great tactical mobility, possess no great strategical mobility. There is an element of truth in this statement, but it omits to allow for the great superiority in the management of riding and transport animals and for the simpler commissariat of a Boer force. It is equally true that the Boers had no leaders who had experience in leading large bodies of men. Unfortunately the report does not go on to inquire what proportion of British generals had had occasion to command large bodies of men against modern weapons. The report also doubts if the large forces of the Transvaal will be able to keep together, owing to lack of higher organization and staff, and considers that their "batteries" of field artillery will only embarrass the Boers by obliging them to modify their loose tactics. As a matter of fact, the Boers never employed batteries, but adapted their artillery system to their tactics, and the very decentralization of battles helped enormously to compensate the defects of their organization, whereas the excessive centralization of our own system often paralysed a large part of any force engaged. Of the artillery in general the report says, "It is very improbable that either in *matériel* or *personnel* it will not be very inferior to ours in action." Speaking generally, it declares that the Boers –

Will have but little chance of success if compelled to meet in the open plains of the Free State or Transvaal an adequate force of disciplined troops complete in all three arms, and it appears certain that, after serious defeat, they would be too deficient in discipline and organization to make any further real stand.

A few remarks at the end of the chapter are devoted to the strategical course the Boers would probably pursue. The report rightly judges that the Pretoria forts will have no practical influence on the campaign and doubts the possibility of the Boers' shutting themselves up in them. The most likely course, it considers, is that the Boers will elect to hold their frontier, though it is not improbable that they will at the outset boldly take the offensive against Natal and Kimberley.

A serious engagement would necessarily come before our columns have penetrated far into Republican territory. Defeat in such an engagement would involve such disintegration of the Boer forces as to terminate the war.

The possibility of their not being driven back into Republican territory and heavily defeated is evidently not contemplated. The remaining chapters contain a description of Delagoa Bay and the railway to Machadodorp in case circumstances necessitated an invasion of the Transvaal from that side, and a sort of short guidebook description of the principal towns and villages of the two Republics and of the climate and seasons in South Africa.

Such, in substance, is the much-discussed report of the Intelligence Division. It contains a great deal of useful and fairly accurate information, and a certain amount of advice which it would have been well for our Army to have followed. And yet it cannot be considered a satisfactory product of our military system. The fault lies not with the officers of the Intelligence Division who compiled it. They were told to collect certain information, and they did so to the best of their ability. The fault lies with the headquarter organization of our Army, as at present conducted, with its complete divorce of information from action. To the observant reader almost every line of it reveals the absence of a real general staff, of a consultative department such as was advocated by the Hartington Commission, and such as Lord Wolseley, it was once hoped, might have created – a general staff in which the Intelligence Division should have its proper *status*, instead of being a mere office for the drawing of maps and the compiling of unauthoritative memoranda. The present volume contains no authoritative discussion of the relative value of British Regulars and Boers under the conditions of South African warfare. It expresses a belief that an "adequate" force "complete" in the three arms would make short work of the Boers, but it gives no standard of adequacy; still less does it attempt to fix a proportion of the three arms most suitable to South Africa. It gives a good account of Boer tactics, but it does not endeavour to think out what modifications ought to be introduced into British tactics to meet so peculiar an opponent. It gives a sufficiently correct estimate of the Boer forces, but it hardly enters into the question as to what the Boers might do with them, on what frontiers they would distribute them, or what British forces they might have opposed to them at the outbreak of war. One cannot help thinking that a real general staff, within whose scope lay both the collecting of information and the applying of that information to the actual strategical plans to be carried out, in fact to the whole military policy, would have produced very different publications. It would, in the first place, have produced for the use of senior officers a full authoritative study of the possibilities of a conflict with the Republics, giving a definite estimate of the total force necessary for success, of its composition, and of the tactics it ought to adopt. Such a work might have contained errors of judgment, but not nearly as many as were made by generals unprovided with anything but an unauthoritative handbook, to which they paid attention or not as it pleased their fancy. In the second place it would have also produced, at the outbreak of war, for the use of all officers, a short handbook describing the military characteristics of the country in which the war was to take place, and of the enemy who had to be met, and suggesting the proper measures to be taken in order to ensure success in those circumstances. Such a manual, at least as regards the features of the country, was written by Captain Chester Master and proved most useful to those who chanced to come across it, but the task ought not to have been left to private initiative. To sum up, the "Military Notes" reflect reasonable credit on the members of the Intelligence Division who compiled them. They reflect little credit on our existing arrangements for providing for the contingencies of war in time of peace.

This report is remarkable not only for the accuracy of some of its assessments, but also because of its publication in book form before the war and the way in which *The Times* was able to reproduce it during the war.

Notes

1. John Carey, ed., *The Faber Book of Reportage* (London, 1987), p. 68.
2. Ibid., p. 116.

3. The first newspaper to appear in England, in 1620, was called *The Corrant out of Italy, Germany etc.*, and was in fact printed in Amsterdam. The first newspaper to be printed in England was the literally titled, *The Heads of Severall Proceedings in this Present Parliament*, which first appeared in 1641.
4. John Carey, 1987, p. 199.
5. Trevor Royle, *War Report* (1987), pp. 16–17.
6. *The History of The Times*, 5 vols (London, 1935–52), vol. 2, p. 168.
7. Oliver Woods and James Bishop, *The Story of The Times* (London, 1985), p. 77.
8. Ibid., p. 75.
9. Ibid., p. 69.
10. Royle, 1987, p. 20.
11. *The Times*, 12 October 1855.
12. *The History of The Times*, vol. 2, p. 177.
13. Royle, 1987, p. 24.
14. Woods and Bishop, 1985, pp. 70–1.
15. Ibid., p. 127.
16. For a comprehensive picture of Britain at this time see R.C.K. Ensor, *The Oxford History of England, 1870–1914* (Oxford, 1980).
17. Woods and Bishop, 1985, p. 171.
18. Ibid., p. 167.
19. Thomas Pakenham, *The Boer War* (London, 1991), p. 53.
20. Rayne Kruger, *Goodbye Dolly Grey* (London, 1983), p. 45.

The War Begins

'Defy the truth whose witness now draws near.
To scourge these dogs, agape with jaws afoam,
Down out of life. Strike England, and strike home.'

(Algernon Charles Swinburne, from 'The Transvaal')

The war began with the Boers invading British territory in four places: into Natal in the east, towards Mafeking in the north-west, south-west towards Kimberley and across the Orange River into the Cape Colony. Denys Reitz, a young Boer soldier, has left a vivid account of the first sight the Boers had of Natal, 'After a long ride we emerged into open country and there, winding across the plain, lay the Buffalo river with the green hills and pleasant valleys of Natal stretching beyond. With one accord the long files of horsemen reined in, and we gazed silently on the land of promise. General Maroola, with a quick eye to the occasion, faced round and made a speech telling us that Natal was a heritage filched from our forefathers, which must now be recovered from the usurper. Amid enthusiastic cries we began to ford the stream. It took nearly an hour for all to cross, and during this time the cheering and singing of the "Volkslied" [the Boer national song] were continuous, and we rode into the smiling land of Natal full of hope and courage.'[1]

All the Boer invasion routes were aimed at strategic railway lines, the central aim of the Boer plan being to cut railway communication with the coast and thus prevent the British from moving their troop reinforcements from the ports to the main theatre of operations. Three towns were singled out as key points of attack for the Boer strategy, Kimberley, Mafeking and Ladysmith. The names of these small South African towns were to become famous all round the world in the months to come. Of the three, Ladysmith was the central point of the whole Boer plan. Ladysmith, the main town on the railway line to Durban, was also the headquarters of the main British force in South Africa, some 12,000 troops led by Sir George White. White was just able to stop the Boers from pushing straight into Durban, but his indecision led to his whole command being in imminent danger of being cut off in Ladysmith. One of the first reports published by *The Times*, sent by its correspondent in Ladysmith, describes the early Boer moves in the region of the town.

PIETERMARITZBURG, OCT 11.

At last the long weary crisis seems about to culminate, and before the end of the week it seems probable that a state of war will have begun. The diplomatic situation in face of the Boer ultimatum makes this almost inevitable, and the reported movements of Boer commandos point to the same result.

It is stated that the Boers have raided Zululand, and that a train to Ladysmith with Natal rolling stock has been seized at Harrismith.

An enthusiastic meeting of Uitlanders desirous of serving in the proposed infantry corps was held this afternoon under the chairmanship of Mr. Hosken.

LADYSMITH, OCT. 11.

Rumours of a movement of both the Volksrust and Van Reenen commandos caused considerable unrest and activity at Pietermaritzburg yesterday. These movements seemed to indicate that the strategy of the Boers contemplated an attempt to work round both flanks of the strategic line of defence now drawn across the Natal frontier. A movement of Free State burghers was reported from the vicinity of Olivier's Hoek, threatening Colenso and our left flank. On the east flank a concentration of Utrecht and Vryheid commandos was reported towards the drifts on the Buffalo river east of Dundee.

A Boer commando of 200 men is stated to have visited Newcastle yesterday. This probably accounts for the reported military occupation of Langs Nek. These men simply made purchases and withdrew, the place being practically deserted.

While the Boers remain inactive, the military defensive measures approved by Sir George White are being completed with all despatch. If the report of an ultimatum be true, an armed occupation of the northern passes by the Boers may be anticipated, but this is an eventuality for which we now stand prepared. The military situation is on a much firmer basis than it was when Sir George White landed.

LATER.

The outlook is more serious. The Harrismith mail is overdue, and it is reported that it has been commandeered by the Free State across the border, and that four railway servants are detained. If the news is confirmed this is equivalent to a declaration of war, as the whole line to Harrismith is the property of the Natal State Railway.

In the first couple of weeks of the war three battles were fought, at Talana Hill on 20 October, at Elandslaagte on 21 October and at Dundee on 23 October. All three battles resulted in the Boers retreating, but they could hardly be called British victories. Both sides lost large numbers of men and even though the Boers withdrew this was more in line with their traditional method of fighting than an admission of defeat. When they came under pressure the Boers invariably withdrew, to regroup and continue the fight under more auspicious circumstances. Boer courage and tenacity is apparent in the first descriptions of the action at Talana Hill that *The Times'* readers found in their newspaper on 23 October 1899.

GLENCOE CAMP, OCT. 20, 6.35 A.M.

B reak of day this morning disclosed the fact that the Boers were in great force all round Dundee. It was seen that they had taken up a position on a hill behind Peter Smith's house, and had posted cannon there.

An engagement was immediately opened with rifle fire, which in a few minutes became general. Then, to waken us up, the enemy put several shot and shell slap into our camp, causing its speedy evacuation and the forming up of all ranks outside.

Our guns were soon in action, and replied to the Boer artillery with telling effect. The whizzing of the enemy's shots as they passed over our heads had music in it, but beyond a natural dodging of heads the enemy's artillery fire produced no result.

So effective, on the other hand, was our reply that in ten minutes the enemy's guns were all but silenced. From a position I had taken up a little way in front of our guns I could plainly see how telling it was. I was also able to observe the movements of the British Staff officers, who were going about their duties as coolly as if the engagement were merely a sham fight.

As soon as the Boer fire slackened our artillery, which had been beautifully served, trotted into the town and posted themselves there. From their new position they soon compelled the enemy to retire, but they still appeared swarming like bees on every place of vantage along the ridge which skirts the town, while others were driven towards the coalfields.

Our guns continued to play on Smith's Hill, where beautiful practice was made. As the shells burst on the top the Boers could be seen scampering for cover. While the guns were so engaged the Hussars deployed on the enemy's left flank. After five minutes' sharp work the cannonading ceased and all was over for the present, the enemy having withdrawn.

This may be put down as the first battle of Dundee. We fully expect another attack, however, in the afternoon.

7.25 A.M.

I had hardly sent off my last telegram before the battle was renewed with increased vigour.

Soon after firing ceased our scouts brought in a message stating that a body of 9,000 Boers was marching on us with the intention of attacking us in the rear. A heavy mist capping the surrounding hills obscures their approach, and it is expected that they may be on us at any hour.

10.20 A.M.

The battle was renewed at half-past 6 with great vigour on the part of the Boers.

Casualties then began on our side, and the Indian hospital corps, with their doolies, under Major Donegan, attached to the 18th Hussars, were run out, keeping in rear of the advancing infantry.

The artillery, meanwhile, had galloped from their second position through the town amid the cheers of the citizens.

The movements of the Boer force were erratic at this period of the fight. They had returned in great numbers to the hill and were being vigorously engaged by our artillery. Their return fire did very little damage.

Talana Hill, site of the Battle of Dundee, 1899

For some time the enemy kept up an incessant fire from the hill, but the shrapnel from our guns soon began to tell its tale, with the result that the Boer fire visibly slackened, and from a ceaseless rattle of rifle fire it gradually dwindled down to straggling shots.

While the artillery in front were shelling the hill, the King's Royal Rifles on the right front were busy with their Maxim and were evidently causing the Boers considerable anxiety as to their position. Their artillery had been completely silenced by the splendid service of ours.

A squadron of the 18th Hussars, with the mounted company of the Dublins, were meanwhile creeping round the enemy's left flank, and a battery of artillery, supported by another squadron of Hussars and a mounted company of the King's Royal Rifles, had deployed on the right flank at the coalfields.

The artillery in front continued to play on Smith's Hill at a range of nearly 3,000 yards, while the Dublins and King's Rifles, under cover of the guns, pressed forward.

It was in the execution of this manoeuvre that the casualties to the infantry regiments occurred, several in their ranks being killed and wounded.

The firing presently eased off on our side and only a solitary shot was returned now and again by the enemy.

General Sir William Penn Symons, taking advantage of the lull, rode forward with his staff in front of the guns and took cover in the rear of a plantation at the base of the hill.

The infantry, in extended formation, were all this time gradually pressed forward. I watched the Boers from the rear of the artillery and could see them massing on the extreme left of the hill, and I observed three of our shells in quick succession either shift them or cut them to pieces.

2.45 P.M.

The fire of the Boers at this juncture was becoming hot, yet, despite this, the 1st Battalion King's Royal Rifles and the Irish Fusiliers, led respectively by Colonel Gunning and Colonel Carlton, continued to mount the hill gradually.

They were extended all along the hill, and at 10 o'clock, after four and a half hours' fighting, the firing screen of infantry managed to reach a wall which runs parallel to the ridge and is about 600 yards from the top of the hill.

This position was gained owing to the magnificent shooting of the artillery, who placed shells at the spots where the Boers were massed with amazing accuracy, compelling them to retire, but on again the determined enemy would come, only to be beaten back time after time by the excellent shooting of the 13th and 69th Batteries, under command respectively of Major Dawkins and Major Wing.

At 11.45 the firing almost ceased, and in a twinkling the infantry were over the wall. With the utmost gallantry they rushed the plateau at the base of the top ridge.

The defence made by the Boers was most determined. They again and again poured into our men a long fusillade of fire, which was well returned in splendidly directed volleys by the Dublins and King's Rifles.

A large party of Boers who were driven from Smith's Hill took refuge in a cattle kraal with the intention of cross-firing upon the advancing firing screen of infantry, but the 13th Battery opened fire upon them and quickly shifted them.

The enemy had so far displayed undoubted courage. Though lacking in the organized discipline of trained European troops, they had stood up to our scattering artillery fire with great determination, and there on the Talana Ridge, standing clearly out on the sky line, they still appeared, unbeaten and defiant.

The battle had raged for six and a half hours when the 69th Battery were ordered to limber up and advance. They galloped into their new position and into action like lightning, and the effects of their fire at the closer range were at once noticeable, so much so that the 13th Battery were also ordered up.

After two rounds from each battery, perfect silence reigned for a considerable length of time in the enemy's ranks. It was broken only by the "whirr-whirring" of the Maxims of the Dublins and Fusiliers, who had secured a good position on the right and who were concentrating their fire on the Boers as they came in view on the hill away to the right flank.

During the cessation in the bombardment the enemy had taken up a position on the hill to the right of the road to the Marina colliery. The 13th Battery soon opened fire on them and compelled them to retire.

Meanwhile the two infantry battalions continued to climb the hill, and at 1.30, after eight hours' hard fighting, the position was gained, the Boers having precipitately evacuated the hill.

What had commenced with the battle of Dundee ended in a glorious victory for our arms, which must be known as the battle of Talana Hill.

Just as the King's Rifles and the Dublins gained the top of the hill, the mounted infantry could be seen working round the left flank.

The description of the battle of Talana Hill carried by *The Times*, while stressing the courage of the British troops, has ominous undertones, and the correspondent seems almost surprised that the Boers have a sound grasp of tactics. Meanwhile ominous reports of mobile Boer commandos closing in on the main railway centres continued to flood into *The Times*, and it was becoming increasingly obvious that the three towns of Mafeking, Kimberley and Ladysmith were in serious danger of being cut off and captured.

MAFEKING (via BEIRA), OCT. 12

The position is critical. Colonel Baden-Powell has warned the inhabitants to expect an attack.

The Boer force near the British position is estimated by spies at 9,000, including a detachment of heavy artillery. The Boers have advanced upon our telegraph extension wires from bases at Maritzani, on the south, and at Malmani, on the east. South of Mafeking, there are 4,000 Boers concentrated at Maritzani, through which runs our line of communications. They have captured Kraaipan and Maribogo, points within our 40-miles southern radius.

The Boers at Malmani, under Cronje's command, when an exterior line is established with the Maritzani column, will attack our position at Mafeking. Our defences are completely organized. Every available man has been mustered, and the women are in laager. A native tribe, the Baralong, under Chief Wessels, are co-operating in outpost duties.

Colonel Hore took up a position at dawn to-day, but, the enemy not advancing, he retired upon the town.

Natives report that the Boers are in a strong position upon the border. A magnificent fight is anticipated, but all that can be expected is that the British force will hold the position.

Commandant Cronje's supineness has been giving dissatisfaction, and it is reported that he has been superseded at the demand of discontented young Boers.

The Boers' supplies are short, since they are cut off from the Mafeking stores; dysentery is setting in, and dissatisfaction and desertion are resulting from the deferred movement.

Martial law has been proclaimed at Mafeking.

4.15 P.M.

It is reported that 500 Boers, with a commissariat train, crossed the border to-day at Maritzani, 20 miles south of our position at Mafeking, *en route* for Kraaipan to seize our communications.

All the wires are cut to the southward. The Cape express from here was unable to get through.

Three hundred of Colonel Hore's force have taken up a strong position flanking Mafeking. An attack is anticipated.

4.35 P.M.

The report that the wires have been cut and that our line of communications is held by the Boers is confirmed.

LADYSMITH, OCT. 18, 12.15 P.M.

The Boers are showing an inclination to attempt to work round our flank, as I forecast in a previous telegram. They were reported to have occupied Helpmakaar, but the information is premature.

The Free State burghers yesterday evening opened fire with 9-pounders on Major Adye's second reconnaissance to the Tintwa Pass. They fired three shells but without effect. The reconnaissance found the enemy a few hundred strong, six miles within the border.

A Boer agent, enlisted in the ranks of the Imperial Light Horse, was detected this morning in possession of incriminating documents.

3.50 P.M.

The situation on the eastern border is developing a more serious aspect. The Vryheid and Utrecht commandos, after looting on the Zululand border, are reported to be in the Umsinga district threatening communication between this place and Dundee.

On the western frontier, Free State patrols are now reported to be in possession of Acton Homes, a farm 24 miles west of Ladysmith, our patrols having fallen back.

The situation at the front is reported to be growing more acute. I am leaving to ascertain particulars.

The following statement was issued by the War Office last night:–

"No news of importance has been received from Natal to-day. The cavalry with the forces at Ladysmith and Dundee is engaged in observing the enemy's movements. Steps have been taken for the security of Pietermaritzburg and Durban against raids. The remainder of the 5th Dragoon Guards is expected shortly to arrive at Durban.

"On the western frontier there is no recent intelligence of a reliable character from Kimberley and Mafeking, both places being cut off from communication by rail and telegraph. It is, however, believed that on Sunday there was a skirmish six miles south of Kimberley, and that the Boers were beaten off with some loss by an armoured train. There was also some fighting at Mafeking on Friday or Saturday, ending in the repulse of the attacking force.

"Opposite Aliwal North and Bethulie, on the Orange River, a considerable number of Boers are assembled.

"Railway communication with the Orange Free State and Transvaal has now ceased, and the remaining refugees have been warned to leave *via* Delagoa Bay. . . ."

The British continued to be cheered by news of 'splendid' battles, which seemed to show that the Boer irregulars could not stand up to the regulars of the British Army in pitched battle.

MODDER'S SPRUIT, OCT. 21, 11.30 P.M.

General French took the Imperial Light Horse and the Natal Volunteer Artillery, with six guns, and supported by four companies of the Manchester Regiment, in an armoured train and made a further reconnaissance to Elandslaagte Station.

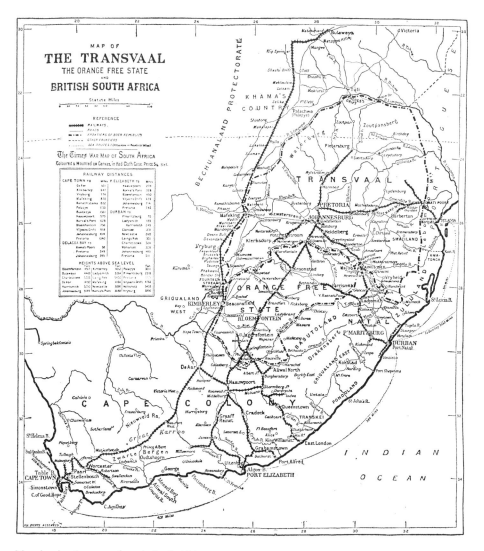

Map showing the arena of war in South Africa

After sighting a small Boer patrol and wounding one man of it, the cavalry and battery arrived on a plateau overlooking the dip in which the station and coalfields are situated. The Boers were apparently surprised. A cloud of mounted men left the station and its environs, making for a ridge about 2,000 yards distant on the opposite side of the valley. Our scouts had almost entered the coal mines when the Natal battery came into action, bursting two shells in the station buildings.

As soon as our battery had thus disclosed our position on the plateau, the enemy opened an accurate fire with two guns from intrenched works on the ridge to which the mounted Boers had galloped. The enemy's gunners evidently had the range marked, for shells fell around the battery in action, crippling one ammunition wagon. The 7-pounders of the Volunteer artillery were unable to return this fire, the range being 4,500 yards, so General French withdrew slowly, abandoning the crippled wagon.

As our battery withdrew the enemy played their guns on the armoured train from which our infantry had detrained. This fire, however, was ineffective. The whole reconnaissance then withdrew with the train for five miles, General French having wired for supports. A few of the mounted enemy attempted to cut the train off, but were out-manoeuvred.

Reinforcements arrived at midday, and their arrival precipitated a sanguinary engagement which lasted two and a half hours, the Boers being driven from their position.

OCTOBER 22, 7.25 A.M.
It was about 11 when a battery of artillery and a portion of the 5th Dragoon Guards arrived, having come out from Ladysmith with double teams. Shortly afterwards another train arrived with more infantry from Sir George White.

Some fugitives, including the manager of the coal mines and the *Standard* correspondent, who had been captured on Wednesday in the held-up train, reported that about 1,100 Boers were in position on the range from which they opened fire in the morning.

The force consisted mainly of two commandos, under Koch and De Million(?), who had two Maxim-Nordenfelt guns and two Maxims. They had marched right down the Biggarsberg Pass, having crossed into Natal by Botha's Pass, and had met no British patrol at all before occupying Elandslaagte. They set themselves to intrench the end of the spur covering the railway and coalfields from the west.

Working on this information, and on the fact that the Boers had had three days to complete these works, General French determined to await reinforcements.

While General French's force with the trains retired to Modder's Spruit, the enemy's scouts were seen circling the hills on the left. Following our retirement these became bolder, firing into the Volunteer Light Horse which covered the party. A troop of the latter promptly dislodged them.

After halting till 2 at Modder's Spruit, it was considered that we were strong enough – having been reinforced with the Devons and the Gordons – to advance. Then a second field battery and the 5th Lancers arrived. The scouts at 3 o'clock, when the 5th Dragoon Guards began to move along the road by which our force had advanced in the morning, reported that the enemy were in force on the ranges on the left. The enemy suddenly opened Maxim fire on the extended Dragoon Guards at short range. The fire was ineffective, however, and our battery immediately shelled them out. They were reported to be a party of Free State Boers, attracted by the early morning's firing. The whole of our infantry, now under General Ian Hamilton, detrained a mile north of Modder's Spruit.

The enemy's position now requires some description. They had intrenched and laagered on the northern edge of a range running at right angles to the railway. The height of the highest spot was about 800ft. above the level of the permanent way. The range itself is a succession of hillocks, one commanding another so that when viewed from the flank they looked something like the teeth of a saw. To the front and on the flanks of this position stretched the rolling veldt, without any considerable cover, for at least 5,000 yards. From Modder's Spruit to the front of the Boers' position lay an undulating five-mile plain, divided by a long shoulder of hill about 4,000 yards' range from the enemy's position.

Shortly after 3 a squadron of the 5th Lancers and of the Imperial Light Horse were sent to clear this shoulder for occupation by infantry, the latter arm marching upon it from the vicinity of Modder's Spruit. The Imperial Light Horse and Lancers speedily gained possession, the enemy's scouts falling back.

The infantry advanced steadily in extended order, the Manchesters leading, followed by Devons and Gordons. It was a long and slow march, and it was nearly 4 o'clock before the infantry could extend along the shoulder of the hill. The Manchesters took the right of the line, and the Devons the left, the Gordons coming up in support. A covering party of the 5th Lancers and Imperial Light Horse were on the right.

As soon as our infantry were well on the hill the enemy opened and shelled the crest with accurate fire. At 4 o'clock our first battery came into action, between the Devons and the Manchesters. The enemy were nothing daunted, and returned the fire of the latter with vigour. Their range was excellent, and, though in the first place they only remained in action six minutes, they upset an ammunition wagon and caused several casualties, especially to horses.

In the meantime clouds of the fleeing enemy were seen, as it appeared, leaving the field and escaping on the right of our advance. This retreat of the mounted enemy was a ruse by which the Boers hoped to draw off part of the attacking force, themselves galloping back to a position on the reverse of the hill.

After the enemy's guns had ceased firing, our artillery, having now two batteries in action, began to prepare for the infantry assault, bursting shrapnel all along the Boer position.

Thunder clouds gathered behind the hills and made an ominous background, against which the lurid light of the bursting shell showed as if it were already night. It was evident that the attack must be pressed home before night, so, with half an hour's preparation, the infantry received orders to advance.

The Devons were given the task of delivering a semi-frontal attack with the Manchesters, supported by the Gordons on the right flank, for which they had to make a wide *détour*. This was at half-past 4. At this period rain fell in deluges for a quarter of an hour.

As the infantry attack began the enemy's guns came into position and shelled the advancing lines of the Devons, who were now stolidly pushing across the open, cutting the wire fences that impeded them. They were extended as much as possible, this being the only method by which the men could face the Mauser and Maxim fire. Nothing could have been finer than the undaunted front of this battalion edging forward against the fire of modern arms.

Having seen the Devons on their way, I joined the Gordons as, skirting the batteries in action, they cut in on the left of the Manchesters. We marched steadily on in columns of companies, until the bouldered nek of the enemy's ridge was reached. This was about three-quarters of a mile from the position of the Boer guns. In front of the Gordons were three successive kopjes, or rather ridges, running diagonally across the flat top of the hill. Each was commanded by that behind it, and the hill was one mass of the typical boulders of the country.

[The section of our Correspondent's telegram which should come in at this point has not yet reached us.]

Many times foiled in places, driven back yet righting themselves, and steadily pushing forward, the troops on the summit pushed on. The first kopje was already a shambles. Men had fallen fast, but the weight of numbers carried our troops on.

It had ceased to be a general's battle; everything depended on company and even on section commanders, and gallantly the officers and non-commissioned officers did their work. If the men wavered and stuck under cover, the officers sacrificed themselves to furnish an example. The fighting on the ridge summit was of this description; it is impossible to give it in detail.

The enemy stood to their positions with a grim persistency which was magnificent, and their stand at the last kopje above their camp and laager was one of the finest pieces of fighting recorded in modern wars. In spite of the united attack of the storming regiments, training their guns at point-blank range and discharging the magazines they checked the advance for half an hour.

It was now 6 o'clock. There was only half an hour's more light, and shattered battalions were lying around the kopje where the Dutch were making their final stand.

Our bugles rang out the advance and other buglers took up the call. Fixed bayonets gleamed amid the boulders through the fading light, and the men sprang up to the well-known notes – sprang up to fall like rabbits.

Again and again sounded the call. Somehow I found myself with a company of the Devons. A fence stopped us. We fell or threw ourselves over it. Still sounded the call.

The Highlanders were shouting above. Cheering madly, we were over a breastwork, and passed a quick-firing gun still smoking. A Dutchman at my feet was calling for mercy. We were in – were there. Some one shouted, "Remember Majuba!" Over the brow there was the sound of skirling pipes. The main kopje was taken.

9.30 A.M.

There was still firing below. With "Majuba" still on their lips, our men dashed forward to carry the laager with bayonets. The officers held them back, and a voice in command said "Cease fire."

Again the bugle rang out, and a white handkerchief fluttered at the end of a rifle. The enemy had surrendered, but the main remnant were pouring over the hillside, where our cavalry pounced upon them.

It was half-past 6. I had just time to look round the laager below the hillside, strewn with dead and wounded, the Dutch and German gunners being distinguishable by their brown uniform. They had fought their guns splendidly. Two of their guns I saw with "Maxim-Nordenfelt" and the direction in English on the carriages. I had to leave at once, as it was already night and we were 20 miles from the telegraph.

It is impossible as yet to furnish details of our losses or those of the enemy, but they must be heavy. At midnight the hospital train came back carrying 90 of our

6th Dragoon Guards on board the
Wakool

wounded, but I am afraid the total will be double that. This must have been a
terrible night. Many of the wounded could not have been found till the morning.
Glencoe was a sanguinary engagement, and this was in every respect equal to it in
bloodshed, but, though the price was high, the defeat was absolutely crushing, and
the moral effect will now be felt all through the Republics.

General French was in command throughout. Our strength was about 3,200. Sir
George White was present during the engagement. General Ian Hamilton
commanded the infantry.

These reports of British victories failed to take into account the fact that the Boers were
fighting an entirely different war from the British. A clue to this mutual
incomprehension can be found in the differing reactions of the two peoples to the
British use of lancers at Elandslaagte. The Boers thought it was barbarous to fight with
'spears' while the British thought the lancers were the cream of British 'chivalry'. In
addition, the Boers had an instinctive grasp of the benefits of mobility, coupled with a
sound knowledge of the best tactics to be used in the terrain of South Africa.

On 26 October 1899 the Transvaal and Free State commandos linked up, and by
30 October the largest British force in South Africa was trapped inside Ladysmith. The
towns of Mafeking and Kimberley were now cut off from the outside world. The Boers
were jubilant and it seemed briefly that victory was within their grasp, but for the
indecision of commanders such as General Joubert, who, when presented with an
opportunity to smash General White's forces at an early stage of the siege, refused it
saying, 'When God holds out a finger do not take the whole hand'.[2]

The situation was thus dangerous, but not catastrophic, for Britain. The Government in London did not lose its head. It has always been a characteristic of the British Army that its campaigns start badly, but it loses very few wars. The most obvious problem faced by the British was a lack of troops in the theatre of operations, and this problem was about to be rectified as Britain was in the process of sending a whole army corps of nearly 47,000 men. The pages of *The Times* were full of reports of troop departures for South Africa.

SOUTHAMPTON, OCT. 22.

To-day the sailing of the Pavonia has been the great event. She went from the Empress Dock, conveying two strong battalions, the 2nd Royal Scots Fusiliers and the 2nd Royal Fusiliers, both in their scarlet serges. The former were stalwart fellows – 682 men and 25 officers; the latter were not very great in point of stature, but a wiry-looking lot of men – 753 of them, with 29 officers. An hour or two later the Malta went, also taking out Reservists of the 1st Coldstream Guards as far as Gibraltar, from whence she will proceed with the full battalion. She takes out, also, some Engineers and a strong body of mounted infantry, who, by universal consent, are the men most needed in South Africa. She took out, also, some 2nd Cameron Highlanders and some Royal Highlanders to reinforce the garrison at Gibraltar. So ended a second day of unbroken success, and the scene in it which will live in memory is the departure of the Pavonia, cheered to the echo by thick crowds lining the dock and the passage into Southampton Water on either side, with poop and forecastle and waist one sea of faces and scarlet, with the thud of the big drum just penetrating the din to remind us that there was a band, and with the strains of "Auld Lang Syne" echoing at the end. The last cheers came from the passengers of the North-German Lloyd steamer Friedrich der Grosse, the biggest ship they possess, and then all was over. Perhaps I may add one personal note. "A splendid sight and a noble one," said an old and gallant soldier who had been my companion during the afternoon. "But," he added, "there are sad losses to think, too." He had three soldier sons whom he was giving to his country, and he was grave and anxious. But he felt that the work had become necessary, and he joined with the rest in the cheering and the waving of hats, and even in the hurling of apples into the crowd of laughing soldiers on board the Pavonia. And his case was by no means singular, but rather typical. We all cheer, we are confident of the issue, but there is hardly one of us who has not also personal cause for anxiety.

Sir Redvers Buller arrived in South Africa on 31 October, to a tumultuous welcome from the inhabitants of Cape Town.

CAPE TOWN, OCT. 31.

The arrival of General Buller evoked one of the most striking popular demonstrations ever seen at Cape Town. The Dunottar Castle was expected yesterday afternoon, but, to the disappointment of the crowd, she failed to appear. Late at night the steamer was signalled, and she was safely docked at 9 this morning.

Troops just arrived at Cape Town

Sir Redvers Buller, who was received by General Forestier-Walker, commanding at the Cape, entered a carriage and drove rapidly to Government House, preceded by a detachment of mounted police and escorted by Cape Mounted Volunteers. The reception accorded to the General was a splendid one. Cheer upon cheer was raised, and the enthusiasm displayed was in every way remarkable for its intensity. Shouts of "Bravo, General!" and "Avenge Majuba!" were frequent. The General, whose face remained impassive, acknowledged the cheers with a military salute.

The whole town is lavishly decorated. The assembling of such a great multitude at the present juncture is regarded as very significant and as confirmatory of the opinion that even the Dutch element regard General Buller as the embodiment of British power, the display of which is now more than ever necessary in Cape Colony and elsewhere.

Buller was an experienced soldier who had seen service in the China War of 1860, the Red River expedition in Canada, the Ashanti Campaign of 1873, the Zulu War of 1879 and the First Boer War. He also had the bearing of the typical stoical British Victorian officer. Personally brave, Buller was a winner of the Victoria Cross, but in his case both his appearance and experience concealed vital flaws. Despite an appearance of outward calm, Buller was indecisive and given to panic. Perhaps this was a reflection of the fact that, although he was a practical soldier, he had no experience of commanding large formations; all his experience having been in the brush wars that abounded during the Victorian era.[3]

On his arrival in Cape Town, Buller was to carry out the explicit instructions that he had received in London. He was to attack, using all his strength, along the railway line from De Aar to Bloemfontein and then on to Pretoria. But Buller never carried out his orders. The tide of bad news about General White's position in Ladysmith had convinced him that he had to divide his forces and move out as quickly as possible to the relief of Ladysmith. The reports of the action at Nicholson's Nek in particular caused Buller to believe that Ladysmith was close to surrendering.

LORENZO MARQUES, NOV. 9.

Father L. Matthews, chaplain of the Royal Irish Fusiliers, who was captured at Nicholson's Nek on October 31, has given me the following account of the disaster:–

"We were sent out to occupy the position with the object of preventing the two Boer forces from joining. We started at 8.30 on Sunday night, marched ten miles, and got to the hill at 1 a.m. The first mishap was that the mountain battery stampeded and scattered the whole lot of mules. We formed up again and gained the top of the hill. The guns were gone, but not all the ammunition. I do not know what stampeded the mules. They knocked me down. It was pitch dark.

"We had one hour's sleep. Firing began just after daylight. It was slack for some time, but the Boers crept round. Then the firing became furious. Our men made a breastwork of stones.

"After 12 o'clock there was a general cry of 'Cease fire' in that direction. Our fellows would not stop firing. Major Adye came up and confirmed the order to cease fire. Then the bugle sounded the cease fire. In our sangar there was a rumour that the white flag was raised by a young officer who thought his batch of ten men were the sole survivors.

"We were 900 alive, having started perhaps 1,000. I think that many of the battery men escaped. Our men and officers were furious at surrendering. The Boers did not seem to be in great numbers on the spot, but I heard that the main body had galloped off.

"The men had to give up their arms. The officers were sent to Commandant Steenekamp. The officers then ordered the men to fall in. The officers were taken away from the men and sent to General Joubert. On the same day the officers went in mule wagons and slept at some store *en route*, and next day took the train at Waschbank for Pretoria. The officers are very well treated, and so, I have heard, are the men. There has been no unpleasantness in Pretoria. The officers are in the Model School, and are allowed to walk as they please in the grounds.

"I think that the surrender was a great blunder, and was caused by a misunderstanding. Major Adye was much put out. The white flag was not hoisted by the Irish Fusiliers."

Having made the decision, Buller acted quickly to carry it out, leaving Lord Methuen, commander of the First Division, to move along the pre-ordained route of advance to the relief of Kimberley and then Mafeking. Buller left for Natal with 12,000 men to attempt the relief of Ladysmith. He shipped a large number of his troops to Durban, and moved the rest of them along the railway to Chieveley, where he set up his base of operations. In front of Buller lay a wide open expanse of plain, through which flowed the Tugela River. Behind the river lay the town of Colenso at the base of a series of hills. In the distance to the north, Ladysmith waited, besieged by the Boers who had began to shell the town in earnest.

LADYSMITH, NOV. 6.

To-day is the fifth day of the siege. On Friday evening the town was heavily shelled, especially when the cavalry reconnaissance had returned to camp after a satisfactory brush with the enemy in the vicinity of the western approaches to the town.

On Saturday Sir George White opened negotiations with General Joubert with a view to the removal of the sick and the women and children to a place of safety. The negotiations culminated in a cessation of the bombardment, which has not been resumed up to the present. In the meantime, all precautions have been taken for securing the safety of the garrison. The wounded have been removed to a neutral zone.

For reasons unknown, the enemy failed to renew the bombardment to-day, and only fired two shells at our balloon. It is supposed that some damage was done by our naval guns to the enemy's position gun in the last twenty rounds on Friday. Possibly the enemy is awaiting the arrival of other position guns before tackling the work in earnest.

Every one is cheerful and confident that we can show a rigid front for weeks to come.

Hitherto the bombardment has done little damage. Yesterday the enemy sent in eight wounded from Dundee.

I have been by train down to the Boer advanced post. The Boers consider that their success is due to the justness of their cause. They have been guilty of abusing the Red Cross flag.

A heavy day is expected to-morrow. News from the south is scanty. Guns are in position all round us. It was difficult at first to locate them, as they use smokeless powder, but the balloon managed to find all the positions.

The fighting continued at Mafeking and Kimberley, but both sets of defenders were in good spirits, and the commander of Mafeking, one Robert Stephenson Baden-Powell, was beginning to emerge as the hero of the hour.

KURUMAN, OCT. 21.

No important movement has occurred at Mafeking since the Boers attempted their previous bombardment of the town. The efforts of Mafeking are directed to constant sniping of the Boer force at the water springs. Nothing definite has resulted beyond the expenditure of ammunition. Commandant Cronje has sent a letter to Colonel Baden-Powell stating that, since the present Boer artillery is ineffectual, he has sent to Pretoria for heavy siege guns, and will bombard Mafeking on Monday. Colonel Baden-Powell replied that the bombardment by the Boers of an inoffensive town packed with non-combatants would be held to constitute a precedent when British troops entered the Transvaal.

OCTOBER 23.

Tropical storms have delayed the conveyance of the enemy's heavy guns, and with them the attack which was promised for to-day. The resumption of the Boer bombardment is therefore deferred. Two seven-pounders under Lieutenant Hutchinson and Captain Williams engaged the Boer battery at the water springs from the reservoir early this morning. The Boers exchanged shells with us from a cannon on a kopje this afternoon. Otherwise the day has been quiet here, but there is tremendous activity in the Boer camp where they are building emplacements for siege guns to the south-west of the town. Meanwhile the enemy continue to direct their energies to unnecessary pillage and to raiding cattle, looting and wantonly destroying the homesteads of inoffensive whites and the kraals of natives. The natives accuse the Boers of outraging their women.

OCTOBER 24.

The enemy continue the work of getting their siege guns into position. A few shells have been thrown into the town to find an effective range. Every one here is prepared, and all our defences have been strengthened. The new Boer guns are reported to be a 64-pound howitzer and a 94-pound muzzle-loading siege gun.

OCTOBER 25.

This is the first day of the actual bombardment. Two hundred shells have been thrown into the town from their 7, 9, 12, 64, and 94 pounders at between 2,000 and 6,000 yards range. We have two men wounded, but none killed. Several buildings, however, have been wrecked, and the streets are ploughed up. Mafeking owes its salvation to its mud walls and tin roofs. We are completely surrounded by the enemy's position guns and intrenchments. The concussion of the explosion of the heavier shells shook the town, creating confusion, dust, and nervousness, but the panic subsequently subsided, and the townsfolk enjoyed comparative immunity from the effects of the shell fire by remaining within the shell-proof shelters. The women have already retired to a laager. About noon the Boers advanced to within 900 yards of the native stand on the west side of the town and 2,000 yards of the east side. Under the protection of their heavy guns they opened fire with their rifles. The natives behaved well. The Boers afterwards retreated with loss, and their fire was silenced. The bombardment ceased early this afternoon, the enemy effecting several reconnaissances to draw our fire. Our fire, however, was withheld, and the proceedings closed with the throwing of a few shells into the town during the night.

OCTOBER 26.

The enemy's siege guns resumed firing at daybreak, but only the buildings and the streets suffered. Their attack was directed against our redoubt and the redans which are constructed at prominent corners. Their rifle and shell fire was heavy on the east side, and we were unable to reply as the range was 3,000 yards. The steady downpour of rain interfered with any definite attack.

OCTOBER 27.

The town is holding out well, and shows great courage and determination. The enemy reopened their heavy bombardment at daybreak. The siege guns ceased firing at 9 o'clock to assume a position on the east side of the town as the buildings there are denser. There is no sickness here, and no cause for despair. The town is ignoring the Boers futile attempt to reduce it.

The scene was now set, with Buller moving to the relief of Ladysmith and Methuen marching towards Kimberley and Mafeking, for one of the worst series of disasters in British military history.

Notes

1. Deneys Reitz, *Commando* (London, 1950), p. 26.
2. Ibid., p. 43.
3. Pakenham, 1991, pp. 160–1.

Black Week, December 1899

'Today the God of our Fathers has given us a great victory' (Louis Botha after the Battle of Colenso).

As the British prepared their offensive, the Boers regrouped to meet the onslaught. General Joubert, injured in a riding accident, was replaced by Louis Botha, a much younger and more energetic man, who was well respected by all the elements of the Boer army. Botha took command over the key area along the Tugela River, where he dispersed his men in a line of commandos to await Buller's advance. However, it was Lord Methuen's command that was in action first, fighting three bloody, but indecisive, engagements at Belmont, Enslin and Modder River. These actions followed the pattern of all the previous engagements, with the Boers retreating to new lines of defences after inflicting heavy casualties on the British attackers. But *The Times* continued to place more emphasis on the gallant conduct of the British troops than on the tactical astuteness of the Boers.

NOV. 25.

Huge bonfires of scented mimosa scrub and night-long choruses with spasmodic instrumental accompaniment hailed the order for a 4 o'clock parade on Tuesday morning in marching order. Life in camps that had been monotonously alike and varied only by the nature of their discomforts suddenly received an impetus, and the welcome with which the men received at last the order to begin the march on Kimberley was universal.

In the earliest grey of the morning the camp was astir and the clanking wagons of the transport were already being shouldered through the deep ruts of the sand by the mules before 4 o'clock. The latter body was sent to our first halting place, Witteputs, by the north-western route, which struck the high road from Hopetown four or five miles out of Orange River. The troops, headed by the Grenadier

Guards, wound out of camp in a long sinuous line some three miles long, and followed the line of the railway for some eight or nine miles. A sharp turn to the left brought us to Finchams' Farm, a small oasis of green, with plenty of water, in the wilderness of karroo. Here we encamped and spent the night, starting in the early part of the following afternoon for Belmont, where a reconnaissance a week earlier had assured us that the enemy was to be found. Later in the day the sound of guns was heard two miles off, and upon arriving in camp at sundown we found the place deserted and the enemy reported near. *Reveillé* was ordered for half-past 1 on the following morning, and the two brigades under General Methuen moved out in silence in the darkness. As soon as the railway was reached the Northumberland Fusiliers moved off to the left, the Northampton men and the Yorkshire Light Infantry occupying the central position of a line of attack two miles long, the right of which was occupied by the Brigade of Guards. One of the features of the attack was the silence with which this extended body moved over the veldt without a word spoken or a verbal order given, in excellent dressing, and without a stumble or a careless clank of a bayonet or rifle to give an alarm. Perhaps the extreme caution was, in this case, superfluous. It became necessary, about a mile from the kopjes occupied by the enemy, to cut the wire fencing of the railway, the same fence that later in the day interfered fatally with the movements of our pursuing cavalry. This was done with a few sharp blows of an axe, but the sound must have been audible for a long way. Some time before I had ridden forward some two miles, crossing the railway near the platelayer's cottage, and listened. The utter silence was broken only by a few distant croaks from a buzzard; the strokes of the axe must have been as audible as pistol shots. The Boers had no pickets or patrols, and as the thin attacking line drew nearer and nearer uncertainty as to the presence of the enemy mingled unpleasantly with the feeling that if the Boer of the western border reserved his fire until his enemy was close he was a different and a more dangerous foe than the Natal sharpshooter at 2,000 yards. Still there was complete silence until we were within 250 yards of the line of kopjes. Then a star of white flame and a "phit" in the ground behind us told us that the hills were indeed occupied. The whole line from left to right broke at once into rifle fire together, and a series of flashes, poured out without intermission of time or space, outlined the crest of the enemy's position, now faintly discernible in the growing dawn.

The fire was indeed hot and was answered as long as our men were on the flat, but when the rocky ascent of the kopjes was reached there was no chance of returning the fire, as hands and knees and feet were alike used in the climb. Here the severest loss of the day was suffered, the Grenadier Guards in the centre of their brigade losing here some 40 or 50 killed and wounded.

When we reached the top the enemy had retreated to their second position, and were pouring bullets into their late stronghold. Lieutenant Russell's was only one example among many. Seeing that half his face was covered with blood I moved up to him and asked him where he was hurt. "Mere scratch," he answered, and went on. I passed a sergeant in the Scots Guards limping down hill as hard as he could; I wondered if he could keep it up much longer. Here and there were Boer wounded lying in pools of blood, but, according to their custom, the enemy had carried off most of their losses. The right of the line had also been carried by this time, and the Fifth were carrying on a sturdy assault on the left, where they were losing a good many under the well-covered fire from "Table Mountain". The Yorkshire Light Infantry moved up between the two positions to the relief of the Fifth and of the Guards, who were moving off the right hand spur of the second position to take the third. Here the fire was very severe; from every side the bullets were showering upon them, and of cover there was practically none. At this point the artillery opened fire, and with comparative ease the last third row of kopjes was taken, though the steepest and actually the most defensible position of any, was very remarkable. Here I noticed that the Guards were delivering volleys, the only instance of a variation from independent firing that I have yet noticed. On the left and centre the shooting was steady on both sides, one small sangar with about 30 men in it keeping at bay half a battalion. Eventually the usual white flag trickery was repeated, but a storm of British bullets greeted the treacherous fire of the Boers, who soon surrendered and crawled out unarmed. One of the saddest incidents of the fight was the death of Lieutenant Blundell, of the Grenadier Guards. Seeing his men firing at a man above him whose foot had been broken by a bullet, he called out to them to cease firing and went forward to help the Boer. The latter's only answer was to raise his rifle and shoot him through the body. An incident like this makes it hard for the officers to keep a hand over the men in battle, and these incidents have occurred in every fight of the war. Colonel Crabbe was wounded in a similar way, and Mr. Knight, correspondent of the *Morning Post*, suffered for responding at once to a flag of truce by standing up out of cover. Of individual gallantry there was much. The cool courage of both General Fetherstonhaugh and Colonel Arthur Paget deserves more than this passing mention. The quiet obedience to orders of the men was most striking, and the courage of the men then for the first time under fire promised much for the success of the march. In truth the division created by brigading together the Guards with such old campaigners as the Fighting Fifth and the Yorkshire Light Infantry possesses every possible advantage that prestige, experience, and pluck can give, and the hard fight they had is witness to the tough nature of the assault.

At 8.15 the firing, which from 4 o'clock had been incessant, showed some signs of decreasing, and bodies of mounted Boers crept away from the fighting line and galloped away northwards. The white flag was at last shown in earnest, and a burst of cheering greeted the first success of our journey. Details as to the numbers engaged have long ago been telegraphed home. Casualties, too, have been recorded, and there is perhaps no better summing up of the chief lesson of the fight than that of a corporal I heard expressing, in other words, his opinion that the rules of war had not been invented to be used as weapons by unscrupulous combatants. Admiration at the pluck of men who stand up against us, sympathy with an out-of-date but undoubtedly genuine national spirit, however badly expressed, even a willingness to give them the advantages of an etiquette they in turn are certain to deny to us vanish before the actual presence of these outrages, however we had come to expect them, and the actual sight of a dying officer butchered in return for his own eagerness to help the wounded is an argument that would convince the most sceptical that the Boer race is unfit for the ascendency it claims.

From a military point of view the experiment of carrying strong positions without previous shelling is, especially in view of recent losses in Natal, open to criticism, in spite of the fact that in this case the inevitable loss has been cheerfully accepted. Also the cavalry was not in a position to turn the defeat into a rout when called upon. Having said this much by way of criticism, it only remains to put on record the redoubled confidence in themselves with which the general's division resumed their march on the following evening, the last offices for the dead having been performed, and the last of the mimosa bonfires stamped out on the camping ground one mile south of Belmont.

At the Battle of Enslin the British continued to follow the same tactics of a heavy artillery bombardment followed by a frontal infantry attack, and again it resulted in a Boer retreat at the cost of heavy British casualties. From the despatch sent the following day we learn that the Army has limited the correspondents to despatches of 300 hundred words or less and we finally have some mention of conditions in the field. But we still have a failure to recognize the Boers' tactical plan.

MODDER RIVER, DEC. 1.

From the battlefield of Belmont, where the great aasvogels were slowly wheeling with motionless wings in huge circles through the blinding glitter of a South African sky, the division made its way on Friday to Graspan with the Yorkshire Light Infantry as advance guard.

It was a short march, and, like that from the Orange River, uneventful. Now and then the ground scouts in extended order flushed a covey of partridges or beat up a herd of sprinbok; once a flock of Kaffir cranes passed overhead with hoarse, gull-like cries, and always the quick lizards flashed in and out of the scrub under foot, but of the enemy there was no sign, though the entire line of march passed between kopjes some two thousand yards apart, and the cover afforded was perfect.

Graspan is a curious reminder of early volcanic activity now completely extinct in the continent. Few strata in the geology of the earth can exhibit a uniformity as universal as those of South Africa. Evidences of seismic disturbance, faults due to volcanic action, even gradients caused by subsidence are rarely seen, and the long extinct crater of Graspan, now a perfect circle of kopjes carpeted with the smoothest and softest of white sands, seemed almost out of place.

The scene at night in this huge Coliseum was extraordinary – the camp fires blazing round the mouth of the "pan", and the alternate dark and vividly lighted figures moving round them, the stars in the fleckless purple above, the dark forms stretched in rows upon the sand, and over all the half-pathetic beam of violet-white haze that now and again lighted the northern horizon, lending to the composition of the picture a note of human interest, and an insistent reminder of the end and aim of our journey.

To the last moment the position had been kept warm for us. Pickets were sent up at once to the surrounding heights, and in one of them was found, in a newly made sangar, a field-glass and a walking-stick still lying in an undusted state that proved that the Boers had occupied the place a few minutes before. Supper was

Methuen's infantry storming a
kopje at Gras Pan

soon cooked and eaten, and the column, wrapped in blankets, slept in the fast
cooling night.

Up betimes, indeed, and on to Enslin, some five miles on, which was reached in
the earliest dawn, the last two miles being covered in fighting formation, the naval
detachment and the 5th Fusiliers being supported by the Yorkshire Light Infantry
and the Northampton Regiment.

On this occasion the Guards had no share in the fighting that ensued, indeed, it
was not till late in the morning that they appeared. The Navy and the Y.L.I. won
the laurels of as hot a fight as Belmont and as plucky a storming of a fortified
height as stands to the credit of any regiment in the list.

The engagement began with a sharp artillery duel between the western batteries
on either side. There was no attempt to scale the kopjes at this end of the position,
a row of five heights – interconnected by neks – of which all except one, a small
hill commanded from either side, were strongly occupied. The armoured train was
met by a hot fire as it moved up, and retired, disgorging part of its crew to help in
handling the naval guns. From the railway eastwards to the last kopje, which lay
almost on the border of the Free State, the fighting was for a long time desultory,
but it was soon seen that this latter hill was the strongest position held by the
enemy, and was occupied by a stronger garrison than any other. It was necessary
that this position should be taken, and taken before a cloud of horsemen hovering
upon our flank could concentrate its strength upon our single brigade. The second
battery shelled the elaborate sangar at the top; for half an hour the bombardment
was kept up, with what result it is even now difficult to say – and a sustained, but

badly-aimed, fire was directed upon the guns and the supports in answer. The rifle fire – here as elsewhere – was evidently under no control. There was a great waste of ammunition, and a wish to make fancy long-distance practice on the part of the Boers was soon obvious. While riding up to the battery at work upon the hill, and while still at a distance of at least 1,600 yards, a steady "sniping" at me was indulged in by the Boers. It is sufficient for any one to be riding or not carrying a rifle to make him a target for long-range independent fire. The rule of the enemy to pick off officers is still fully enforced wherever there is the slightest chance of distinguishing one. Of course the late regulation forbidding officers to wear or bear anything marking them out from their men has had the best results. It is not too much to say that as the Zulu war stopped once for all the carrying of colours into action, so the present war will finally have forbidden officers to be in any way marked or distinguished from their men. Even the red chevrons of the non-commissioned officers have been found at Orange River too certain a mark, and they now wear on their sleeves a lightly ink-outlined indication of their rank.

The Naval Brigade that now moved up to the foot of the hill was destined to receive a terrible lesson. They advanced in extended order, but in converging upon the position to be taken they unconsciously found themselves closed in, and in that formation attempted the ascent. The fire directed upon them was terrible, and, distinguished by their swords, the officers were the first to fall. Commander Ethelstan was mortally wounded 50 yards from the first slope, and one by one the rest fell as they advanced, many with two or three bullet wounds. The slaughter was appalling to watch; the gallantry displayed was useless under the pitiless iron hail that was but slightly checked by the redoubled shelling of the reinforced battery. With a cheer the Yorkshire men – by a curious coincidence they had been conveyed from Mauritius by the very men to whose help they now came – ran up, pouring upwards a tremendous fusillade towards the crest of the sangar. Of course they lost heavily, but their open formation and the impossibility of distinguishing officers saved them from the concentrated fire that had deprived the naval detachment of their leaders, and little by little the thin line of khaki crawled up to the top.

The activity of the gunners was now extraordinary. Shell after shell burst upon the very edge of the sangar and the fire slackened perceptibly. The rampart that they had constructed now proved a serious disadvantage to the Boers. Except by leaning head and shoulders over the breastworks and exposing themselves to the storm of shrapnel that safeguarded the upward climb of the two regiments now reinforced by some of the Northumberland Fusiliers and the North Lancashire men, the Boers could deliver no effective fire, and many cautiously retreated to a second position from which they could fire upon the first of our men who reached the summit. The storming line was now so near the crest that the guns could only be directed upon the Boers enfilading the position from the spurs of the kopje on the left, and almost in a calm Lieutenant S.C. Taylor, closely followed by Lieutenant Jones, of the Marines, reached the outer works of the sangar and made their way over.

In the next half minute fifty men tumbled over and immediately rushed forward to clear the position in rear. This was, however, stubbornly held for a quarter of an hour, more, perhaps, as a screen than anything else to cover the retreat of the Boers, many of whom had already fled, broken into small parties hastening to their horses, which stood in safety some fifty yards down the hill on the other side. Whatever the cost, the position had been taken and the enemy fled almost simultaneously from the whole line. The artillery galloped round in rear of the position and shelled the crowds of flying horsemen that spotted the north roads, driving an arc of shells into the dense mass with astounding rapidity and accuracy.

Above, the hill-top was almost dripping with blood; not a boulder escaped its splash of crimson, and the innumerable splinters and chips of the ironstone blocks indicated the terrific nature of our fire. Most of the dead or wounded Boers were carried off – 50 of the more severely wounded were found in their hospital a quarter of a mile away – but here and there a dead man proved that here the Transvaal had sent its men down for the first time to meet the oncoming column. The rifles – carried away with even more sedulous care than their dead owners – were of German make, and two at least of the dead were members of Albrecht's foreign legion.

The skill and labour with which the summits of the kopjes had been prepared and fortified were extraordinary. The embrasures and head protections were most cleverly constructed, and the means of retreat – now a matter of no small importance for the Boers – had been as carefully provided for as the ground allowed.

Of the courage of the naval detachment and of the Yorkshire Light Infantry too much cannot be said. Man by man they climbed in the fiery hail and returned it with a steady courage and carelessness of loss that cannot be overpraised. Of the latter regiment, it is enough to say that E Company lost so many that it formed up after the fight under the command of the senior corporal. The wiry Yorkshire stock, confident in its continuous experience of war, and hard with a steady training of months, makes a man into a soldier after the heart of Napoleon, and the silent pride of their motto "Cedo nullis" was more than justified as they swung back into camp as steadily as though the loss of 53 of their best men were no great price to pay for work as well done as theirs.

On the other side, there were the same disgraceful scenes of cowardly firing upon the Red Cross that have become the rule and not the exception. Major Beevor, R.A.M.C., was fired upon as he conducted his bearers with laden stretchers from the field, and in one vile instance the fire came from a Boer ambulance wagon.

At night the troops bivouacked by the railway siding, the camps separated by the torn-up rails and broken and bent telegraph posts and rails, and already the aasvogels, summoned from some invisible quarter, were circling round the second battlefield of the relief.

But the Battle of Modder River was, in particular, a chilling warning of what was to come. One of the Boer commanders, De La Rey, brought into play the idea of utilizing the natural defensive strength of river barriers, but in a novel manner. Instead of constructing his defensive line of trenches behind the river, De La Rey dug his trenches a few yards in front of it. As the trenches were well concealed this gave the Boers a

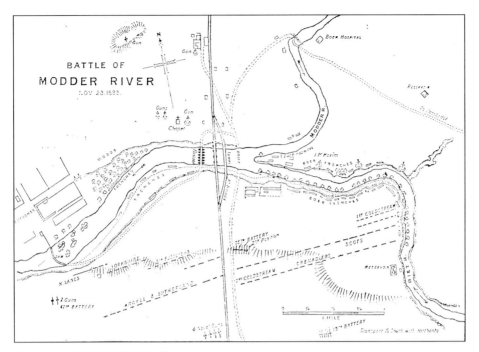

Plan showing the Battle of Modder River

strong element of surprise. It also dissuaded their men from retreating from the field
before heavy losses had been inflicted upon the enemy, as they needed the confusion
caused by such losses to make good their escape across the river. The Boers hidden in
the trenches were ordered to hold their fire until the British were well within rifle
range. The ground in front of the trenches had been carefully prepared. Coloured
marker stones were carefully laid out at accurately measured distances so that the
Boers' rifle sights could be adjusted for range before any firing began. In the previous
battles the Boers had been firing downhill, so that bullets which struck a target emerged
to hit the ground. At Modder River, because of the short range and level field of fire,
one bullet often injured more than one man. Finally, *The Times*' reporting of the battle
begins to acknowledge that the Boers had won at least a tactical victory, in that the
relief of Ladysmith had been delayed.

From Enslin, the column pushed on to Klokfontein, a halting place that
possessed the double advantages of good water in plenty and of being within
easy striking distance of Modder River. Water, of course, is, more than any other,
the question that decides the halting-place of the men; the colour of the water is of
no consequence – much of it on the march has been mahogany coloured – but free
from enteric germs and abundant it must be. With each battalion goes a water cart
that has pre-eminence above any transport except the ammunition carts, and the
need of it was never better shown than after the storming of Rooilaagte at Enslin.
Men lay down at the bottom of the hill on their stomachs and lapped up diluted

red mud, churned and fouled by a hundred mules, and scarcely fit for animals to drink. It is almost impossible to prevent them after the fever of excitement and a hard morning's work in the sun has gripped them. Luckily the ochreous mixture was pure enough, and no harm resulted.

Klokfontein is merely a farm upon a bluff surrounded by four vleis of varying degrees of muddiness. It had been deserted by the owners in the face of the British advance – a symptom of disloyalty that is no unfair test – and the general took up his quarters for the night in a room with a broken-in door, littered with many scattered photographs of the family of De Jongh. Everything of the least value had been removed.

Reports came in of the peaceful state of the neighbourhood; and the Boers were reported to be clear north of the river preparing for a last resistance at Spytfontein. Half way through the afternoon, however, a Rimington scout returned with a story of a skirmish and a retreat from an apparently empty cottage that proved to be a well-fortified block-house. This threw some doubt upon the rumours of serenity, and as the most careful examination of the spies failed to shake their contrary testimony, the general himself determined to reconnoitre the situation. Accompanied by but one or two of his staff he advanced to within a few hundred yards of the position at Modder River unmolested.

Nothing was more peaceful; a few Boers might be lurking in ambush and caution was therefore necessary, but the long descending sweep of the veldt towards the tree-lined course of the river – or rivers – betrayed nothing. There were no men to be seen, no earthworks, no unusual number of horses grazing, no banners floating from the tin-roofed white houses near the head of the bridge.

At 4 o'clock on the following morning, an hour before the time appointed, the column broke up the camp and moved forward, the Northamptons acting as advance guard, with the Yorkshire Light Infantry at the head of the main body. It was only a short march of some five or six miles, and before 7 the first shots had been fired by the artillery on the extreme right. The attack was answered at first vigorously, and the general, standing on the edge of a disused quarry, watched the practice of the guns with interest. One shell from the Boers fell among the artillery spare and reserve horses. But there was soon a lack of energy about this long range skirmish that made one contented to leave the spot and make one's way towards the Modder River Bridge, which was reported to be damaged by the Boers in a curious and effective manner – as indeed it is – firmly believing that the engagement could last but a few minutes longer. Leading my pony behind the second line of the Scots Guards, I was preparing to unstrap a camera from the saddle to take a photograph of the destruction when suddenly, without warning of any kind whatever, there burst out the most appalling fusillade from the immediate front. The Mauser bullets swept the field in thousands; half the leading company fell at once; the Maxim gun remained with its crew of men fallen round it, not one escaping. Every man at once threw himself on the ground except a few who took cover on the river bank on the right flank. For a moment nothing could be done, and the silky whistling of the Mauser bullet continued in unabated vigour sweeping the veldt for some 1,800 yards, and even wounding some of the staff, who must have been at least 2,500 yards from the firing line. Then an attempt, led by Captain Lowther, to collect a flanking force and join Colonel Paget and General Colvile was made in the cover afforded by the willows and the sandhills of the river bank.

This manoeuvre was, however, prevented by a well-directed enfilade, and it was felt that nothing could be done on the right flank until the guns had cleared the situation. These, which had been concentrated on the right, quickly came into action, and for the remainder of the day poured a continuous fire of shrapnel into the shelter trenches and embrasures of the Boers.

But so well had the fortifications been carried out that it was long before the rifle fire of the enemy was considerably affected, and even until sunset it was held impossible to risk the renewed disaster that must have followed any exposure whatever, and for the whole of the day the Guards Brigade lay on the open veldt in a heat that was actually 110deg. in the shade at midday. Meanwhile the left flank had not been idle, and after the general had personally led them to the summit of a slight rise that commanded the only possible means of crossing the river – the dam that had been built to turn the Modder River into an ornamental water for the picnics of the Kimberley excursionists – they moved in echelon towards the edge of the river bank on the enemy's extreme left.

That it could even be attempted to cross the river sliding sideways through the rush of water over the paddles along a rickety iron bar, one by one, clinging to the short supports in full view of the opposite shore, was an act of reckless heroism against which even the wary Cronje had not provided. This, however, is what was actually done, and it would be difficult to find a parallel for the stubborn pluck of the men who accompanied Colonel Barter across the 300 yards of dam and weir. One by one some 400 of them crossed. Then a detachment of the Royal Engineers, showing how well they could take their part in the forefront of the fighting line, followed them, after that some more of the Yorkshire Light Infantry. Little by little a force was collected which cleared several of the nearest houses on the right and effected an occupation of an irrigation patch from which they were never dislodged. Shortly before this Colonel Northcott, the general's *alter ego* and right hand, had been mortally wounded while riding away from the general's immediate neighbourhood on the latter's horse. To this is probably due the fact that Lord Methuen did not himself observe that the crossing had been effected, and was only informed of it after he had given an order for the left flank to retire to a position less swept by the iron hail that never ceased from the other bank of the river.

This, however, was fortunately not carried into execution, and there came almost immediately a lull in the firing. This curious suspense, in each case followed by redoubled activity, was repeated twice later in the day, and probably indicated physical weariness as much as anything else on the part of the enemy. To fight for thirteen hours is an ordeal that in any kind of warfare would be a terrible strain; but, out on the treeless, shadeless veldt with the thermometer at the degree above mentioned, the exhaustion suffered by our men was so great that in hundreds of cases men and officers alike slept as they lay in the scrub, careless of the shell and rifle fire that surged over them. To provide them with food was impossible, to bring a water-cart on to the field – as the Coldstream Guards found by bitter experience – was only tempting men to expose themselves to death,

Bivouac of General
Hamilton's mounted infantry
at the Modder

rushing for the water at all hazards, and leaving the cover, such as it was, afforded by the nine or ten inch growth of mimosa scrub.

Early in the afternoon the general was shot through the thigh, and for some time the two brigades, in the absence of orders, were compelled to act independently of each other, the only communication being a warning to the 9th Brigade not to fire upon the first, of which there was some danger. General Colvile, whose headquarters were in the laager on the right almost touching the river, then assumed command in the field, and a question arose as to the course to be pursued after the fall of dusk. At first the intention was to rush and bayonet the Boers in their trenches under cover of night, but this course was finally abandoned upon receipt of news that half the 9th Brigade were already across the river and safely intrenched. The plan adopted late in the evening was that the 1st Brigade, leaving only one battalion of Coldstream Guards on the right, should make their way across protected by the force already on the northern bank. This, however, was found to be unnecessary when morning came, as the Boers had evacuated the town bag and baggage, and retired to a position halfway between Modder River and Spytfontein.

Worse was to come for the British forces. General Gatacre ('Back-breaker' to his troops) was ordered by Buller to launch an attack in the middle of the Cape line to support Methuen's advance to his (Gatacre's) left. Gatacre advanced on 9 December: his plan was to carry out a night march to Stormberg Junction, an important railway junction on the line from East London to Bloemfontein. When the troops arrived,

Gatacre planned to carry out a surprise dawn attack. In theory the plan was sound; in practice it was a disaster. The men were exhausted before the night march began, and instead of reaching their objective a couple of hours before dawn (thus giving the men some rest), the guides took a wrong turn and the soldiers kept marching until daybreak, revealed them to the waiting Boers. Too tired to put up any real resistance, the British were soon overwhelmed. Although Gatacre's force sustained only 100 casualties, a further 600 men were captured due to an oversight on the part of the commander.

PUTTERSKRAAL, DEC. 7.

The move forward is at last at hand. A strong column will leave here by rail to-morrow evening, and, having detrained north of Molteno, march on to the Boer laager at Stormberg, which it is proposed to rush with the bayonet at 3.30 a.m. on Saturday. Only one field battery is to proceed with the troops, and this, having selected horses, is to be also conveyed by rail. The distance is about 25 miles, and would be far too much for horses only just off the ship, and General Gatacre has wisely decided against overtaxing their strength by such a march. Every one is to go as lightly equipped as possible, the baggage being left to follow the column later on. Sir William has most kindly arranged to have the horses of the newspaper correspondents conveyed with the train which carries the Headquarter Staff, so that it will be our own fault if we are unable to gain a fair idea of what takes place. To attempt such an enterprise on foot is of but little use, since a pedestrian with his limited powers of locomotion cannot cover a sufficiently wide area to gain a comprehensive view of operations upon even a reasonably large scale. We shall have somewhere about 2,500 of all ranks, including two and a-half battalions (less details) mounted infantry and artillery. It is a thousand pities that, owing to the delay in sending him reinforcements, the General is not in a position to do as he would have much preferred – make a decided move with the intention of sweeping the enemy right over the frontier by a continuous advance. But even what is about to be attempted must, if successful, be attended by very important results. The line to De Aar will be reopened within a few days, and the petty commandos in the Dordrecht and Barkly districts will be obliged to fall back as the only alternative to being destroyed in detail. A concentration of the enemy about Burghersdorp and a subsequent fight in that neighbourhood, probably at Albert Junction, may be expected to follow the Stormberg engagement. At all events, the immediate concentration of the enemy is a certainty; but there is of course a chance that his combined strength may be too great for us to tackle with the troops at present available; in which case we shall be obliged to await the arrival of reinforcements. Such delay, if it occurs, will be most regrettable since much moral effect will thus be lost.

DECEMBER 8.

The move northwards has been postponed until to-morrow, the reason being, I believe, that after further consideration it has been decided that an earlier start than that arranged for to-day will be necessary in order to reach the enemy's position before break of day. Under present arrangements, therefore, we shall leave here about the middle of the day to-morrow. The 16th Field Hospital under Major

Lilley, R.A.M.C., only arrived in camp yesterday, and although fully efficient in every way, I imagine that a start off to fight a battle on the very same evening would have been a somewhat severe test.

DECEMBER 12.

I have had neither time nor opportunity to write more until now, and the task before me is a very difficult one.

General Gatacre had under his command in this district only three and a-half battalions, two batteries field artillery, and some 850 mounted infantry and volunteer horsemen. The Colonial Boers were joining the enemy in considerable numbers, and it appeared very needful to strike a blow that would have sufficient influence to check the stream of rebellion. Stormberg Junction had been occupied by the enemy, who had thus cut the lateral communications by rail and telegraph with the British forces under Lord Methuen and General French to the westward. At first sight it may appear as if all Sir William Gatacre needed to do was to move forward his troops north of Molteno to a position of observation threatening Stormberg, and by so doing, even if obliged to delay an attack upon the Boers at that place, overawe the disaffected. But inactivity after a forward movement will generally, and rightly, be interpreted as a confession of inability to proceed further, and such, pending the arrival of reinforcements, would have been the actual condition of affairs. Moreover, with the forces at his disposal the General was not strong enough to maintain himself in the vicinity of the enemy and also to guard his own communications. Something therefore needed most urgently to be done, and Sir William elected to adopt a bold course. Accordingly he arranged for a sudden swoop by rail upon Molteno from Putter's Kraal, followed by a night march and an attack at dawn upon the enemy's position. That the enterprise involved extreme risk, and that such an attack upon a difficult position that had not been properly reconnoitred by efficient staff officers is against the principles of war, it would be idle to deny. Yet there are occasions when the true instinct of a commander leads him to disregard all rules and accept the risks that his conduct may entail upon him. The whole question turns upon the value of the advantages consequent on success in comparison with the losses that may be incurred in case of failure. General Gatacre was quite aware that he might incur disaster, but he considered it his duty to face the risks before him without regard for his own reputation or any other considerations except the immense gains to the British cause that would assuredly accrue in the event of victory.

I am fully persuaded that the decision to carry the Stormberg position by a *coup de main* was justified by the circumstances under which it was arrived at. Certainly, had the enterprise proved successful no one who attempted to pass hostile criticism upon the victorious General could have obtained so much as a hearing. The actual failure was due to a variety of accidents, some of which, it is true, were not unavoidable.

Stormberg Junction, at the foot of the "Rooi Kop," a considerable mountain overlooking the station, is situated about nine miles to the north of Molteno, the magnetic bearing being 356deg. The Rooi Kop has its greatest length north and south, and to the north-west, west, and south-west of it were the Boer positions and the scene of the fight. The intention of the General was to fall upon the south-western portion of the Boer defences by inclining somewhat to the westward and then coming up in a north-easterly direction upon the right front of the enemy. In the event – owing, no doubt, to some extent, to the darkness – the guide at the head of the column lost his way, with the result that the force made a wide detour to the westward, circling completely round until, returning from the north-west, it struck the right rear in place of the right front of the enemy.

Owing to various delays upon the railway, the start from Molteno took place two hours later than had been intended, and this fact, added to the immense increase in the length of the march, deprived our troops of the aid which the moon would otherwise have afforded upon the road to their halting place, and further, which was even more detrimental, necessitated their subsequent advance against the enemy being proceeded with after only one hour's rest instead of three. The infantry had been at work, or in the train in open trucks, or marching since 4 a.m. on Saturday morning. The actual march occupied seven hours, and it is, therefore, little to be wondered at that the men were wholly incapable of making a supreme effort when at last they were surprised by receiving fire at short range whilst marching in fours in fancied security. On receiving the enemy's fire the companies at hand rushed at once against the kopjes from which it proceeded and, advancing from boulder to boulder, swiftly commenced to ascend. Indeed, it is the fact that a considerable number actually reached within a few yards of a lower line of "scanses" which could not, however, be reached without ladders. But at this juncture our own artillery, failing in the yet uncertain light to observe the ascent of the infantry, opened fire upon the enemy, and several shells falling short dealt destruction amongst the assailants of the position. A partial retirement instantly ensued, and, having been brought to a standstill, the attack gradually melted away until, convinced that the case was hopeless, the General ordered the "retire" to be sounded. Had the order been promptly obeyed the troops might not improbably have been withdrawn without very serious loss, and a fresh attempt might even yet have been successfully prosecuted. But it was not to be. Many men were loth to retire because they were anxious to go on, whilst not a few were so utterly exhausted that they simply preferred to stay where they were, at all hazards, than to undertake the ordeal of a rapid retirement over the open ground at the foot of the hills. Eventually over 500 unwounded men were taken prisoners. Steadily, as if on parade, the retirement was executed by those who responded to the order, the soldiers moving back at a steady pace, without the least hurry or confusion, and halting constantly to fire. As an example of rear guard skirmishing the performances of the Northumberland Fusiliers and Irish Rifles could scarcely have been surpassed. Disputing every inch of ground the survivors of the ill-fated attack finally gained a line of low hills, which formed a horse shoe about 1,500 yards west of the scene of their repulse and from which the road by which the column had advanced shortly before was within easy reach. It was indeed fortunate that this most excellent rallying position was at hand. Whilst a sufficient portion lined the crests and easily kept the enemy back the remainder were re-formed in rear. Then, finally, when all hope of collecting more men had to be abandoned, the General gave orders for the retreat upon Molteno.

Fortunate, indeed, was it that at the last moment, before leaving Putter's Kraal, Sir William decided to take both batteries of artillery in place of only one. Had there been but one battery the entire force must have fallen into the hands of the enemy. Never were batteries more skilfully handled. Retiring alternately from position to position the gunners splendidly atoned for the mischance of the earlier morning. The courage and steadiness of all ranks in the 74th and 77th Field Batteries undeniably saved the remnant of the infantry and themselves also from destruction or capture. Even as it was, had the enemy shown the very least enterprise, the situation must soon have become desperate. The mounted troops, too, vied with the artillery in their unflagging energy and devotion, but all would have been unavailing had the enemy pursued his advantages with courage and average common sense. Our line of retreat lay round the circumference of a circle of which the enemy held the centre, so that from first to last the Boers possessed the advantage of working on interior lines. Their heavy guns, themselves in complete security upon account of their superior range, swept the plains over which the tired troops were wearily plodding. The fire was beautifully directed, but fortunately harmless, owing to the shells being nearly all plugged. Bursts were quite the exception. Be all this as it may, it is at least certain that before many miles had been traversed in retreat stragglers were the rule and formed bodies the exception. Amongst the latter a party of the Royal Irish Rifles was most skilfully directed and kept well in hand by the adjutant, Lieutenant Sitwell, whose behaviour was distinctly conspicuous. I am certain that, say, five miles from Molteno, 300 average good men could easily have rolled up the entire column – all that was needed was to head it and swallow it by driblets as it came along.

So far as I can understand the matter the causes to which this most lamentable failure must be attributed are as follows:–

(1) The map of the ground was utterly misleading and worse than useless. Not only was the contouring so incorrect as to give a totally false picture of the configuration of the hills, but the actual distances and the roads were inaccurately represented.

(2) So far as I am aware, no one amongst the responsible authorities had taken any compass bearings, and consequently no one knew where he was being taken in the dark. A knowledge of the general direction in which it was intended to proceed and occasional reference to the compass would have sufficed to disclose the fact that the guide completely boxed the western half of the compass-dial – concluding with a straight shot at the needle-axis – instead of keeping a line pointing a few degrees west of north.*

(3) The Berkshire Regiment, by whom the redoubts now occupied by the Boers at Stormberg had been built, and to whom every inch of the ground was familiar, were left at Queenstown instead of being employed to recapture the works which they had so unwillingly evacuated about a month previously. The consequence of no one knowing where he was going or what he had to attack, or when proximity to the enemy had been reached, was that the infantry, marching in fours, were suddenly fired into at a point where after ascending but a few feet their further advance against the enemy was precluded by an unclimbable precipice. The moment that the first shots were fired companies doubled straight at the points

whence the firing seemed to have proceeded and commenced to scale the hill. Soon, however, they came upon a perpendicular wall of rock, from the summit of which the Boers were plying their rifles at half-a-dozen yards' distance. Here fell Lieutenant-Colonel Eagar, and close to him Major Seton of the Royal Irish Rifles. Colonel Eagar was the man who reached the highest point attained by any of the attackers, and was then shot down, where many another British officer has fallen before now, at the head of his battalion, gallantly leading them as in the days of old when long-range-weapons had not been invented.

(4) Over 500 men, afterwards made prisoners, had fallen into a trap from which they failed to extricate themselves. Consequently when the rest of the force had been rallied upon a defensive position in rear the General had not forces sufficient to warrant a fresh attempt upon some selected point of attack.

(5) In any case the men, who had been by this time on the move for over 24 hours on the stretch, who had just completed seven hours' marching through the night, and who had been actually under arms for upwards of 16 hours, were so dead beat that severe hill fighting was quite beyond their powers. During the actual retirement from the hills attacked – or rather under which we were ourselves attacked in anticipation – men were falling asleep in the open ground, under fire, after or before using their rifles. No sooner did they halt to fire than they fell forward sound asleep. An officer told me that he awoke several such men by kicking them soundly and thus insisted upon their continuing their retreat to a place of safety.

(6) The guns were at first in the same trap as the infantry and were compelled to retreat some distance over very difficult ground before they could come into action upon, even then, a poor position, with most inferior command. During this movement a gun was lost in consequence of being stuck fast and the struggling horses shot down by the enemy. It was a pitiable sight, of which those who saw it cannot speak without emotion.

Finally, to state the case in brief. The position to be attacked had not been reconnoitred by any of those to be engaged against it, and even its exact situation was unknown to any of them. The information supplied by the Intelligence Department was complete and accurate, but owing to the misdirection of the march its value was thrown away. The distance to be marched was nearly doubled. The start was two hours late, so that the moon set long before the journey had been completed to an intermediate halting-place, and the men lost the rest that they so much needed. Day broke without the point of attack having been reached, and at the time when the enemy opened fire the column was unsuspiciously "route marching." Both battalions were winding along the foot of the hill and were fired upon simultaneously; both consequently became at once engaged in a skirmishers' fight, so that there remained no formed body of troops to interpose by any deliberate action in accordance with any fixed idea.

Defeat in such circumstances was the natural consequence. The only marvel is that the force escaped annihilation; certainly but for the good work done by the artillery and by the mounted troops not one man could have reached Molteno, although the shooting of the Boer riflemen was contemptible in the extreme. Worse shooting in action than that of the Boers in the Stormberg engagement has, perhaps, never been seen in war. Moreover, the failure of the enemy to make any determined attempt to cut off the straggling procession of worn-out troops denotes either strange want of confidence or incompetence. That we should have been beaten by such an enemy renders our case the more deplorable. Our retreat was molested merely by "snipers". Upon the other hand, the Boer artillery practice was splendid. They had no field artillery, and apparently not more than two mobile guns. Some say that they had but two guns in all, including the 40-pounder in a fixed position. Yet they succeeded in teaching most of us what it is like to come under a well-directed shell fire. Luckily, however, we had our instruction at small cost to ourselves, since few of the Boer shells burst. This was no doubt a cause of disappointment to their gunners – but not to ourselves.

It was, I think, a pity that the two companies of the Royal Scots and the 12th Company R.E., who remained in Molteno, were not ordered out to cover the retirement of the troops. The occupation of one very awkward position about three miles from Molteno by fresh troops was most desirable. Had the Boers been enterprising and made use of this position, we should have been cut off when actually in sight of our goal.

STERKSTROM, DEC. 13.

I omitted to mention that the armoured train which advanced toward Stormberg from Molteno had a narrow escape. The Boers had laid a pretty little trap by partially removing fish plates and getting ready a big gun to open on the train as soon as it got into difficulties. The sharp eyes of those in the train were, however, destined to perceive the trick, and a halt in time saved the situation. No sooner had the train come to a standstill than the gun opened fire, the range evidently having been measured, since the first shot was pretty close and the second and third within a few feet. The range was about 7,000 yards. Lieutenant Gosset did not wait for more. Forty-pounder shells cannot be digested, even by armoured trains.

It should also be noted, in order to show how early in the proceedings misfortunes commenced to befall, that the field hospital, bearer company, Maxim gun of Royal Irish Rifles, with sundry ammunition wagons and other vehicles, lost the column at the very start, and pursued the direct road to Stormberg, upon which they bivouacked at the point C, shown on the accompanying rough sketch. At dawn, this detachment, guided by a native policeman, moved round to the west, and eventually rejoined the column during its retreat. Until this reunion took place, the troops were absolutely without any hospital or ambulance.

*[Note. – Our Special Correspondent at Cape Town, in forwarding this account of General Gatacre's repulse, makes the following interesting comment:– "Your Correspondent with General Gatacre, I think, exaggerates this point. Owing to the abundance of magnetic ironstone all over South Africa (and the name "Rooi-kop", "red-head", probably indicates its presence near Stormberg) compass bearings are liable to be all over the place, especially at night, when it is impossible to know how near one may be to magnetic rocks. At Chieveley one day I was taking some bearings which made Colenso lie due east instead of north, north for the nonce happening to be a large stone a yard or two away."]

As a postscript to his report of the battle, *The Times*' correspondent gives a vivid description of what went wrong on Gatacre's night march, and in doing so provides an insight into the perils of war reporting.

STERKSTROM, DEC. 13.

Since concluding my letter this afternoon, in which I endeavoured to describe and to some extent account for the disaster which we have experienced, it has occurred to me a narrative of my own adventures during the eventful 10th of December and the night of the 9th might be interesting to some of your readers. The infantry marched off at 9.15 p.m., and, as we were unwilling to give our horses unnecessary fatigue by a long march at infantry pace, two other Correspondents and myself waited half an hour with the intention of accompanying the artillery. The latter, however, not being ready to move so soon as we had expected, we followed after the infantry, whom we supposed to have proceeded by the Stormberg road which runs in a northerly direction from the town of Molteno. We did not hurry ourselves, but rode at a leisurely pace, making about five miles an hour. At the end of a little more than an hour and a quarter we began to wonder why we had not overtaken the column, and shortly after one of us dismounted, lit a match, and examined the road in search of footprints. There was no fresh "spoor" whatever, of horse or foot, except the tracks of our cart; all else was quite stale. What, then, were we to do? That we were on the direct road to Stormberg was certain, and also that this road was the one which we had been informed would be used by the column. Naturally, we concluded the infantry must have moved off the road by some Kaffir path which we had failed to notice. After a brief consultation we decided to return and meet the artillery; and this we did in some haste lest they also might perhaps elude us. At the end of about two miles we heard wheels, and supposing the sound to herald the approach of those whom we sought we halted and dismounted to await their arrival. To our surprise the supposed artillery turned out to be the hospital and bearer company, with sundry ammunition wagons, a Maxim gun, and other odds and ends. At the head of this conglomeration rode Colonel Edge, R.A.M.C., to whom I addressed myself. He had been ordered, he told me, to "follow the artillery," and he was naturally astonished when I explained to him that he was actually following nobody. At this juncture there arrived two sergeants of the Cape Mounted Police, who were likewise under the impression that they were following the detachment of their own corps. From these we learned that the nearest Boer laager was about two miles beyond the point from which we three Correspondents had just returned. The time was now 11.30 p.m.

After a consultation it was agreed that we should ride back to Molteno and report to Lieutenant-Colonel Waters, D.A.A.G., who had been left in command, and from him learn what was to be done. It was at least obvious either that the column had taken the wrong road or else that the detachment which we had encountered had lost its way. The moon had now set, and we could not ride very fast. However, at the best pace that we could muster we hurried back to Molteno, the police who accompanied us examining the tracks they knew of, so as to detect the spoor of the column in case it had anywhere left the road. Our impression, however, was that the troops must have taken the Steynsburg road direct from Molteno, and this we eventually found was the case. It may here be mentioned that Molteno is generally placed wrong on the maps of South Africa. It is the first station south of Stormberg Junction, from which it is nine miles distant. Having arrived at Molteno Station, we speedily roused Colonel Waters and explained the situation. One of the chief *employés* of the Intelligence Department was present, and he assured the colonel, from our description of where we had been, that the detachment was on the right road. Naturally, therefore, Colonel Waters could do no more than request us to tell Colonel Edge to proceed. In short, the officer left in command at Molteno was not aware, nor was his civilian assistant in the Intelligence branch, that the general had changed his plans and elected to march by the westerly route.

We felt very small and very much annoyed. We had deliberately undertaken a task which involved adding 12 miles or more to our night's journey – for nothing – and, what was worse, we had no idea where to find General Gatacre's troops. However, there was nothing for it but to return to Colonel Edge, as we had promised, so away we went. Within a mile and a half we met the entire detachment marching back towards Molteno! Colonel Edge and those with him, instead of remaining where they were until we returned, had decided that they must clearly be on the wrong road, and they preferred therefore to anticipate the order to return which they expected us to bring. This gave the wretched mules an extra six to seven miles' work. Once more the column reversed and set out for the second time towards Stormberg.

Leaving the wagons to follow at their own pace, we trotted forwards, accompanied by the policemen as a sort of advanced guard. Just before we reached the furthest point to which we had attained on the previous occasion we heard wheels and voices from the westward, and, riding up, found one white and four black policemen with two mule, wagons, one of which carried the reserve ammunition of the Northumberland Fusiliers. In answer to our inquiries, the constable, who did not strike me as an intelligent man, stated that he had lost the column in the dark and had struck across the veldt so as to find the main road – and, in short, here he was.

The time was now 2.30 a.m., and it was decided to wait where we were until dawn. The drivers of the wagons were told to outspan and feed their mules. At 3.45 we got ready our horses and, accompanied by the police, cantered forward to reconnoitre. The police sergeants went to the westward, while the three correspondents and four blacks went east at first, and then, working gradually north and west, on hearing the firing to our left front, we cautiously approached the Boer positions amongst the kopjes west of Stormberg. By 4.30 we had clearly located the scene of the fighting, upon which I sent back one of the blacks who knew the road to tell Colonel Edge what we had discovered and to guide the lost detachment into the region where its various contingents would find their proper spheres of usefulness. The black faithfully and successfully performed his task, and consequently the wounded men eventually had one ambulance, otherwise there would have been none. A civilian, whose name I regret having forgotten, drove out with a Cape cart from Molteno and did excellent service, disregarding his own safety and deliberately remaining for many hours under shell-fire conveying wounded men from the rear.

But to return to my story. Having duly sent off the black to Colonel Edge, we continued upon our way, winding in and out amongst the kopjes opposite to those along which we could see the Boers hurrying along towards the scene of the fight. So intent were they upon this that they disregarded or failed to see us. At all events, we were only once fired at throughout our progress from opposite the centre of their position until we passed round the western flank and there joined the right of Gatacre's troops on the defensive position to which we had observed them retiring. Up to this point we had no reason to suppose that any greater evil had happened than that the attack had failed. For this we were in a measure prepared, as the firing had not commenced until after daylight and had not been heavy. We, therefore, supposed that, having arrived late, our people had found the enemy wide awake and had merely done some little skirmishing in order to disengage themselves. The regular and leisurely mode of retirement which we had observed naturally encouraged us in this belief. As I stood under shelter of a friendly boulder on top of a convenient kopje watching the retirement, I almost forgot my disappointment at the failure which it indicated in my admiration for the manner in which it was being carried out.

A few hundred yards before we reached the right of our firing line on the ridge of low kopjes where the defensive position had been taken up we met Captain Amphlett's company of mounted infantry galloping forward to seize a favourable covering position further to the right of the British force. This proved an excellent move. The line of retreat for our men was on the circumference of a semi-circle, the centre point of which, together with the entire diameter, was in the hands of the enemy. The resistance offered by the mounted infantry for a long time prevented the enemy from utilizing some of the most favourable ground that would otherwise have been at his disposal upon our exposed flank. Riding up on to the ridges I met Captain Riddell, of the Northumberland Fusiliers, whose company was deployed along the crest line, and at his request cantered further to the right in order to ascertain whether some men whom he had observed coming back towards that part were actually arriving, he having lost sight of them. Just as I reached the kopje, which had hitherto hidden them from view, I came upon the party coming in all right, so was able to return and reassure Riddell as to their fate. Little, however, did either of us then realize that not less than 500 men in addition to the killed and wounded were boxed up in a trap and were shortly to be made prisoners. The few regarding whom we were at the moment interested represented merely a tiny fragment that had succeeded in breaking loose.

It was curious how few at this time seemed to have grasped the fact that we were in an extremely tight place, but by degrees it dawned upon us. I talked for some time with the men of the Northumberland Fusiliers who were lying down in quarter column about 200 yards in rear of the ridges, my object being to get the soldiers' idea about what had taken place. That there had been very bad luck and that they wished that they themselves had been in front at the time seemed to be the only ideas prevailing. That there might be any further danger or difficulty did not seem to have crossed their minds. By degrees, however, from what I heard from various officers I came to understand that we had had a very serious beating, and that more excitement would assuredly follow. Accordingly, I rode back towards the ridges, intending to have a good look round and obtain some notion of the general situation. Just, however, as I arrived, the troops received the order to retire on Molteno, and various local matters put general considerations out of my head. First there was a sergeant of the Northumberlands who dislocated his ankle amongst the boulders, and immediately afterwards there was a young subaltern of the Irish Rifles, named Stevens, who had been shot through both lungs. The latter, under the circumstances, naturally interested me most, but my relations with the former resulted in an amusing incident which is worth telling, and to which I shall therefore refer presently. Meanwhile, the career of Lieutenant Stevens was remarkable. From the ridge he walked down for several hundred yards supported by two men of his regiment. Then for about three-quarters of a mile four riflemen carried him in a blanket. From the blanket he was transferred to an ammunition wagon, upon which he was carried about a mile or more. His next conveyance was a hospital stretcher, and, finally, after a still longer interval, he reached the ambulance. Nothing but the marvellous pluck and endurance of the man could have saved him. Hurt as he was nine men out of ten would have sunk from exhaustion. But Stevens had always a cheery smile as one rode up to see how he was getting on, and as he jolted along upon the ammunition wagon he laughed heartily when I told him how the black police who had been with me in the morning had deserted me in order to steal Boer horses that had stampeded during the firing. I was delighted to hear yesterday when the P.M.O. returned from Queenstown that Stevens is doing well and likely to recover. The sergeant also, I was rejoiced to learn, had reached the hospital. I was afraid that, after all, he might have been left on the road for reasons that will presently be explained.

From the ridges this sergeant rode my horse to the rear with strict injunctions to send it back immediately, so soon as some other means of conveyance had been reached. My meaning, of course, was that a mounted man should lead back the horse. But it so happened that when my friend the sergeant caught up the ambulance the horse was handed over to some man or other belonging to I know not what, but, at all events, a man who had no rifle. This worthy, finding himself in possession of a horse, preferred to ride it himself to returning it to its rightful owner – and he rode it accordingly. Retribution, however, was speedily to fall upon him. Taking a short cut round a kopje, I intercepted him when emerging from a defile and had my revenge. Observing that he was unarmed, I thrust into his unwilling hands the rifle I had taken from the sergeant and also made him take over a couple of handfuls of ammunition which I produced from my pockets. He had made me walk perhaps two miles with a rifle, but in the end he himself had to tramp 12 carrying the same weapon into Molteno! It was, perhaps, two hours later when I again met my sergeant. Major Lilly, R.A.M.C., had asked me to ride forward to catch the ambulance and, having turned out of it any men who could bear travelling on carts or wagons, to bring it back to pick up some bad cases in rear. Amongst those whom the non-commissioned officer in charge of the ambulance caused to dismount was my sergeant, who inquired anxiously after his rifle. I reassured him as to this, and then left him sitting at the side of the road whilst I returned with the ambulance. When riding back once more I did not see him, so assumed that he had been picked up, but was much troubled about him and naturally thankful when next day I was able to ascertain for certain that he had safely reached his journey's end. It would have been hard had I, after being instrumental in his being originally enabled to leave the field, been the cause of his being hereafter left behind and made a prisoner.

During the rest of the march I do not think that any further proceedings of mine are worth writing about. I watched our artillery practice, and observed how excellently our mounted troops anticipated the enemy by taking possession of successive kopjes from which to keep him at a distance. The enemy, moreover, was, I thought, most unenterprising, and, except by the fire of his big gun of position, did but little to interfere with our retreat. This gun was well placed to command the road, and its fire was admirably directed. Fortunately, its shells generally failed to burst, and I do not believe it succeeded in doing us any damage. Finally, having been with the troops from about 5.30 a.m. until 10.15, I trotted along for the last couple of miles to Molteno and dismounted at the Central Hotel at 10.45. I have seen in my life one or two ticklish fights, but at Stormberg for the first time I was enabled to realize what actual defeat means. It was, indeed, a case of *vae victis*. The hopeless exhaustion of the unhappy soldiers was terrible to see.

After the Battle of Modder River, Cronje the Boer commander moved his forces back to a line of kopjes at Magersfontein, where the Boers proceeded to construct a defensive position of great strength and sophistication in front of this line of low hills. Dispensing with their traditional method of fortifying the hills themselves, they dug a series of concealed trenches at an angle, so that any troops advancing on them would be channelled into the centre of the Boer line and would thus have to face the heaviest possible concentration of fire. After a day's rest Lord Methuen decided to move against the Boer position in a surprise night attack. He ordered the Scottish Brigade led by General Archie Wauchope to carry out this attack. Wauchope was a genuine Victorian hero; in the three previous colonial wars that he had fought in he had received severe wounds and survived. Late in the afternoon of 10 December, Wauchope led the Scottish regiments forward but their advance was impeded by a furious thunderstorm accompanied by heavy rain. As dawn broke over the plain in front of Magersfontein, the Scots unknowingly arrived in front of the Boer trenches. As they moved forward to attack the supposed Boer stronghold in the hills, the Boers opened fire from their concealed trenches almost at the feet of the advancing Scots. The result was predictable devastation and confusion. Wauchope and numerous other officers were killed in the first minutes of the attack as they sought to lead their men forwards.

MODDER RIVER, DEC. 14.

Perhaps I had hardly expected to write this letter from the same place as the last, but the issue of the battle at Magersfontein last Monday has postponed the actual relief of the diamond city for some days, perhaps weeks. Before I attempt any comment upon it the actual sequence of events in the engagement must be remembered. During a halt of 12 days at Modder River, during which our forces were reinforced by the Highland Brigade, one howitzer battery, one horse battery, the 12th Lancers, a balloon section, and a 4.7 naval gun from her Majesty's ship Doris – promptly christened "Joe Chamberlain" by the entire division – the work done by the Royal Engineers in throwing across the Modder a temporary railway bridge and a pontoon bridge, each a fine piece of engineering completed within seven days from the battle, had made the advance of the reinforcements possible. In the former case the old gradients from the level of the existing railway to the level of the river have not been used, a new cutting being made 50 yards up stream on either side of the river, and the rails carried across on cairns and sleepers, where they will remain until the floods wipe them away. Even then the cuttings will still represent this curious substitute for the steel bridge now daily falling into a worse state of twisted uselessness and danger.

On Sunday afternoon warning was sent round to the troops to hold themselves in readiness for an advance, and the 30 oxen that draw the 4.7 gun plunged and swerved away to an eminence a mile from the station, marked by a platelayer's hut, from which point the whole of the enemy's centre, some three and a half miles distant, was within easy range. The howitzers moved out and the field and horse batteries, convoyed by the Highland Brigade, took up positions about 2,800 yards from the kopjes that had been surveyed for days beforehand and known to be heavily intrenched. Fire was opened about half-past 4, and until nightfall a steady and, as was afterwards found, a most effective, bombardment was kept up.

The Boers themselves have admitted that their losses were far heavier from shell-fire on Sunday than on the following day, giving as the reason that the effect of lyddite acting upon the ironstone rock had been infinitely more widely spread than when, on Monday, aim was particularly directed upon the trenches constructed some hundred yards from the foot of the kopjes.

Cronje is credited, with perhaps some truth, with having purposely dug his outworks at some distance from the safer ground of the kopjes themselves in order to prevent a certain unwilling part of his army from bolting back when our fire became too hot. Certainly it was impossible for any Boer to retreat without being instantly shot, and, heavily mauled as they were, the trenches were throughout manned without reinforcements by the men who filled them in the morning. Another reason that will occur as likely to prompt the device is the well-known attraction that any elevated object has for a gunner. It is more difficult to drop ten shells a hundred yards short of a conspicuous object than to send 30 into it.

There was little fire in answer, and no lights appeared on the crests of the hills during the evening.

From the extreme left of the position it was possible to see small bodies of Boers watching this artillery duel from a kopje in safety until a shell from the heavy gun sent them cantering towards Douglas, a place that may give us some trouble yet. The belief that the trenches were but thinly occupied was by no means held on the left flank, and General Pole-Carew fully recognized the seriousness of any attempt to storm the fortifications which, as usual, were designed with extraordinary skill by Albrecht, the German expert.

Since the fight took place the intrenchments have been greatly strengthened, and it is doubtful whether the loss of life that must be suffered in any attempt to take the position is worth incurring for a victory which can be achieved in any other way. From west to east the kopjes are fringed with intrenchments, carried on their eastern extremity across the plain of slightly rising ground, dotted with shrubs and small thickets, as far as the river. Thus, some five miles of earthworks from the south-east spur of Chief Kopje have been constructed, and the enemy were certainly occupying the entire line from end to end, besides the large bodies under cover upon the sides of the kopjes, in the sangars built upon the crest of the hills, and in reserve behind the heights.

Estimates of the numbers of the Boers present vary considerably, but all things point to 15,000 as being approximately correct. Our forces numbered about 11,000 of all arms, including reserves, Army Service Corps, and others who had no place in the fighting line.

This force moved forwards under cover of the night, and the Highland Brigade, to whom was entrusted the duty of making the first assault, soon vanished in the darkness. They had been expected to make their way to the south-eastern face of the kopjes and then extend for attack as soon as there was light enough to see their way, but by a mistake the entire brigade, still in quarter-column – the least effective of all formations, and that affording the most certain target, in fact, a formation that should never have been used within the range of the largest ordnance possessed by the enemy – found itself within 400 yards of the southern face of the enemy's position opposite to the barbed wire entanglements of the strongest intrenchment of the entire line of defence.

A moment later a single shot was followed by a fusillade that must have emptied the magazine of every Boer rifle for a space of a quarter of a mile. Beneath this hell of fire discipline vanished, the men broke and fled, leaving on the field dead, dying, or wounded, one man in every five of the 3,000 men who but 30 seconds before had been marching at ease, trusting absolutely to their leaders, and thinking of nothing less than that, in march-past formation, they were to be instantly called upon to face at point-blank range the most devastating volley that has probably been poured into any body of men. Recharging magazines delayed the Boers a moment, but in the Mauser system this operation wastes much less time than our own. The darkness, more than any possible cover, saved our men from a second catastrophe, and there was entire silence as the shattered remnants of the brigade made their way back. This silence was broken at last by a huge lyddite shell from the naval gun, bursting on the spur to the left of the scene of disaster. From that time onwards artillery became the chief feature of the day, and the accuracy and steadiness of their fire while within rifle range of the shelter trenches and the promptness and energy with which they eventually covered the retirement of the troops deserve the highest praise.

A few shots, not perhaps 50 in all, were fired by the enemy, but their guns were quickly silenced, and the only fighting that took place for some hours was on the right. Here the mounted infantry and cavalry were early in touch with the Boers, backed by Major Allason's Horse Battery, which galloped forward and took up a position a mile and a half east of the kopjes enfilading the trenches on their left, and sweeping the containing line of intrenchments running eastward to the Modder. The mounted infantry early in the day pushed forward too far, and were at one time cut off by a body of horsemen who intercepted their retreat. A bold

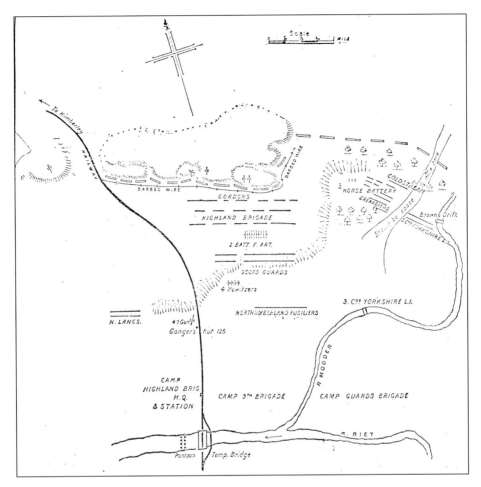

Plan showing the Battle of Magersfontein

dash, however, cleared their way with the loss of one man only, Private Lazenby, brought into camp under fire by Lieutenant Riley, the retreat being covered by Sergeant Cassen, Lance-Corporal Bennett, and Private Mawhood, who dismounted, without cover, and under a hot fire knelt and kept off the Boers for some minutes.

The 12th Lancers under Lord Airlie did well on the same flank and under similar conditions. Meanwhile, the Yorkshire Light Infantry stormed a house, and occupied the drift over the Modder on the extreme right of our line, three companies being left as guard of a second drift half way back. Some of the Grenadier Guards came to their support, there being a considerable gap between this small force on the extreme right and the right of the main body, which was composed of the Coldstream Guards and Grenadier Guards, with a small sprinkling of Argyll and Sutherland Highlanders. The Highland Brigade reformed, reinforced, and, led by the Gordons (who had but arrived the day before, and whom it had not been intended to use), approached the kopjes in open order without suffering any great loss. The Scots Guards acted as guard for the central artillery and two batteries of field artillery and a howitzer battery, and the extreme left was protected by the naval 4.7 gun and the North Lancashire Regiment. There was little incident to note throughout the day, except on the extreme right, where the Yorkshire Light Infantry expended 22,000 rounds. There was little rifle fire from us, and what there was from the Boers came chiefly from a strong contingent of sharpshooters who crawled among the bushes in front of their left extension and sniped at anything that showed itself.

Towards 2 o'clock the monotony and heat combined with the terrible shock that had been suffered in the early morning, and little by little the Highland Brigade came back, the movement culminating in a general withdrawal under cover of a terrible fire from our guns, front and flank, which, however, was unable to reduce greatly the redoubled fire from every yard of breastwork and every boulder on the hill sides.

There were, however, fewer casualties than might have been thought, though again and again, a man flung up his arms and fell. The retirement was an obvious mistake, as the men were in no danger where they lay, and by remaining where they were would, as the Boers have subsequently admitted, had persuaded the already intimidated and decimated enemy to retire from the trenches under cover of night exactly as had previously happened at Modder River. It is, however, only just to General Lord Methuen to state here, on the highest authority, that this retirement was in direct opposition to his definite orders, given earlier in the day to the Highland Brigade, to remain until nightfall in their positions. As there has been some uncertainty on this point, it is necessary to lay stress upon the truth.

The probability, already referred to, that in future civilized warfare endurance in awaiting evening in extended order under cover will be a considerable factor in success receives additional support from the action at Magersfontein. It is a higher trial of condition than might be supposed to lie for 13 or 14 hours under a semi-tropical sun without more food or water than has been carried into action, and the need to obey rules laid down as to emergency rations and water bottles has become urgent.

With this retreat the battle ended, except that the artillery, covering their own retirement, fired continuously for some 20 minutes, ending with a salvo of lyddite shell from the howitzers that shook the ground.

The Guards were left to bivouac as they lay, and continued their line to the left to occupy the position left by the Highland Brigade. Some of them advanced during the night far enough to see that the Boers were still manning their intrenchments and refreshing themselves out of the gin-bottles that always form a striking feature of their evacuated earthworks.

Desultory shelling from the Boers' extreme right had marked the close of the day, and with the morning it again began. Presuming on the military traditions of the Boers, the artillery had remained all night on the field, and recommenced fire, but this lasted for a short time only, and by 9 o'clock the brigades were on their march back to the river, leaving only the ambulances at their dreary work.

Then occurred the incident that attracted some notice. Under a flag of truce the

Boers asked that stretcher-bearers should be sent to take away the wounded and dead British that still dotted the veldt close under their trenches, and the request was instantly complied with, Major Beevor taking a large force of men with him under the Red Cross. On our extreme left the naval gun regarded the approach of a small body of Boers with mistrust, and, in ignorance of the armistice, fired two or three times. This the Boers regarded as bad faith, and as a reprisal shelled the horse battery several times. This, considering itself bound by the armistice, made no answer, and the Boers then ceased fire.

It is difficult to sum up impressions of an encounter which has resulted badly without referring again to the continued lack of information which caused the initial blunder and consequent slaughter. It is not too much to say that no troops could have retained their *moral* in a situation for which not the slightest palliation has yet been offered. Whose is the fault is not the question to raise yet, but it is only fair to the men who were thus shaken to state frankly that it was by no fault of their own that they were compelled without alternative to begin an arduous day by retreating in disorder; and it must not be forgotten that for the rest of the day the brigade was practically without officers in a position in which men require leadership more than usual.

This reverse has checked the advance, postponed almost *sine die* the relief of Kimberley, which was the end and aim of the movement, and has placed the division in a position of which the Boers will not be slow to take advantage. But the soul of goodness was in the evil thing, and many a quiet act of heroism and steady unselfishness marked the day. No words can be too high in which to praise the medical staff, who in the hottest fire, which their presence always attracted, carried through their work as coolly as though in hospital, and conducted their transport operations, heavy as the strain was, with such perfection that 500 wounded were sent off by train to Cape Town before 10 o'clock on the following morning.

Of the artillery I have spoken. It remains yet to note the excellent work done by the extreme right – recognized by the General in orders on the following day – and to put on record the exhibition of the same desperate pluck of the same men who but a twelvemonth before had carried the heights of Dargai.

At Magersfontein the British suffered over 1,000 casualties; some of the Highland regiments lost 60 per cent of their officers. Coming so soon after the defeat of Gatacre at Stormberg, the news of Magersfontein was greeted with dismay in Britain, but the country consoled itself in the knowledge that Buller would not let them down. On 15 December, Buller led his troops toward the Tugela River and the town of Colenso beyond it. Botha, the Boer commander, had adopted De la Rey's idea and had dug lines of trenches on both sides of the river, leaving the hills behind his position lightly manned. When Buller commenced his attack he shelled the high ground behind the river, in the mistaken belief that the Boers were adhering to their traditional tactics. This mistake led to the British advancing towards the river confident that the Boers were undergoing a very heavy bombardment. As at Stormberg and Magersfontein, the first intimation the British troops had that this was not the case was a withering fusillade of rifle bullets delivered at almost point-blank range. Fortunately for Buller

The burial place, at
Modder River, of the
Highlanders who fell at
Magersfontein

someone in the Boer lines had commenced firing before the appointed signal, otherwise
the British losses would have been much greater. As it was, British casualties were
more than 1,000 killed, wounded or captured, coupled with the loss of ten guns. The
Boers sustained only 40 casualties. This was a disaster for British arms.

CHIEVELEY CAMP, DEC. 21.

By the beginning of last week (December 11) everything was at length ready
for an advance on Colenso. A force, whose fighting strength was nearly
20,000, had during the past fortnight concentrated at Frere Camp. The infantry
consisted of four brigades – namely, the 2nd, under General Hildyard, consisting
of the Devonshire, the Queen's, the West Yorkshire, and East Surrey Regiments;
the 4th Brigade, under General Lyttelton, composed of the 1st Battalion Rifle
Brigade, the 3rd Battalion of the 60th Rifles, the Durham Light Infantry, and the
Scottish Rifles; the 5th Brigade, under General Hart, consisting of the Dublin and
Inniskilling Fusiliers, the Connaught Rangers, and the Border Regiment; and the
6th Brigade, under General Barton, which was composed of the Royal, the Irish,
the Scots and the Welsh Fusiliers. This force numbered approximately 16,000
men. The cavalry and mounted infantry brigade, under Colonel the Earl of
Dundonald, included the 1st Royal Dragoons, the 13th Hussars, Bethune's
Mounted Infantry, Thorneycroft's Mounted Infantry, each about 500 strong, three
squadrons of the South African Light Horse under Major Byng, and the composite
regiment under Major Watter, made up of a mounted company of the 60th Rifles
and the Dublin Fusiliers under Captain Eustace, a company each of Natal

Carbineers, Major McKenzie, and Imperial Light Horse, Captain Bottomley. The whole mounted force numbered about 2,600. There were five batteries of field artillery, the 7th, 14th, 63rd, 64th, and 66th; and besides these there was a naval battery consisting of two 4.7 guns, capable of firing lyddite, and 14 long-range 12-pounders. The guns all belonged to, and were mounted by, the Terrible. They were all drawn by oxen, the two big ones requiring 28 each. The naval contingent consisted of 254 men, 200 of whom belonged to the Terrible. Captain Jones, of the Forte, was in command.

On Tuesday, December 12, the first move was made. At dawn General Barton's brigade, with the two large and six small naval guns, marched out and occupied a position about three miles from Colenso. The position chosen was a stony kopje directly in front of the village of Colenso, just to the east of the railway line. From this kopje the country slopes gradually down to the river, and is absolutely open except for a few small dongas intersecting it. The river cannot be seen from the kopje for the reason that it has high, steep banks, and that along them there is a good deal of brushwood. The road bridge, however, which till yesterday stood intact, can be easily seen. Colenso village lies on this side of the Tugela, and close to the river on the far side rise abruptly the line of steep little kopjes which the Boers have been busy fortifying ever since they recrossed the Tugela at the end of last month. They extend about half-a-mile east and west along the river, and about the same distance north and south. On the westernmost and nearest to the river is situated Fort Wylie, a position completely commanding both bridges. Fort Wylie was held by the Dublin Fusiliers and Durban Light Infantry whilst they were in possession of Colenso. On both sides lies the flat plain through which the Tugela winds, but behind them line after line of kopjes rise in steps till they culminate in a range of hills which approach the river to the westward of Colenso, and form the two dominating positions of Grobler's Kloof and a hill that has been christened Red Hill for want of any other name. This formed the centre of the Boer position. The two kopjes which they had fortified elaborately completely commanded the approaches to Colenso, the more so as the plain opposite sloped gradually down towards the river, and was entirely devoid of cover. Behind these kopjes a retreat if necessary was easy. An attacking enemy would have to storm kopje after kopje, whilst all the time he would be under fire from Grobler's Kloof and Red Hill. In fact, to hold Colenso he would have to hold all the hills in a ring round it, and if the possession of them were disputed it would entail more than one day's fighting. To the east of Fort Wylie the river bends sharply northward, and here the left flank of the Boer position is on the south side of the river on a solitary hill called Hlangwane. This is, doubtless, the weakest spot in the Boer position, for if an enemy could take it by storm or otherwise he could render the kopjes north of Colenso untenable.

At 7.15 o'clock on Wednesday morning the naval guns commenced the bombardment of the Boer position on the kopjes north of Colenso, which was continued till midday. The range was 7,200 yards and the practice was extremely good. One line of intrenchments, in particular, had two great gaps, each about 30 yards long, knocked in it. This was done with lyddite, the power of which was terrific. Not quite so high a percentage of the lyddite shells burst as of the ordinary kind, but this is due to the fact that the fuse of a lyddite shell cannot be charged with fulminate, and so needs to strike harder ground to cause it to detonate. To the fire to which they were subjected for nearly six hours the Boers made no attempt to reply, although it was evident they were manning their trenches, for when a shell fell in a new place they could be seen scattering in all directions.

The next morning the entire force moved out of Frere Camp at 4.30 and marched to Chieveley, where they pitched their camp on the west side of the line and about a mile nearer the river. Meanwhile, the naval guns had moved forward to a slight hill on the west side of the railway, about 1,000 yards further forward, and again shelled the kopjes behind Colenso, sending a few shells into a small camp visible about three miles away from the river, which was reported to be General Botha's. Again the Boers made absolutely no reply, and it was pretty generally supposed either that they did not intend to hold the position or at least that they had withdrawn their big guns. The bombardment ceased at midday, but was continued at intervals during the afternoon whenever the enemy were seen attempting to mend the breaches in their earthworks. That evening it became known that a general attack would take place next morning, and orders were sent round that camp was to be struck and the baggage packed and troops to be in their allotted positions by 4 o'clock next morning. The disposition of the troops was as follows:– On the left General Hart's brigade was to cross the river at a bridle drift about three miles above Colenso at a curve in the river, in approaching which General Hart's men would be exposed to flank fire from the enemy on the other side. He was supported by the 63rd and 64th batteries and his flank covered by the Royal Dragoons. Next to General Hart on the right came General Lyttelton's brigade, with orders to act as supports to General Hart's and General Hildyard's brigades. On General Lyttelton's right a long low spur of hills, scarcely more than an undulation, with a broad flat top, ran gradually down from the high ground at Chieveley to the Tugela. On the western side of the flat top, about 2,000 yards in advance of their position of the previous day, was the chief naval battery consisting of two 4.7 guns and four 12-pounders, under Captain Jones. The range to the kopjes north of the Tugela was between 3,000 and 4,000 yards. About a quarter of a mile away the railway ran along the eastern edge of the flat top of the spur. Between the two General Hildyard had orders to advance directly upon Colenso bridge. His left was to be supported by the 14th and 66th Field Batteries and a battery of six naval 12-pounders, under Lieutenant Ogilvy of the Terrible, the whole under Colonel Long. To the east of the line lay a broad flat plain intersected by a few dongas. Across this General Barton's brigade was to advance and co-operate with General Hildyard's, whilst on his left Lord Dundonald had orders to attack Hlangwane Hill with the 7th Field Battery and the whole of the cavalry and mounted infantry, except the Royals, who were on the left, and Bethune's mounted infantry, who were guarding the baggage. The formation was, brigades of infantry, alternating with batteries of artillery, the two flanks being covered by cavalry, and our front only extended about three miles to the Boers' fire, though this was not discovered until the battle was in progress.

At dawn, on Friday, the 15th, the troops were filing slowly out of camp to their respective positions. There was no wind and not a cloud in the sky. By a quarter to 5 there was sufficient light for the main naval battery to open fire, which they did upon Fort Wylie. For three-quarters of an hour only an occasional gun was fired on our side, but at 5.30, when all was ready for an attack, the bombardment became brisker. The Boers made no response whatever. Shortly before 6 the 14th and 66th Batteries and the naval 12-pounder battery advanced across the plain to the right of the railway. Colonel Long, Colonel Hunt, and Lieutenant Ogilvy (commanding the naval battery) were riding in front, and Colonel Long selected a position about 800 yards from the river and 1,200 yards from Fort Wylie, more than a mile in advance of the infantry. He had scarcely given the order to unlimber when a single gun was fired from one of the kopjes behind Colenso. This was evidently the signal for the Boers to commence firing, and immediately a tremendous fire began from the intrenchments on the kopjes, from Fort Wylie, and from trenches along the river, all directed upon the two field batteries. Just behind the batteries lay a small donga, and 300 yards behind that a larger one. The naval battery drawn by oxen was in the middle of crossing this donga when the fire commenced. Two guns under Lieutenant James were already across, and they got into action behind and to the left of the field batteries. Two more were in the middle of the donga and two more had not yet entered it. When the fire began the native drivers of the last four guns at once ran away, but the sailors manned the oxen and at length with great difficulty got their guns into action behind the donga. Meanwhile the other naval battery and Colonel Long's two batteries were directing a tremendous fire upon Fort Wylie. The 14th and 66th were themselves the object of a most deadly musketry fire from the enemy, who were sheltered under the bank on the near side of the river at a range of about 800 yards, as well as a tremendously heavy, but not so effective, shell fire. At about a quarter past 6 Colonel Long was wounded and was helped back into the donga behind the artillery. Shortly afterwards Colonel Hunt, commanding the two batteries, was also hit. The rifle fire from the enemy's trenches was terribly effective and our casualties were very heavy, but the men served their guns with the utmost gallantry and coolness. At 7 o'clock, the ammunition train not having come up, the ammunition in the limbers was exhausted. Captain Herbert, A.D.C. to Colonel Long, and one of the few unwounded officers left, who had already had his horse shot in going to fetch a doctor, was sent off to ask for reinforcements, and whilst doing so had a second horse shot. The order was then given to retire into the donga behind until fresh ammunition should arrive. This was done, the men carrying their wounded with them. They did not attempt to destroy the guns by carrying away the breechblocks because they expected to return to them as soon as the infantry came up. The naval 12-pounder battery, which was about 400 yards in the rear of the field batteries, continued the bombardment alone under very heavy fire. It is extraordinary that their loss of four wounded was not greater, for they remained in action entirely unsupported until 9.30, when they received the order from General Buller to retire. There were several extraordinary escapes. Lieutenant Ogilvy, after having his horse shot, had the three shells from a Hotchkiss pass between his legs whilst looking through his field glasses.

Meanwhile, on the left General Hart was developing his attack. The bridle drift by which he was to cross was defended by a semi-circular position following the curve of the river. The Dublin Fusiliers were the leading battalion. The brigade advanced in column, and the Dublins had scarcely taken open order when the enemy opened on the column with shrapnel. They were temporarily unable to deploy owing to the nature of the ground, and in the interval the Connaught Rangers, who were now leading the column, suffered heavy loss. At 6.30 the Dublin Fusiliers, with the Connaught Rangers, advanced across the open ground under fire, and as they came into the curve of the river the Boers opened an enfilading as well as a front fire upon them. The ground was very dry, and every bullet could be seen striking up a spurt of dust. The fire was terrific. Besides the musketry fire, the enemy shelled them with three guns, one directly ahead at comparatively short range, one on the flank at the foot of Grobler's Kloof, and a 40-pounder on the top of the Red Hill. The 63rd and 64th Batteries on the left seemed unable to silence their fire, and the naval battery, which was the only one capable of doing it, was concentrating its fire on Fort Wylie. The Dublins and Connaughts advanced magnificently against the almost overwhelming fire, men falling at every step. As they approached the river the enemy's fire seemed to redouble. Every time a company rose to its feet to advance there was a perfect crash of musketry, and the plain all round them became a cloud of dust spurts. It seemed wonderful that any man could survive it. And yet there was nothing to tell where the enemy lay concealed. Not a single head even was visible; nothing but a long line of smoke, scarcely visible, and the incessant crackling roar. The batteries sent shell after shell wherever they could distinguish the line of the trenches, but they failed to silence the terrible fire. At last our men reached the river, but where there should have been a ford there was 7ft. of water. The few who tried to cross it, overcome by the weight of rifle and ammunition, were drowned. The rest lined the bank, and poured in a tremendous fire on the still almost invisible enemy. Then came the general's order to retire, and our men fell slowly back. It was during the retirement that the brigade suffered the heaviest loss. Half General Lyttelton's brigade went out to cover the retirement, but the men had to retire half a mile across the open under perhaps the heaviest fusillade of the day. Even when they at last reached cover the 40-pounder on the top of the hill pursued them with shrapnel until the naval battery eventually silenced it. The day after the battle it was reported that the Boers had dammed the river below the bridle drift, thus making it impassable. It is more probable that the guide, a Kaffir, led them to the wrong place.

In the centre the naval battery had at first directed its fire entirely on Fort Wylie. Under the combined fire of this battery and the batteries under Colonel Long, the small kopje on one end of which the fort stands became completely enveloped in lurid clouds of smoke and red dust, which rose straight up in the air and gave the effect of the hill being on fire. The hill was chiefly used by the Boer riflemen, who, as far as could be seen, retreated very soon after the bombardment began. But there were also two or three small guns mounted on it. Under the tremendous fire the gunners worked their guns bravely for a time, but at the end of half an hour no reply came and the bombardment ceased. Fort Wylie was silenced. One of the last shots from the 4.7in. guns, a lyddite shell, struck the corner of the fortification and knocked the whole end of the fort shapeless.

Meanwhile the central attack began to develop. General Hildyard's Brigade on the left of the railway was advancing in extended order along the flat top of the spur straight on Colenso bridge, and the Irish Brigade a little behind them was crossing the plain on the right of the railway in the rear of the now silent 14th and 66th batteries. The Queen's were the leading battalion of Hildyard's Brigade supported by the Devons. From the manner in which they advanced they might have been taking part in a field day at Aldershot. The country over which they advanced was absolutely devoid of cover, and they were subjected to a heavy shell fire from the kopjes behind Colenso which the naval battery did its best to silence. Nevertheless they advanced in perfect order, maintaining absolutely perfectly their intervals and their alignment. As they approached Colenso the enemy opened a heavy musketry fire upon them from the banks of the river. It was now that the want of artillery was most apparent. The naval battery, the only one supporting the advance, was unable to get at the enemy, who were down in the hollow, and there was nothing to check the latter's fire. Still the Queen's pressed on. They checked a minute in a Boer shelter trench, and then with a series of short rushes the leading company gained the edge of the plateau and disappeared over it into cover in the scrub that grows all round Colenso. Company after company succeeded them, and down below we caught glimpses of men running across the open from one patch of cover to the next. The roar of musketry swelled louder and louder, and then it died away into single shots. Then it suddenly rose again, and a swarm of brown figures were seen swarming up the steep sides of Fort Wylie and disappearing on the other side. The naval guns behind were trained on the struggling mass, when the word went round that it was our men storming the fort. But it was not, it was the Boers evacuating their positions along the river and falling back to their second line of defence, and the sudden storm of musketry was our men firing on them. Previous to that they had not seen a single Boer to fire at.

During the advance two companies of the Devons had crossed the railway with their colonel, Colonel Bullock, to support the 14th and 66th Batteries. They and two companies from the Scots Fusiliers, who had advanced on the right side of the railway, took shelter from the Boer fire in the larger of the two dongas behind the guns. At 9.30 General Buller and General Clery rode down to the guns and remained there some time under a heavy fire. It was here that both the generals were wounded. General Buller was hit in the ribs by a fragment of shell, which, fortunately, did not penetrate his coat, but gave him a severe bruise, and General Clery was grazed right across the chest by a Mauser bullet. It was here also that Captain Hughes, R.A.M.C., staff-surgeon to General Buller, was killed, being hit in the chest by a rifle bullet. General Buller then ordered the naval 12-pounder battery, which had remained in action all the time, to retire. They had lost 32 oxen, and their Kaffir drivers had long since run away. With infinite difficulty it was done, however, but the spare ammunition wagon was left behind. A Natal farmer and transport-rider named Pringle, the owner of the wagon and span of oxen, then went out quite alone, his Kaffirs having deserted him, and under heavy shell fire at last inspanned the oxen, and brought back the ammunition. A little later two exceedingly brave attempts were made to recover the lost guns. Captain Schofield, A.D.C. to General Buller, Captain Congreve, temporarily acting as Press censor, and Lieutenant Roberts, A.D.C. to General Clery, with about six men, harnessed two teams of horses to limbers and galloped out to the guns with them. On the way out Lieutenant Roberts was wounded in three places, and Captain Congreve was hit in the leg as he dismounted. The rest were not touched, although they were under a terrific fire, and succeeded in bringing back two guns, the only two saved from the 14th and 66th Batteries. A message was then sent to the 7th Battery, which was on the right asking for assistance in getting the guns out. Captain Reed, of the 7th Battery, rode down with a team of wagon horses; but while they were being harnessed to one of the ammunition wagons they were almost all shot, and Reed was forced to retire, being himself wounded in the thigh. After this General Buller gave orders that no more attempts to save the guns were to be made.

On the extreme right Lord Dundonald was attacking Hlangwene Hill. He went round to the east side of the hill, and then, dismounting his men, advanced with the South African Light Horse on the left, the composite regiment in the centre, and Thorneycroft's Mounted Infantry on the right. The 13th Hussars were left in reserve, and the 7th Field Battery, under Major Henshaw, alternately shelled Hlangwene Hill and Colenso. Under cover of this fire Lord Dundonald attempted a flanking movement on the east side of the hill, and was advancing up a narrow valley when his flank was turned by a party of Boers who had moved down off the main hill on to a spur and engaged Thorneycroft's. This movement of the enemy prevented further advance, and the mounted infantry could not do more than hold their ground for a considerable time. At length the order to retire came, but for two hours it could not be obeyed owing to the heavy fire the enemy poured in whenever they tried to move. At about 3.30 the 7th Battery, by well-directed shelling, had sufficiently silenced the enemy's fire to allow the retirement to take place. Even as it was, however, the losses during the retreat were far heavier than they had been during the attack. This was the first time the South African Light Horse had been under fire, and they behaved splendidly under it.

About midday by General Buller's orders a general retirement began all along the line, except on the extreme left, where the retirement had already taken place. General Hildyard's brigade, pursued by a deadly fire, retired in just as good order as when they advanced, the Boers reoccupying the positions they had vacated, but not attempting any pursuit. By some mistake the order was not communicated to the men who had gone to the support of the disabled batteries, and when the Boers crossed the river in force at about 4 o'clock to take possession of the abandoned guns the former were surrounded and made prisoners. Most of the wounded, including some wounded officers, were left for our ambulances, and their sufferings were intense, for they lay in the donga without shade or water for about six hours before help came.

Our losses in killed, wounded, and missing were 1,114, but the proportion of killed to wounded was fortunately extremely small. Many of the men were very slightly wounded indeed, the most frequent wound being one in the foot. This in the majority of cases was not serious, as many of the men so wounded hobbled to the ambulance without assistance after having had the first dressing applied.

The extreme strength of the Boer position it is almost impossible to exaggerate. Men who know the country well say it is by far the strongest position in Natal;

Langs Nek, they say, cannot compare with it. The Boers held an exceedingly strong position, and no one can deny that they made an exceedingly able defence. To have lain low for two days when they saw our camp within easy reach of their big guns, and to have forborne to fire on the morning of the battle until they had us within easy reach whilst they themselves were all the time under shell fire, was a thing many more disciplined troops could not have done. Their position was excellently planned, their trenches and gun emplacements were extremely well hidden. All day we were fired at by guns whose position we could never find, and through the heat mirage we were never sure exactly where the musketry fire came from. It was one of the conditions of modern warfare. We had to attack an invisible enemy whose position could not even be fixed by the smoke of his rifle. It was rifle fire that caused our losses. Their shell fire, though accurate enough, was not deadly, and during the advances men did not drop till they had come within effective rifle range. This was the case in spite of the fact that by far the greater number of the Boer shells burst, and burst accurately too, sometimes right in the middle of our men.

The extreme heaviness of the enemy's fire often at what is now considered close range induces the question, Are the Boers really such good shots as they are made out to be? Perhaps when there are shells bursting over their heads they are not quite so steady; but, considering the amount of firing, one might reasonably have expected that had those trenches been manned by British infantry the casualty list of the attacking force would have been heavier.

Our big naval battery, after its first success against Fort Wylie, seemed unable to repeat the performance on the guns on the other kopjes immediately behind Colenso. It was reported the day after the battle that the enemy had erected bomb-proof shelters over their guns, from which they only emerged to fire. It is impossible to say whether or not this is true. Several times our shells pitched right into the emplacements and burst there, and usually after that the gun was silent for from half an hour to an hour, but almost invariably at the end of that time it would commence again. It was as if the gunners had fled on the explosion of our shell and only returned when they considered it to be quite safe to risk another shot. There were two Hotchkiss guns which could never be located all day.

The following day an armistice was agreed to for the purpose of burying the dead. The Boer loss is quite impossible to estimate. It is extremely difficult even to guess at the numbers engaged, as they were never seen and only the intensity of their fire gave any clue.

During the night of Saturday, the 16th, after the conclusion of the armistice, camp was shifted about a mile back out of range of the enemy's big guns.

Buller's reaction to his defeat was to panic. In the depths of despair, he sent a message to White in Ladysmith, ordering him to surrender. 'As it appears certain that I cannot relieve Ladysmith for another month, and even then only by means of protracted siege operations . . . you will burn your ciders, destroy your guns, fire away your ammunition, and make the best terms possible with the general of the besieging forces, after giving me time to fortify myself on the Tugela.'[1] Fortunately, White ignored this order and pressed on with the task of defending the town.

The Warwicks at De Aar hear
that Lord Roberts is coming
to take command

At home in Britain, the reaction to the news of this week of defeats was predictably severe. On 18 December Buller was replaced as Commander-in-Chief by Lord Roberts. Lord Kitchener was appointed as Roberts' Chief of Staff and the Government called up the remaining reserves. Fearing that this might not be sufficient to achieve victory, the Government set about raising new regiments, such as the Mounted Yeomanry, and began to accept more and more troops from the Empire, particularly Australia and Canada. As the British field forces found themselves pushed back on the defensive, any hope for the relief of the three besieged towns was postponed indefinitely, and automatically the eyes of the world came to focus on Ladysmith, Kimberley and Mafeking.

Note

1. Quoted in Kruger, 1983, p. 143.

The Siege of Ladysmith

Once the initial British reverses had taken place, the Boers were in a very strong position to win the war. At Ladysmith the Boers had boxed in the main British force in South Africa, and it is possible that, if they had simply left a masking force in place around this town, they could have gone on to deliver the *coup de grâce* to British rule in South Africa. They might have used their mobility and temporary numerical superiority to capture the major sea ports such as Durban and Cape Town. Instead, the Boers sat down before the three towns of Ladysmith, Kimberley and Mafeking, and tried to capture each town by engaging in regular siege operations, a task for which the Boers were singularly ill-equipped, both in terms of armament and mentality. The Boer experience of warfare had equipped them with two stock tactical systems: using the mobility conferred by their horses, they could conduct lightning raids to dislocate the enemy's coherence as a force and thus defeat them; or, when faced by a stronger force, the Boers would retreat into either a manufactured defensive position, the laager, or a defensive position provided by nature, a kopje or a river. Much has been written about the British inexperience in dealing with European foes in the period leading up to the Second Boer War in 1899. However, while this is true it tends to overshadow the facts that the Boers were not really a European fighting force, and also that it was the Boers' inexperience of regular tactics, and their inability to adapt to the demands of regular warfare, that was to lead to their ultimate defeat.

So, although the sieges of the three towns form the dramatic centre-piece of *The Times'* reporting of the war, they were by no means the close investments that European readers imagined they were. The following extract from Denys Reitz's diary gives a graphic picture of the Boer approach to siege warfare: 'This time I rode around the western circle of Ladysmith in order to visit the Free State Commandos guarding that side of the cordon, as I had many friends and acquaintances there, and after spending a pleasant day among them, I timed my journey to reach the Kroonstadt camp by sunset, as I wished to put up in a night with my Norwegian uncle. I found him making ready to accompany a picket to the plain towards the English lines. His preparations for going on duty were unusual, for he inspanned an American buck-board on which he piled a feather-bed, blankets, and pillows, and as soon as the rest of the picket moved out after dark he told me to leave my roan horse in camp, and he and I drove in state to the place where we had to do guard for the night. The spot was not more than four hundred yards from the nearest English sentries, but this in no way disturbed my uncle's serenity. He unharnessed his two animals, hitched them to the wheels of the buggy, and giving one of the younger fry half-a-crown to do his sentry-go, he spread his bedding and was soon comfortably snoring within earshot of the British.'[1] Although this is obviously an extreme example, it nevertheless captures the essential feel of the Boer approach to seige warfare.

In all of the besieged towns the biggest hardship was boredom. The diary of A.J. Crosby who served with the Natal Carbineers throughout the siege of Ladysmith, captures the mood of resigned boredom that was prevalent throughout his time in the town, 'Roused at 2.30 exercising horses. On fatigue cleaning up sick horse lines. Little doing in afternoon, heat again tremendous. At 8.30 were sent out to support piquet. Thunder and dust storm, rain commenced between 9 and 10 and continued several hours making it disagreeable for our bivouac.'[2] This was clearly not a comfortable experience, but nothing to compare to the hardships of, for example, the siege of Sebastopol during the Crimean War, or the siege of Paris during the Franco-Prussian War. Yet the sieges of these small African towns became Victorian epics. The reason for this apparent incongruity lies in the coverage that the sieges received in the press: the excitement and dangers of the siege were emphasized and the boredom and lack of significant military action played down. *The Times* was as guilty of this approach as any of the other newspapers. Why was this done? A combination of factors led to the manufacturing of the 'siege epic'. The early set-backs led newspapers to concentrate on the gallantry of the besieged because precious little else was happening elsewhere. Also, and perhaps more importantly, newspapers were not sold by tales of early rising and boring days. Editors realized that the public craved excitement as well as information, and so reports that told the *true* story of life in the besieged towns were suppressed in favour of tales of gallantry and suffering. *The Times*, despite its reputation for accurate reporting of events, followed the general trend and concentrated on 'action' reports to the detriment of the truth.

Much has been written about Sir George White's critical blunder in allowing himself to be surrounded in Ladysmith. This seems to be a somewhat unfair criticism in the light of the report of the enquiry that met in 1902 to discuss the conduct of the war. Lord Roberts, giving evidence before the enquiry, stated that, 'when Sir George White arrived in Natal, he had no instructions in regard to the wishes of the government as to any particular plan of campaign, nor was he aware of any general plan of operations in South Africa.'[3] It is therefore no great surprise that White should find himself cut off by a foe that not only had a plan of action, but who was also in possession of an intimate knowledge of the terrain. White, once he found himself outmanoeuvred, set about defending Ladysmith in a professional manner.

Wednesday, Nov. 1. – Although the communications with the south are still uninterrupted to-day, the town was practically in a state of siege. The commissariat department have been busy commandeering foodstuffs from all the stores, the banks are closed, and bread has risen to 1s. a loaf. The unofficial armistice has continued, as the ambulance parties of both forces were still out searching for wounded. One battalion (the Dublin Fusiliers) was despatched to

AT LAST!

Sir George White. "I HOPED TO HAVE MET YOU BEFORE, SIR REDVERS."
Sir Redvers Buller, V.C. "COULDN'T HELP IT, GENERAL. HAD SO MANY ENGAGEMENTS!"

Cartoon from *Punch*, 7 March 1900

The Warwicks unloading
Maxim Guns from the *Gaul*,
Cape Town

Colenso with the Natal Field Battery, as it was reported that the enemy were
moving down upon the Tugela in force. The situation had proceeded so far that in
Ladysmith it was accepted that the closing of all communication could only be a
matter of hours. The situation in which Sir George White found himself was this.
He had at his disposal to defend Ladysmith a force of 9,000 men, 36 field guns,
and a naval contingent with two heavy position guns. Of foodstuffs and small arm
ammunition he possessed a supply which would not, under ordinary
circumstances, become exhausted in three months. But the artillery were not so
well placed. The supply of shell worked out to a little over 300 rounds per gun for
the field batteries and, even with the naval guns, it was evident that expenditure
would have to be made with a sparing hand. Ladysmith does not lend itself readily
to defence. Roughly, the town lies in the bend of a horseshoe. But the hills which
make this formation are disconnected, and the ranges and spurs straggle over a
large area. Not only are they uneven, but their continuations stretch away in every
direction, and form positions which in the majority of cases actually command the
town. With the force at his disposal it was, of course, absolutely impossible to
hold every hill, and, even contracting his front so as to hold the majority of
strategical points, Sir George White found his 9,000 men, of which only 5,000 odd
were infantry, holding a line of posts extending over 11 miles. Against this the
enemy have brought at least 20,000 men, this being the very lowest figure at
which the estimate can be placed, there being every reason to believe the
combined force under Joubert, now occupying Natal, to be between 25,000 and
30,000 men.

But this is not all; the experience of the last three weeks has shown the enemy to be not only numerically superior, but also possessed of arms which outrange anything that we can bring against them. If it had not been for the timely arrival of the naval guns it is impossible to conjecture what the consequences would have been. Take, for instance, the most important arm – the artillery. We have 36 guns of the best-manned artillery in the world, but at the very outside, however well served our guns may be, they have not an effective range above 4,500 yards. Against this the Boers have brought into the field guns fitted with the latest telescopic sights, and having a range of 7,000 to 8,000 yards. However devotedly our gunners may manoeuvre their weapons, they cannot dislodge an enemy in action against them whom they cannot see. This of the field artillery; and while I write a 6-inch position gun is shelling the town and defences from about 8,000 yards. If the naval guns had not arrived, if the Boers had cut the communication three days earlier, we should have been powerless to reply. As it is we have been forced to take most of their bombardment sitting. With regard to the infantry arm, the discrepancy is not so great. But the Mauser rifle with which the Boers are armed is the better weapon, and has a greater range. With a good pair of glasses and a Mauser it is possible to make tolerable practice at 3,000 yards. No British infantry is trained to these ranges. Our men know nothing of glasses; yet the farmer-soldier, our enemy, would not think of taking the field unless one man in four possessed powerful binoculars. Thus, at first sight, the task set Sir George White and his little force seemed stupendous. But there are saving contingencies, the first being the dislike which the Boer has ever shown to take the offensive. He will defend a position stoutly, but until he is absolutely certain of the success of a forward move he is loth to undertake it. This was proved in the engagement on Monday (October 30), and at Rietfontein, when opportunities were given to the enemy to follow up a retiring force. It has been proved in the half-dozen outpost affairs which have taken place throughout the campaign. Moreover, the South African Republic has been served badly by its agents, for if their ammunition had been as serviceable as their guns our casualties would have been three times as heavy as they have been. Their shrapnel is poor. On Monday, when the 42nd Field Battery moved up to within 3,000 yards of the enemy's position, well-fused shrapnel burst in front of the battery time after time. If these missiles had been from our own arsenals it would have been impossible for the men to have faced them and worked their guns. As it was, though they lost severely, they were able to make the enemy's position untenable. Since the bombardment shell have been picked up filled with extraneous matter, proving the duplicity of the contractors who supplied the war material.

To-day the loyal town guard of Ladysmith was disbanded. A fortnight ago the members of this corps were enrolled, and the youth of the town embarked upon their duties with great enthusiasm. But when once the Boer guns found the range of the town, the majority of the Town Guard removed to Maritzburg.

Thursday, November 2. – At dawn the enemy recommenced to bombard Ladysmith from Peppworth Hill. They only had one large calibre gun in position, "Long Tom," who is destined to be famous. The first shell fell into the town, and a fragment killed a Kaffir. Shortening their range, they continued to play with this

Map showing Ladysmith and district

solitary gun upon the Naval Battery, which was our nearest artillery defence. The sailors replied shot for shot, but the enemy had utilized the delay caused by the armistice in strengthening their redoubt, and it is doubtful if our return fire was very damaging. Our own men, as soon as they had laid their guns, retired to cover on the reverse of the hill, one man remaining to fire each gun. In all probability the enemy's gunners did likewise. Unfortunately, Lieutenant Egerton, R.N., while directing the guns, was hit by a shell, losing both his legs. He succumbed in the evening.

The enemy had not closed in on the west, and Brigadier-General J. F. Brocklehurst was sent out to make a reconnaissance with the 5th Lancers, some Volunteer Cavalry, and the 69th Field Battery. To the west of our position stretches a large rolling valley, covering the Maritzburg and Van Reenen's pass roads, a country eminently suitable to cavalry. This reconnaissance was successful, for it came upon a Free State laager, and so surprised the enemy that the battery was able to shell them while they were at breakfast. The Boers streamed out from the wagons and made for the hills under which the laager lay. We were not in sufficient strength to dislodge them, but the Volunteer Cavalry succeeded in rounding up about 50 of their ponies, which were brought into camp.

Trains were still leaving for the south as fast as the railway officials could get them clear. Major-General J. D. P. French and staff left in one about midday, General Buller having summoned the general to join at the Cape. This was the last train that succeeded in getting away. Subsequently we learned that it was fired upon by the enemy in the vicinity of Pieter's Station, but, running the gauntlet of this fire, reached its destination. About 3 o'clock the telegraph wires were cut, and from that moment the siege proper of Ladysmith may be said to have commenced. Hundreds of inhabitants who had been patiently waiting for accommodation in the downgoing trains were thus cut off, for when it was found that the hospital train, which had been due to arrive at Ladysmith in the evening, did not arrive no more trains were despatched.

In the afternoon the firing slackened, and a Boer ambulance came in under a flag of truce, bringing Major Riddell, of the K.R.R., and other wounded. The Boer doctor brought a letter from Joubert asking for an exchange of prisoners. This was allowed, and every courtesy was shown to the Boer hospital assistants who accompanied the ambulance. They freely entered such stores as remained open and made considerable purchases. One tendered Transvaal gold in payment. On being told that it was not current coin he replied laconically, "It soon will be."

There was a very grave subterfuge in connexion with this ambulance. Unfortunately the discovery was made too late to prevent the harm. It appears that the Boer commandant, Van Dam, who despatched the ambulance, sent as the driver one of his artillery officers. This man was allowed the freedom in the town which is extended to those who claim the protection of the Red Cross, and he deliberately spent his time in taking note of various vulnerable points. On the morrow, when the bombardment reopened, there is no doubt that, influenced by this man's information, the fire was directed upon the ordnance park and the house occupied by the Headquarters Staff. This is not the first history which I shall have to relate of Boer juggling and duplicity in connexion with the Geneva flag.

Friday, November 3. – As I said before, the hills which enclose the valley in which Ladysmith lies roughly form a horseshoe. It might, perhaps, be better said that Ladysmith valley is a triangle, with our northern picket as its apex and the M'Bulwana range as its base. This base and apex are joined by ridges varying in altitude above the plain of Ladysmith from 300ft. to 500ft. The centre of M'Bulwana, where one of the enemy's batteries is situated, has been ranged by our gunners as 11,500 yards from Observation Hill, our most northern post. M'Bulwana itself is a tableland about 1,100ft. above the level of Ladysmith. The Klip river cuts through the triangle about three miles from the apex, and it is in the small triangle thus made that the town lies. Half-way between the river and the most northern posts runs a low range of stone kopjes. This is Convent Hill, and on its western slopes are the Naval Batteries and Cove Redoubt, the main positions of our heavy guns. North of Convent Hill lies a large plain, a square mile in extent;

A Boer mortar outside Ladysmith

this is known as the old camp, while right in the apex of the triangle are the
corrugated iron huts which constitute the lines of the permanent garrison of the
station. South of Convent Hill, nestling well into its side, is the town proper, the
railway station being on the east, with the principal street running west. The
eastern side of the hill triangle continues south of the town for a matter of two
miles, when it abruptly dies away into the bush-covered veldt which leads up to
Lombard's Kop. Lombard's Kop is a conical hill with a flat top, standing detached
from M'Bulwana range, but making the eastern angle in the imaginary triangle.
Between Lombard's Kop and the end of M'Bulwana passes the Helpmakaar road.
On the west the side of the triangle is made by a bold, even ridge, known as
Caesar's Camp. It does not stretch quite so far south as the eastern side, but
branches out into another heavy spur, which is the first of a succession of hills
which bound another valley somewhat similar to that in which Ladysmith stands.
Between the termination of Caesar's Camp range and the western limit of
M'Bulwana are a number of low ridges occupied by the enemy, covering the
Maritzburg railway in the vicinity of Pieter's Station. The Maritzburg–Ladysmith
line passes out of the valley at the point of the left angle of the triangle.

　　As near as can be judged, a line drawn from the apex of the triangle to the
centre of the base, M'Bulwana, would measure $8\frac{1}{2}$ miles. The base itself being

practically the same length, some idea of the area of the valley can be formed. With the present garrison it is impossible to hold more than a portion of the triangle, and our infantry is distributed along a line commencing from the abrupt termination of the Caesar's Camp range on the left, right round the old camp, including the detached post known as Observation Hill, to the point overlooking the Helpmakaar road where the eastern ridge drops into the veldt before rising again to form Lombard's Kop. This gives us a very fairly defensible front of ten or 11 miles, which the defending battalions themselves have intrenched as necessary. But, though the front as it faces the lower spurs of the Biggarsberg and the intrenched position of Peppworth Hill is strong enough, the rear and both flanks of the line would be exposed to artillery fire if the Boers occupied M'Bulwana and succeeded in getting artillery into position on its summit. The extensive plain saves us from infantry fire, and the Klip River from direct assault. At the present moment the main strength of the enemy seems to be concentrated at Peppworth Hill, where it is believed that Joubert and Erasmus have their camps. The Peppworth guns have been ranged at 7,500 yards from our batteries in position on Convent Hill, and, taking this as a centre, it may be said that there are no Boer guns within that range. But, of course, this brings many of the Boer positions to within 4,000 yards of our posts. For instance, field guns placed on outlying kopjes constantly drop shell into the old camp, while other artillery engages the posts on the Helpmakaar road and Caesar's Camp at ranges suitable to our own field artillery. But, as a rule, the Boer gunners are quick to gauge the capabilities of the 15-pounders, and retire to positions from which the superior range of their own weapons gives them the advantage. With the exception of Peppworth Hill and the nek between Lombard's Kop and M'Bulwana, it is impossible to say which are the Boer positions, for they have proved a mobile enemy, and each day they open upon the town or posts from positions newly occupied during the night. So well do they choose their ground that, as they use smokeless explosives, it is often several hours before our men are able to mark down the exact knoll or eminence on which the guns are placed. This morning the Boers began a desultory shell fire into the town from three batteries. Peppworth Hill still fired "Long Tom", the high velocity field battery from the nek below Lombard's Kop entertained itself with the picket posts of the Devonshire Regiment and the balloon, while a second field battery about 3,000 yards to the right of Peppworth dropped common shell into the open plain constituting the old camp. The effect of this shelling was more disastrous to the town than it had been on previous days. The field gun from M'Bulwana had found the range and wrecked the front rooms of two private houses. A projectile from Peppworth exploded in a house a few yards from the Royal Hotel during luncheon. The dining room was crowded with guests, windows were shattered, splinters fell upon the tables, and the room was filled with smoke, but no one was hurt. If the shell had fallen half a dozen yards further the results would have been appalling.

We were not yet tied up altogether, and a strong cavalry reconnaissance went out early in the morning under the command of Brigadier-General Brocklehurst. The column consisted of the 18th and 19th Hussars, two squadrons of the Imperial Light Horse, under Major Davis, commanding in the place of Colonel Scott Chisholme, killed at Elandslaagte, some mounted infantry, and the 53rd Field Battery. The cavalry found the enemy with one gun in position, about four miles north-west of Ladysmith. The battery came into action, and the cavalry, dismounting, lined the crests of the range of kopjes which run parallel to Caesar's Camp on the far side of the Van Reenen's road valley. The battery silenced the enemy's solitary field gun with half a dozen rounds of shrapnel, and also succeeded in checking the head of a large column of mounted enemy who were seen working southwards. But while the position taken up by our cavalry precluded any chance of a frontal attack, the enemy brought artillery to bear on their left flank from the succession of high knolls which jut out for about five miles at right angles from Caesar's Camp. General Brocklehurst sent in to Ladysmith for reinforcements. The 5th Dragoon Guards, one squadron each of Natal Carabineers, Natal Mounted Rifles, and Border Mounted Rifles, and two more batteries of artillery were sent out to support the column. Sending one of the new batteries of artillery to cover the position which the 53rd Battery was holding, General Brocklehurst withdrew the latter and brought it into action against a low knoll on a ridge to the left from which the enemy had opened with a field gun. The position which General Brocklehurst found threatening his left flank was peculiar. The enemy were in possession of three flat-topped hills, each with a valley between them, covering a front of about two miles; at right angles from the most western of these kopjes ran the low knoll against which our battery had come into action. Between the kopje and this knoll was a valley, perhaps 1,500 yards across, leading, it was believed, to a large Free State laager. General Brocklehurst brought two batteries into action against the knoll, and their fire speedily silenced the gun in position there, which, it is believed, was abandoned by the enemy. In the meantime the Mounted Infantry had been sent to scale the centre of the kopje on the left, two squadrons of Royston's Volunteer Cavalry being deputed to turn the enemy out of the main and largest kopje. The men were forced to gallop under fire before they could dismount. This they gallantly did, and, leaving their led horses in various kloofs, worked up to the summit of the hills, driving the enemy before them, with trifling loss to themselves. The Imperial Light Horse and 5th Dragoon Guards remained as escort to the guns. As the movement developed the firing on all sides subsided. The two cavalry regiments and battery on the right sufficiently secured that flank.

Thinking that the enemy had evacuated their position, Major Davis sent a squadron of the Light Horse up the valley before mentioned, doubtless with the object of securing the laager presumed to be there. The squadron gaily trotted across the veldt to find itself suddenly in a *cul de sac*; for, waiting until they were conveniently within 1,200 yards of two fires, the enemy opened on them. The Light Horse appeared to be absolutely caught; to turn was out of the question, and they were forced to gallop forward for shelter, the hill side itself and boulders giving partial cover. From the position of the guns and the intensity of the fire it seemed that the squadron must be annihilated. Artillery fire was directed against the surrounding hills, and under its cover a squadron of the 5th Dragoon Guards, under Major Gore, was despatched to extricate them. In the meantime the mounted infantry and dismounted Volunteers had made the summit of the kopjes on the left and were engaging the enemy, whom they had driven out of the position into the succeeding hills. This distraction on the left, with the concentrated fire of two batteries, enabled the squadron of the 5th Dragoon Guards to extricate the Imperial Light Horse, and both parties galloped back across the enemy's front by troops in extended files. Marvellous to say, the losses were trifling. Captain Knapp, of the Light Horse, was killed, and there were half-a-dozen minor casualties. During the return gallop a troop horse was shot, throwing its rider. Lieutenant the Hon. R. L. Pomeroy pulled up and, taking the dismounted man up behind, brought him safely out of range – a plucky action, since for 300 yards the fire was heavy. It was now 4 o'clock in the afternoon, and the enemy having been driven from his original positions there was little left to be done. The Brigadier-General did not think that he was justified in ordering a dash for the laager. The price in casualties so late in the day would have been too great. A general retirement was therefore ordered. As Royston's Volunteers led down from the hill-top, the two long-ranged guns which had been in action on our far left earlier in the day again reopened, but their fire was practically harmless. There were no further casualties until close to camp, when the troops returning from this reconnaissance were accurately shelled by the guns which the enemy had now got into position at the foot of M'Bulwana. It has been suggested that the artillery officer who entered Ladysmith with the ambulance had marked down the range of the bridge over the Klip River, on the Van Reenen road, for the enemy had shelled the ammunition train which had followed the batteries out, and on the return of the column succeeded in causing a few casualties by well-burst shrapnel.

From M'Bulwana the enemy had perceived the column and its reinforcements leaving along the Van Reenen–Maritzburg road, and doubtless believed it to be a column moving to reinforce Colenso. Seeing the garrison thus weakened a considerable body came forward to within range of the pickets on the Helpmakaar road. But when they realized how strongly these pickets were held they immediately fell back. It has been characteristic of the Boers until the present that they will not close to the attack of a position unless they are confident of success. Time after time have they had opportunities in which bold enterprise might have been crowned with success. But on every occasion they have received our offers of battle with extreme caution.

It has been necessary to make mention of the dishonest use to which the Boers have put the white flag. At Talana Hill they are reported to have saved their guns by displaying it. At Elandslaagte they treacherously fired upon the Highlanders and Light Horse after having shown it and caused the "cease fire" to be sounded. The incident of the artillery officer has already found mention. The following letter marks the culminating point:–

Naval Brigade Camp, Ladysmith, Nov. 3, 1899.

Sir, – I have the honour to report that about 2.15 p.m., the Boer large calibre gun having been struck by one of my small 12-pounders, a man jumped on to the parapet of the gun and vigorously waved a white flag which he kept displayed for at least 15 minutes. My gun immediately ceased fire. To my astonishment this

Boer gun had the wickedness to recommence firing, and as I write is throwing shells with great accuracy into the cavalry camp. I desire that you will communicate this cowardly breach of warlike etiquette to that noble and high-minded officer, General Joubert. By all the rules of civilized warfare this Boer gun and the officers and men working it are my prize; the gun should be dismantled and the officers and men sent into Ladysmith as prisoners of war.

I have the honour to be, &c.,

(Signed) HEDWORTH LAMBTON, Captain
    Royal Navy.
To H. E. Lieutenant-General Sir George White,
    V.C., K.C.B.

Monday, Nov. 6. – On Saturday, Sunday, and Monday there was practically an armistice. The bombardment of Friday, small as it was, had thoroughly unnerved the civil inhabitants of the town, and induced the Mayor to address Sir George White on the subject of the removal of non-combatants, women, and children to some place of greater security. Sir George White, on consideration, despatched a letter to General Joubert under a flag of truce suggesting that hospital trains, conveying the wounded and all non-combatants, should be allowed to proceed south unmolested. A reply to this letter was received to the effect that it would be impossible to permit any one to pass through the Boer lines, but that the wounded and such non-combatants as had never borne arms against the South African Republic might be removed to a place of safety in the plain in front of M'Bulwana, where they would remain unmolested under a neutral flag. On the receipt of this news the Mayor convened a meeting of residents at the Town-hall. It was a strange crowd which attended. Every denomination of South African white man was represented. The Church sent a heavy contingent; half a score of women with blanched faces swelled the gathering. Respectable merchants, casual loafers, trembling natives of India all jostled each other to hear the words of wisdom which dropped from the lips of his worship the Mayor. Never before have I seen a crowd into the hearts of which terror seemed so firmly struck – terror bred of modern explosives. The most piteous face in the throng was that of a Maritzburg barrister, who had visited Ladysmith with the view of seeing war as one attends a picnic. A bursting shell unnerved him, and to complete his misery the enemy cut communication. The Mayor opened the meeting; men roused to a patriotic fervour hurled heroics to the crowd. The only dignified speaker was Archdeacon Barker, who closed his address with the peroration, "that if he was to die, he would die under the Union Jack in preference to the white flag." The crowd applauded; some one suggested the National Anthem. It was sung in chorus over and over again. Not a man would flinch from his post, the townsfolk of Ladysmith were of one mind. The meeting closed with a bar of "Rule Britannia," and then every one dispersed to pack his bag and to accept Boer magnanimity.

Thus it was resolved, and on the following morning Colonel Ward arranged for a camp at Intombi, about four miles south of the town, on the railway. Trains were run down to a convenient point, hospital tents pitched, and during Sunday and Monday the majority of wounded were transferred from the town. Men with families carried their homes out in wagons, and, I regret to say it, dozens of able-bodied men accompanied these caravans who might have borne arms in the defence of the town. The camp was placed under the control of the resident magistrate of Ladysmith. Hitherto the Boers have respected the camp, none but medical officers being allowed passes to visit the neutral zone. A train leaves every morning to ration the refugees. On Sunday Joubert sent in about 90 of our wounded from Dundee. They were trained down to Modder Spruit, with their attendant medical officers. All windows in the train were shuttered to prevent the passengers from realizing any of the enemy's movements. These officers report that they and the wounded have been treated with every courtesy by the Boers, Joubert himself having constantly made the round of the hospitals. The details of General Penn Symons's death show that he met the end calmly, dictating a last message to Lady Symons half-an-hour before he died. Few realize the serious effect which General Symons's loss had upon the early issues of the campaign. His services were lost to the country just at the moment they were most required. A victory won is a little thing in comparison with a victory driven home.

Although a number of the residents of Ladysmith sought the protection of the neutral flag, there were quite a number who remained. These people spent the three days of armistice in discovering situations which promised to secure them against shell fire. The Klip River which encircles the town with many bends commended itself to most, and by Sunday night its shelving banks presented a pathetic, yet almost amusing, spectacle. Every civilian adult, white and black, capable of wielding pick or shovel had bent his back in honest toil, and the gravel cliffs of the streamlet will remain a lasting testimony to what man can do when moved by a sense of physical danger. The majority of delvers were able to secure some mining talent to aid them in their work. Others with longer purses enlisted the services of soldiers, who brought the rudiments of military fortification to bear upon their labours. Others, imbued only with the instinct of self-preservation, burrowed shafts perpendicular to the bank, so that the cliff face bore the appearance of a nesting home of mammoth sandmartins. On every hand were gabions, sandbags, and sangars. But the greatest defence of all was that of the Imperial Light Horse. The majority of these men are Johannesburg miners, and they at once began to undermine their camp with shafts and galleries. Commandeering every coloured man that ventured near their camp, they cut ten shafts in the river cliff, and working night and day for 48 hours constructed an underground gallery capable of holding half the garrison. The sequel to their industry was amusing, for as soon as the last barrowful of earth had been thrown to the surface, down came a staff officer, and the regiment was sent to support the Manchester Regiment on the most exposed crest line of the defences. But there was a pathetic side to all this labour. The poor women and children were terrified out of their lives. Exposed to the most erratic climate in the world, old dames, young mothers, and delicate women left their homes to grub out an existence in damp holes and dirty subterranean passages; conscious of the din of arms above them, their anxiety for the safety of fathers, brothers, sons, and husbands was intensified by the lying reports which reached and circulated even in the level of the river bed. Such is the history of a beleaguered town.

But while the civilian population were hard at work upon their private defences, the military intrenchments were being pushed forward with wonderful despatch. The three days of grace were a godsend, for, if the Boers had chosen to hurl an organized attack upon any of our most vulnerable posts, it is doubtful whether, during the first four days of the investment, we should have been strong enough to have prevented them from occupying positions from which they could have dictated terms. The post known as Wagon Hill, is extremely difficult to defend, and, if it were once occupied by the enemy and intrenched, their guns would have town and garrison at their mercy. But, happily, as well as being a slow thinker, the Boer is a slow mover, and, while the enemy was occupying himself in completing the investment of the place and building gun emplacements at distant ranges, the defending units worked night and day to place their posts in a thoroughly defensive state. The commissariat and ordnance departments between them were able to supply 12,000 sacks. These were divided between battalions defending posts. Most of the troops, having come from India, had knowledge of the value of stones for building breastworks, and by Tuesday night the defences were so far perfected that every one was confident that the place was secure against infantry attack. The only anxiety lay in the extended front which it was necessary to occupy. Roughly from left to right it covered 11 miles. This used up every infantry battalion, leaving nothing to support a threatened post except cavalry. But as during this campaign cavalry armed with a long-ranged weapon has proved itself quite a new arm, and has constantly been employed as infantry, dismounted cavalry is not to be despised. The defence programme provides dismounted Lancers and Hussars to support the infantry line. On Sunday morning a general commandeering of horses for remounts for the Volunteer Cavalry took place. My animals were seized to make part of the bunch of 300 animals which made the first day's haul. On representation to headquarters my property was released, but the Carabineers succeeded in securing the 100 animals which they required. It was not surprising that there was casualty in the ranks of the Volunteer Cavalry, for ever since Natal was invaded on October 12 this arm has been worked day and night, and practically has been solely responsible for keeping touch with the enemy.

It is impossible to say what the real objective of the enemy is at present. As far as we know they have not detached a very large force to attack Colenso. Probably they hope to reduce Ladysmith before making a definite move southwards. This theory is supported by the intercourse which our medical men have had with groups of the enemy while tending the wounded. A doctor who mixed with the Free State commando on Friday said that the burghers on that side were confident that our garrison lay in the hollow of their hands. These burghers were big, fine men, travelling light, but there was a brightness about them which gave colour to the confidence which they expressed. They were perfectly friendly and outspoken, and greatly elated over the misfortune which had occurred to Colonel Carleton's column. They maintained that the 870 men who surrendered and were trained to Pretoria surrendered to an inferior force. But, however confident of success they may be, they are distressed at the effects of our artillery fire. They openly allowed that they could not face it, but had faith in the guns they were bringing from their base to reduce or silence all the advantage which our gunners possessed.

Of the 5th Lancers they spoke in great wrath, but with bated breath. They aver that they gave no quarter after Elandslaagte, and slaughtered men suing for mercy. The element of a cavalry pursuit was new to them, but they promise no quarter to any Lancer who may fall into their hands. This threat would probably be carried out, for three days after Elandslaagte we had the melancholy incident where a party of Boers allowed a 5th Lancer patrol of five men to ride into their midst, and then, instead of calling upon them to surrender, shot them down. One trooper only managed to escape to tell the story.

To-day, Second Lieutenant Hooper, of the 5th Lancers, arrived in camp, having come through the Boer lines from Estcourt to join his regiment – a very plucky exploit. He brought the first definite news from below. Our force at Colenso had had a brush with the enemy, and had fallen back on Estcourt. It seemed to bear out the impression that the force detached south by Joubert at present is inconsiderable. In the evening there was a report in camp that the Boers were trekking north. This report is said to have originated from the balloon section, who have done excellent work during the investment, in spite of the fact that they are certain to draw the enemy's fire as soon as they attempt an ascent. But a balloon affords a hard mark, and only once has it been damaged, when a shrapnel burst succeeded in spoiling an ascent.

Tuesday, November 7. – At 7 o'clock in the morning the enemy began an organized fire on the town and defences. The Peppworth heavy calibre gun opened with solemn regularity. A 4.7 howitzer found the town from Surprise Hill, while on the north a battery of high-velocity field guns burst shell in the old camp and Rifleman's Range. It was found that another 6in. gun had been placed in position on M'Bulwana, which, with two 4.7 howitzers and a battery of field artillery on the nek below Lombard's Kop, divided their attention between the Devonshire Regiment's pickets on Helpmakaar and the body of the town. Efficiently served and with sound ammunition this armament should have been sufficient to render the town unsafe. But, though the Boers opened with a heavy fire, the return from the only guns with which we could cope with them, the 4.7 naval guns, seemed a sufficient reply, for after two hours the firing slackened and practically ceased, the net casualties resulting from it being two cows and three horses. One or two buildings were struck. Towards evening a similar desultory fire was again opened, which wounded two men in the breastworks. These two casualties cost the enemy about 400 rounds of shell. The Boer small-calibre guns fired for the most part shrapnel. The position artillery fired common shell with a bursting charge of 50lb. of melinite and an occasional shrapnel in a very thin casing. Occasional pieces of ring and segment shell were found, showing that the enemy varied the missiles which they hurled against us. When the first burst was heard in the morning there was a general rush to earth amongst the civilians; for five minutes the main street was alive with a scurrying crowd. Ten minutes later Ladysmith was clear, except for an occasional staff officer or mounted orderly. In the evening the enemy made a half-hearted attack upon Caesar's Camp and Wagon Hill. But by this time everything there was snug and such of the enemy as came within twelve hundred yards of the post were speedily dislodged. But as it appeared that the Boers had discovered the advantage which would be theirs if they could gain Wagon Hill, Sir

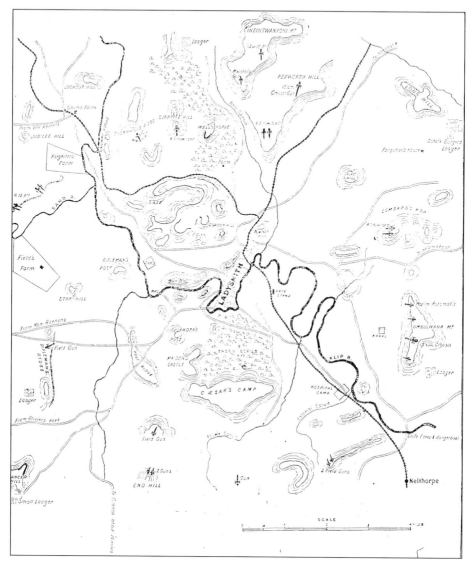

Map showing the position of the Boer guns round Ladysmith

George White considered it advisable to support the Manchester Regiment and Gordon Highlanders with the Imperial Light Horse. As an attempt to rush the post at night was anticipated they were hustled out immediately.

Wednesday, November 8. – The bombardment burlesque was deferred until 9 o'clock. It then recommenced in the same desultory way as on the previous afternoon. By the aid of the balloon and the powerful telescope of the Naval Brigade, the majority of the enemy's positions had been located. But it was with extreme difficulty that some of the batteries using smokeless explosives were discovered. The high velocity battery on a spur of Lombard's Kop, which had been spitting shell into the Devonshire Regiment and the town for 48 hours, was marked down. The sailors plied it with a charge of lyddite. The second burst was accurate, for the guns remained silent, and through our glasses we distinctly saw a group of mounted Boers ride up to the battery, then gallop away as if a cavalry brigade was behind them. The battery never fired again that day, and on Thursday its position had changed. Each day intermittent firing takes place between our cavalry and the enemy's outposts. But it is generally at impossible ranges, and the effect is rarely worth recording. The Boers about this period daily sent in large gangs of Indian coolies. As these men had been employed in working the Dundee and Elandslaagte coalfields, and the Dutch had taken the trouble to rail them down to Modder Spruit, it is probable that they despatched them in the hope that they would help in the reduction of the town by further exhaustion of the food supply. The send off which was given to these wretched Indians was typical of the Dutchman; they were told that "the British flag was lost in Natal, and that they had better go and look for it." To a certain extent they have a right to this pleasantry, as the annexation of all Natal above the Tugela River has been declared by the South African Republic, and Dutch magistrates have been appointed to all the districts occupied.

THE FIRST ATTACK ON THE TOWN

Thursday, November 9, was the most eventful day that we have had since communication was cut. It was the day on which Joubert selected to attempt to force the position. It was also the seventh day of the investment and the Prince of Wales's birthday. At 5 a.m. the enemy commenced the orthodox artillery preparation which should precede an assault. The two heavy calibre guns pitched their 94lb. projectiles into the town at regular intervals of seven minutes. The batteries on Lombard's Kop turned their attention to the Helpmakaar road posts. Surprise Hill and Bell Hill dropped missiles into the old camp, and the bombardment proceeded merrily and harmlessly for about an hour. Our naval guns replied at dignified intervals, and sections of a field artillery battery on Rifleman's Range and King's Post were sufficient restraint for the gunners preparing the position for assault from the north. There is no doubt that Joubert had prepared a simultaneous attack from three points. A pretence at two of these attempts came together, the third, that on the Helpmakaar posts, coming later. It cannot be said that any attack was severe, but, the heaviest firing being directed against Observation Hill, it shall be honoured with the title of the main attack. Early in the morning the 5th Lancers, as usual, patrolled in the vicinity of Observation Hill, which is a detached post held by two companies of the Rifle Brigade 2,000 yards to the direct front of Cove Redoubt. The country in front of Observation Hill is typical of the theatre of the operations. It is approached by rocky succeeding spurs, such valleys as there are abounding in dips and kopjes, affording admirable cover to a skirmishing enemy. But there are certain folds of veldt which it was necessary for the enemy to cross before they could occupy positions within damaging range. The passage of these folds entailed exposure, and it was this exposure that the Boers would not face that morning. The attempts were made in a very creditable manner. Peppworth Hill from 6,000 yards furnished artillery support, and M'Bulwana even from 11,000 yards made excellent practice against the reverse of Observation Hill. A heavy rifle fire was also brought to bear upon the sky-line of our position. But, if theoretically correct, it availed them little. Practice is teaching our men the best methods of meeting an attack of modern arms. The men lay snugly among the boulders while a tempest of lead passed over their heads, and the furious fusillade of the attack was answered by single aimed rounds from between the clefts of cover. Groups of the enemy made repeated bids to reduce the range of the attack. But it is just that discipline and leading necessary to induce men to cross the open under fire that the Boers lack, and time after time they were driven back. So effective was our fire that I can safely say that I never saw a Boer that morning within a thousand yards of our firing line. The expenditure of Dutch ammunition was prodigious; the enemy must have fired 100 rounds to every single round burnt by our men. So heavy was the fire that Sir George White reinforced Observation Hill with four companies from the Rifle Brigade. But this reinforcement was never needed.

The simultaneous attack was made on the western defences, Wagon Hill, Range Post, and Rifleman's Post appearing to be the objective. It succeeded no better than the attack upon Observation Hill. In fact, the well-directed fire of the two field guns on Rifleman's Post were of themselves sufficient to dispel it. The Boers had taken advantage of one of the deep folds in the big open plain which faces our western line, and here two shrapnel found them in rapid succession. In a moment the veldt was alive with galloping burghers putting distance between themselves and shell-fire. The Dutch artillery was more stanch than the riflemen, and for a considerable period an automatic gun and a field battery played on Caesar's Camp. But it made no impression, and the damage to town and earthwork was immaterial. The attack on the Helpmakaar posts came later in the day, and at the best was only a half-hearted movement. If the enemy had been aware of the small effect which their shell-fire had made upon the shelter trenches of the Devonshire Regiment they would never have attempted to attack. Though the most exposed of all our defences, and exposed to artillery fire at short ranges from three points, this battalion have so converted the hillside that they are proof against all attack. The officers and men have grown cunning in the art of war, and, though shell after shell has displaced the earthen dressing of the breastworks, the siege casualties have not yet reached one per company. The enemy came down into the scrub-veldt which fronts the Devons' Post. The one squadron of the Imperial Light Horse which is permanently on patrol on the Helpmakaar road was reinforced by two squadrons of Natal Carabineers, and a battery of artillery stood to arms in camp in case the attack should develop.

But no development took place, and, after an exchange of long-range shots, the great attack of Thursday, which Joubert had promised the President would succeed, dwindled into the usual monotonous artillery duel. When the earnest nature of this attack is considered, a little incident which took place at noon is distinctly humorous. It was the Prince of Wales's birthday, and in orders for the previous day had appeared a paragraph to the effect that a Royal salute would be fired in honour of the Prince and that every man would receive a ration of rum in which to drink his Royal Highness's health. At a quarter to 12, when the artillery fire on both sides had somewhat slackened, Sir George White and staff climbed to Cove Redoubt. Precisely at noon the Naval Brigade fired a salute of 21 guns, directed in turn upon each of the enemy's known works, a percentage of rounds being fired with guns so elevated that they might fall into the valley beyond Peppworth Hill, where it was calculated Joubert and Erasmus had their camp. Immediately after the last round of the salute had been fired, Sir George called for three cheers for the Prince. The sailors jumped to their feet and cheered in ringing chorus. Picket after picket caught up the cry until the whole of Ladysmith was one shout of jubilation. Not content with this, post after post burst forth in the National Anthem. What the feelings of the enemy must have been it is impossible to imagine. They must have interpreted the clamour as resulting from contempt for their concerted effort to reduce us. A pigeon was then despatched conveying a telegram of congratulations from the garrison to the Prince. It was a pleasantry which cheered us all.

Our total casualties throughout the day were three killed and 17 wounded. Five men were hit by the burst of one shell; the remainder of the casualties were mainly rifle wounds. The result of the day's fighting was a great relief to all for it again proved the estimate which we had formed of the Boer – that if he has the heart to come on, he has not the organization and discipline which can turn this courage to account.

Friday, November 10, opened with a heavy thunderstorm, and the Boers made no attempt even to shell the town. In fact, it was at one time supposed that the enemy had drawn off, as the squadron of Imperial Light Horse on the Helpmakaar Road were able to patrol nearer to Lombard's Kop than upon previous days. The patrols also found evidences of a hasty withdrawal of the enemy, saddlery and camp furniture lying about in some profusion. But there had been no change in the main artillery positions, and the 37mm. gun sputtered into groups which advanced incautiously. A report was current in the morning that the Boers were engaged in damming the river above us. This mattered little, as the river came down in spate from the night rains. This rise was not an unmixed blessing, as the rise washed out many of the dwellers in caves in the river bed. But during the last 48 hours a great change had come over the townspeople. They had become reconciled to the screech of shrapnel and faced the bombardment, if not with contempt, at least with composure. When the weather became heavy, such civilians as remained congratulated themselves in that they had not migrated to the refuge camp at Intombi.

An Indian coolie came in in the afternoon from Joubert's camp. He had been detained there eight days. His information was not valuable, but he informed us that the Boers were living chiefly upon slaughter cattle and that three of the shells from the Royal salute had fallen in the vicinity of the camp. He also reported having seen 50 wounded Boers as the result of Thursday's fighting.

Saturday, November 11, the ninth day of the investment, opened with considerable excitement, as a European called Brockie, having evaded the Boer outposts, brought news into camp from Estcourt. On Thursday, just before sundown, heliograph communication had been established with Estcourt, but it was but a flash of a few moments' duration. Headquarters knew nothing of what was passing below beyond the fact that we still held Estcourt. The man Brockie brought the tidings that three brigades under General Clery had left Cape Town to relieve us, that General Sir Redvers Buller had relieved Kimberley, and that there were no Boers south of the Tugela. This news gave us great impetus, for it was felt that the colony was safe and that Sir George White had fulfilled his mission, which was to save the colony until Buller's forces could take action. This messenger had experienced great difficulty in forcing the lines. It had taken him 36 hours, and when travelling by night he had constantly passed through the enemy's picket camps, and on one occasion had been forced to brain a sentry. He reported that the Boers had armed their Basutos and Kaffirs for outpost work. These he had been able to pass by pretending to be a Dutchman, but this native cordon accounts for the difficulty we have had in getting our Kaffir messengers through. I have sent a man out every day, but I fear with but slight success. Two have come back having been captured and their messages taken from them. This point is certain. At the present juncture the Boers find it politic to treat the native of the country well.

About midday the heavy guns opened on the town and shelled for about an hour. Mr. Carter's house was again hit, this making the fifth time; a store in the main street was also damaged. But the net result in loss of life was two mules belonging to the team of an ambulance wagon. A siege baby was to-day born in one of the subterranean passages in the river bank. In the evening a deserter came in from the enemy. He was a colonial born Irishman belonging to the Irish brigade. His information was of some value, and proved that our estimate both of the enemy's positions and of his strength had been comparatively correct. He stated that the Boers expressed great dissatisfaction at the result of Thursday's attack, but were still confident of bringing about the fall of the town. The deserter also reported that the Irishmen were being employed in hauling the ammunition for the big guns up the hills – a risky proceeding, as our shrapnel searches the reverses. One shrapnel alone had killed and wounded 17 of his comrades. His further information was that it was published in the Boer camp that Mafeking had fallen and that Commander Cronje was due in a day or two to arrive before Ladysmith with a reinforcement of over 5,000 burghers.

Sunday, November 12, was another quiet day. Some exchanges in wounded were made, and Joubert sent an apology to General White for his men having fired on an ambulance. The sappers went out to Lombard's Kop and destroyed with dynamite a farmstead which had given cover to the enemy. An occasional exchange of shots took place as usual between patrols.

The Times' report accurately identifies the main threat to the besieged garrison as coming from the Boer artillery. But the Boer artillery, like so many of the Boer martial practices, refused to conform to any of the norms of 'civilized' warfare. One day the garrison might be subjected to a bombardment of infernal accuracy and intensity; the next the Boers might prefer to rest their guns, or fire objects such as Christmas puddings, as they did on Christmas Day 1899, but there was always the danger of real shells and the reminder of mortality that they brought. It was the arbitrariness of the shelling that worked upon the imagination of the garrison and stretched their nerves. One person might be lucky, as was Saddler Sergeant Lyle on 18 December: 'Saddler Sergt. Lyle had a marvellous escape. He was sitting on a milk case about 2 ft. by 1.6 at the opening of his tent a little to the left of where a shell burst, a fragment of which passed through the case between his legs, smashing 4 rifles strapped to the pole and through another man's kit and blankets (Sergt. Major Mitchell who worked for Nicolson in Vryheid) tearing his things to pieces. A farrier sergt. was asleep alongside but neither were touched.'[4] Unfortunately, we don't have a record of Sergeant Lyle's reaction to this incident. Other members of the garrison were, however, not as fortunate. On 30 November a shell hit the Town Hall, which had been pressed into service as an emergency hospital, killing or wounding ten of the patients and staff.

On occasion the garrison ventured out from its fortifications to attack the surrounding Boers. The prime targets for these sorties were the Boer gun positions.

LADYSMITH, DEC. 8.

In consequence of information received yesterday, it was considered that it might be possible to capture at night the new heavy calibre battery recently erected by the enemy on a spur of Lombard's Kop, which had daily been raking the town with considerable effect. The scheme was one in which bold audacity was the chief factor of success. The battery was six miles from our camp and was erected on the summit of a flat-topped kopje, a sheer ascent of 500ft. General Sir A. Hunter had charge of the arrangements. He selected 100 picked men of the Imperial Light Horse, 100 Natal Carabineers, and a few sappers and gunners, with 300 mounted Volunteers protecting the flanks.

With the utmost secrecy the little column of resolute men was led out by Major Henderson. A party of his guides, by admirable leading, brought the force in a bee-line to the foot of the hill at 2 o'clock. It was pitch dark. The men extended and began to creep up. When they were a short way up, they were challenged by a Dutch picket. The challenge was answered by a cheer. In spite of the difficulties of the climb up an almost sheer ascent, the men raced up the hillside, and, time now being everything, rushed the picket, who began firing, giving the alarm to the defenders above. The very precipitous slope for a time gave cover; then, when our men were within 20 yards of the summit, the Dutch poured rifle fire into them. Colonel Edwards shouted "Fix bayonets; let them have it with cold steel." Though the whole force mustered only four bayonets, being mounted infantry, the ruse had its effect. Shouting "Cold steel!" the men breasted the crest, and the Dutch gunners fled into the darkness. Colonel Edwards, at the head of his men, was the first in the gun emplacement. There was no hand-to-hand fighting. The men formed a cordon round the gun parapet, and the sappers, under Captain Fowke, R.E., placed guncotton charges in the two big guns with two-minute fuses. In three-quarters of an hour the whole thing was done. Captain Fowke was the last man to leave the parapet, having waited to inspect the satisfactory results of the bursting charges. The casualties from fire were one severely wounded and eight wounded, including Major Henderson in two places. A 6in. Creusot and a 4.7in. howitzer were destroyed, and a Maxim was captured and brought away.

Our men withdrew in perfect order, covering their retirement with volleys. The success of the operation was due to the magnificent guiding of Major Henderson and the guides and the intrepid leading of General Hunter and Colonel Edwards. The gun parapet sandbags were 31ft. high. "Long Tom's" breech block was brought away as a trophy.

A bold reconnaissance to the north-east came under a severe fire from the enemy's intrenchments. We had about 20 casualties, but succeeded in carrying away much of the enemy's telegraph line.

From a private letter of a Boer gunner which we found it seems that the enemy are less sanguine of reducing Ladysmith. The writer admits that "our burghers are now a bit frightened."

Altogether the garrison of Ladysmith is to-day in higher spirits than it has ever been before.

During the siege the dozen or so correspondents from the British and colonial press lived in relative luxury, often commanding the best accommodation and food: 'Looked up Norton-Smith who has taken up quarters with Mrs Mason. Found him looking a perfect wreck. Had he remained at Intomba Camp I fear he would never have returned. He is very fortunate to get such good quarters, especially amongst such celebrities as several of the war correspondents are making this their head quarters.'[5] Despite the relative comfort of their surroundings, the correspondents were not all immune to the perils of the siege. Although none of the reporters died from wounds at Ladysmith, George Steevens of *The Daily Mail* succumbed to the near-epidemic of dysentry that affected the town, and died just after Christmas 1899.

Morale within the town was generally good for most of the siege, but the repulse of Buller's relief column in December 1899 caused widespread despondency; all the more so because of the garrison's assumption that Buller would inevitably be successful.

LADYSMITH, NOV. 28.

The garrison has been thrown into a great state of excitement by news which came in this morning of the movement of a relief column and of British successes on the southern frontier of the Free State. It is quite time that relief came. The enemy have succeeded in bringing a third gun of heavy calibre into action within 5,000 yards of the western defences. This is a very different matter to the 8,000 yards of the other 6in. guns.

The enemy have now ascertained our most vulnerable points, and the shelling has become disagreeably effective. Rations are reduced, and a certain amount of sickness is prevalent. But the whole atmosphere has changed since this morning's news, and all are prepared for the last effort which it is anticipated the enemy will make before completing the withdrawal to their own frontier, evidences of which withdrawal are now being observed from our posts.

There is no indication that the enemy are preparing to dismantle their gun positions. Shells from the new 6in. battery are falling into the town as I write.

Our guides occupied an empty farmhouse to the north yesterday and found that the Boers had erected a hospital flag above it. This is another example of their misuse of the Geneva flag.

The shell fire has caused an increase of casualties during the last few days, but their number is not serious as yet.

LADYSMITH, DEC. 19.

It is impossible to express the feeling of consternation with which the news of General Buller's check on the Tugela was received in the invested town. All had made up their minds that the period of enforced inactivity was at an end. We were proud to think that we should be able to meet the relieving troops with the little histories of our own regarding the Gun and Surprise Hill batteries. No one for a moment imagined that the Southern force would be anything but successful. On December 12 heavy firing had been heard in the direction of Colenso, while on the following day the pickets on Caesar's Camp and Wagon Hill had seen the smoke made by the bursting shrapnel. Then we waited for news – waited breathlessly for orders to be given to the Flying Column, composed of the Devonshire and Manchester Regiments and the Gordon Highlanders, to leave camp to complete the devastation which the Southern force had begun. Men and women congratulated themselves in the streets when they heard that one of our heavy guns had been sent to Wagon Hill to cover the movement of the Flying Column. But the silence was prolonged, though the helio winked ceaselessly from the hill tops; but rumour had its way and stories were told of a splendid victory, of deserting Boers, of fleeing Dutch and slaughtered burghers. But nothing from headquarters. December 16 was Dingaan's Day, the anniversary of the declaration of independence of the South African Republic by the triumvirate in 1880. It was thought that this would be a suitable date for us to crush the power of the rebel State. Day dawned, and with the advent of the sun the big gun on Bulwana opened a spiteful fire. Twenty-one rounds were fired into the town. The Boers had remembered the salute which we had fired on the Prince of Wales's birthday. Grimly, on Dingaan's Day, they returned the salute. And with effect, for there were three fatal casualties from the fire.

Still the garrison congratulated itself. This salute was but the song of the dying swan. In a fit of bravado the enemy had fired into us before removing the gun to escape the advance from the south. A story came in from Intombi Camp that the Boers had sent a number of wounded Dutch for treatment. Excitement ran high, and a speculative photographer circulated a notice to the effect that now the siege was practically at an end he would be happy to take a mass group of the civilians who had survived. But on Saturday night a sinister order appeared. The batteries attached to the Flying Column were sent back to their positions on the line of defences.

On the morrow the following general order was published to the garrison:–

The General Officer Commanding the Natal Field Force regrets to have to announce that General Sir Redvers Buller failed to make good his first attack on Colenso; reinforcements will not, therefore, arrive here as early as was expected. Sir George White is confident that the defence of Ladysmith will be continued by

Major-General French, the
cavalry leader

the garrison in the same spirited manner as it has hitherto been conducted until the
General Officer Commanding in Chief in South Africa does relieve it.

The news was received with blank dismay. The disappointment was
overwhelming. Then, as the situation began to be studied calmly, the tension was
relieved. It did not really matter if the investment lasted a few weeks longer. We
had few of the luxuries of life, it is true, but there was a full ration of the
necessaries for at least two months. The defences were practically secure against
attack. Our worst enemy was sickness. The situation was anything but desperate.
The men having so long stood to the field fortifications seemed satisfied to remain
on the defensive. The disappointment was acute, but, as far as the garrison was
concerned, the situation remained unchanged. As a whole, the health of the troops
was good. Enteric fever in a virulent form had made its appearance and was
dealing hardly with the younger men. But this was to be expected, after 10,000
men had been cooped up in a small area for 50 days.

Perhaps the most serious question which the authorities had now to face was
that of forage for the cavalry. The garrison, with mounted Volunteers, includes $5\frac{1}{2}$
cavalry regiments and two brigade divisions of artillery. There is a limited supply
of grazing ground within the perimeter of the camp. But it is very limited, and
whenever our animals stray outside to better grass the drovers and escort are
immediately shelled into more discretion. Even if grazing were sufficient the
situation would be serious, as troop and battery horses cannot do their work on
grass alone. To my mind only one course remains open. The cavalry are no good
here; they never have been any good since our communication was cut; they

should go, and make their way down south. It is not a long ride to the Tugela, and once across the Tugela they would be safe. It is a pity that the cavalry has ever been here at all. After October 30 it was apparent to all that the place would be invested. When General French left he should have taken the cavalry, or the majority of the regiments, with him. They would have been of inestimable value to the relieving force. If there had been 3,000 cavalry working from Estcourt no general raiding of the Weenen and Upper Tugela districts would have taken place. They would have prevented the Boers from breaking up into the small parties which have been responsible for the general looting of Northern Natal.

From all accounts the invaders have carried out their devastation with a ruthless hand. Not content with lifting all cattle found on the farms, they have destroyed private property in a shameful and childish manner. When orders were given to leave the homesteads standing, the raiders, after removing everything portable, resorted to the petty spite of slitting pictures and firing bullets into pianos, and in every way trying to do as much annoying damage as possible. In a farm which we have retaken we found the pictures with the eyes gouged out of the portraits, and all the little harmless ornaments, which the feminine mind loves so well, deliberately smashed. A poor revenge!

After the disasters of 'Black Week' the garrison, although unhappy, did not face the prospect of imminent defeat or surrender. The Boers relied almost entirely on their artillery's ability to wear down the garrison, rather than pressing their numerical advantage to take the place by storm. It is true that the Boers did launch a number of fairly large attacks but, despite the bravery of some of their troops, none of their assaults came close to achieving the breakthrough that they needed. The attack that took place on 6 January 1900 was perhaps the closest that they came to victory.

LADYSMITH, JAN. 10.

Saturday, January 6, witnessed the most sanguinary and desperate engagement which has yet fallen to the lot of the troops forming the Ladysmith garrison. Shortly after midnight the Boers, in four columns, attacked our most vulnerable defences, and by daybreak succeeded in effecting a lodgment in two places. So determined was the assault and so tenacious were the enemy that the Boers maintained their hold of the positions won for 17 hours, and were only dislodged after an immense sacrifice of life. The carnage on both sides was terrible. From beginning to end it was a soldier's battle, and our ultimate success lay in the company leading of the infantry.

The enemy had chosen to make their main attempt upon the western face of the perimeter. The defences here are ranged upon the summit of a flat-topped hill which forms a crescent, with the interior slopes facing the enemy. The southern half of this crescent is known as Caesar's Camp; the northern, which rather lies in a westerly direction from the town, as Wagon Hill. From end to end the military crest line is a little under four miles. The summit of Caesar's Camp is a broad plateau some 800ft. above the level of Ladysmith. Wagon Hill is practically a continuation of Caesar's Camp, forming two smaller plateaus connected by lower saddles. These plateaus are known as Wagon Hill and Wagon Hill West respectively. Caesar's Camp is held by the Manchester Regiment with the 42nd Field Battery and a naval 12½-pounder gun, Wagon Hill by half a battalion 60th Rifles, and Wagon Hill West by two squadrons of the Imperial Light Horse. As the position faces the enemy the ends of the hill are very steep and difficult, and under all circumstances would afford cover to an assaulting column. Towards the centre of the crescent the ascent is less perpendicular and has the appearance of a huge grassy glacis. The Dutch, with their natural instinct for attack, ignored the centre slope and simultaneously assaulted both horns of the crescent.

WAGON HILL.

As I have said before, from the very commencement it was a soldier's battle, and it would be impossible to give a detailed account of the action as it proceeded along that long line of front. I will therefore confine my description in the first instance to the sequence of events as they occurred on Wagon Hill. It so chanced that it had been determined to place a gun on Wagon Hill West. This entailed the presence of a working party of sappers and half a company of Gordon Highlanders on the hill. The working party was busy hauling up the different pieces of the gun and carriage when the assault was made. In fact the Kaffirs with bullock teams and carts made so much noise that, according to a story which was told by a prisoner, the enemy believed that we had been informed of the impending attack. So firmly did they believe that we were reinforcing that at one period there was some hesitation whether the attempt should be made. As it turned out, it was providential that this working party was present, for it added 60 rifles to the defence of the post. The Boers apparently collected in Fourier's Spruit, a dry stream bed which runs past the foot of the position. Here they surprised an outlying picket of the Imperial Light Horse. It consisted of four men, whom the Boers overpowered, killing two and wounding the others. The force, which consisted of about 300 picked men of the Harrismith commando, then took off their shoes and split up into two columns. One, under de Villiers and Van Wyk, commandant of Harrismith, commenced the steep ascent of Wagon Hill West; the other column climbed the almost sheer slopes of Wagon Hill proper. This column evidently made its objective the nek which joins the two Wagon Hills, which, if secured, would ensure the isolation of the most western post. They all but achieved their object, and if it had not been for the presence of the working party and sappers nothing could have deterred them. As de Villiers's party was creeping silently up the hillside, Lieutenant Mathias, an officer of the Imperial Light Horse, was descending to visit his posts. He suddenly found himself in the centre of the Boers. They mistook him for one of themselves, and he had the presence of mind to continue to climb upwards with them. When a few yards from his own picket he rushed forward and gave the alarm. But the enemy were already upon them. It was just half-past 2 when this picket was driven in. In a moment all was confusion on the summit of the hill. The working party of the Gordons had left their arms on the nek and rushed to find them. It was pitch dark, and from their similarity of head-dress it was impossible to distinguish the enemy from the Light Horsemen. The sappers, who had their arms, were formed up in some sort of order behind the gun epaulement by Lieutenant Digby Jones. But after a few seconds of indiscriminate firing the mixed defenders were driven over the reverse, and the Dutch were in possession of Wagon Hill West. Luckily the gun had not come up, but was still at the bottom of the hill.

It was an absolute surprise. The chaos for the moment was supreme. Rifles were snapping on every side. The Kaffirs and coolies with the wagons had fled, overturning the lanterns. The vivid flashes of the rifles furnished the only light. Firing now opened along the nek, showing that the Boers had forced the breastworks of the outlying pickets of the 60th Rifles on Wagon Hill. The Naval Volunteers fired half-a-dozen wild and erratic rounds from their Hotchkiss, and evacuated their gun-pit, hauling the gun with them. The little knot of mixed troops driven from the summit of Wagon Hill West was gathered in the dip of the saddle. All were strangers to the position, and they were herded together like sheep. Men were firing blindly into each other and into the darkness. Lieutenant Macnaghten, Scots Fusiliers, commanding the Gordon working party, collected as many of his scattered Highlanders as could be found. Something had to be done, and he shouted out for some one who knew the position. A trooper of the Light Horse volunteered to lead him up to the crest-line sangars. They clambered up amid the hissing of Mauser pellets and the spit-sparks of explosive bullets bursting on the stones. Men in felt hats were firing on every side. "They are our men; for God's sake don't fire," shouted the guide. They may or may not have been Volunteer cavalry. The situation seemed hopeless. Lieutenant Macnaghten stumbled across a breastwork. It was full of prostrate men. One was shrieking in agony, others were groaning. There were perhaps 15 bunched in this flimsy sangar, constructed to hold four at most. All were wounded with the exception of three, and among the grievously wounded was Lieutenant MacGregor, the other officer of the Gordon working party. Macnaghten collected his sound men together, but, though the hilltop was alight with rifle flashes, it was impossible to separate friend from enemy. Fearing to do damage to their own supports if they fired, the little group lay with fixed bayonets until they were surrounded. Then a big burgher loomed up before them and shouted in English "Hands up." With three sound and 13 wounded men Macnaghten could do nothing, and the Boers took the little party below the crest-line. The enemy had won the crest-line, while the two weak squadrons of the Imperial Light Horse had been almost annihilated.

As soon as it had become apparent that the affair was more than an interchange of shots between pickets, Colonel Hamilton, commanding this section of the defences, telephoned down for reinforcements. The first to arrive were two and a half companies of Gordon Highlanders from Fly Kraal, a post at the foot of Caesar's Camp. One company under Captain Hon. R. F. Carnegie was immediately despatched to the support of the Manchester pickets on Caesar's Camp, the remaining company and a half was taken by Major Miller-Wallnutt to Wagon Hill, one half company under Lieutenant Baird being left in a breastwork on the first saddle below Manchester Fort. At 4 o'clock the four companies of the same regiment which were in camp in the town were ordered up to Caesar's Camp. They marched out at 20 minutes past 4, and just as they were across the Klip River bridge, a bullet, which must have travelled over 3,000 yards, struck Colonel Dick-Cunyngham, inflicting a mortal wound. Other reinforcements were on the move. The remaining two squadrons of Imperial Light Horse dashed off to Wagon Hill, where they arrived not a moment too soon. The Dawson City half battalion of the 1st 60th followed them, while four companies of the Rifle Brigade were drawn from King's Post and sent up to Caesar's Camp. As day broke there were indications that the enemy contemplated attacking both Helpmakaar and Observation Hill. The 21st Field Battery was sent out to cover the approaches to Wagon Hill on the west; the 53rd Battery took up a position in the scrub jungle covering the southern slope of Caesar's Camp.

The situation on Wagon Hill at daybreak was strange. The Boers had effected a lodgment on the plateau and the nek connecting with Wagon Hill West. They were lying, some on the reverse of our sangars, others among the stones on the ridge. A remnant of the Light Horse with some stragglers of the 60th were ensconced among the boulders of an eminence to the left of the saddle, from which they checked the Boer advance. Cross fires were coming from every direction, and to show a head was to court instant death. On this part of Wagon Hill proper Boer and Britisher were barely 30 yards apart. Wagon Hill West was clear save for a buck-wagon and its in-spanned team, loaded with the foundation for a gun-carriage. Our men were all huddled in groups along the inside slope of the hill. The enemy occupied similarly the outside slope. The plateau itself had become a "Tom Tiddler's Ground." Neither side dare show upon it, for the 60th Rifles covered it with a cross fire from the reverse of Wagon Hill and the Boers from the boulders on the crest-line of the kotal. But the Boers holding the incline were pushing more men up the waterway by which they had made their way up to the nek. The augmented firing line was sorely pressing the remaining handful of Light Horsemen. The arrival at this moment of their two squadrons from camp could not have been more opportune. Led by Colonel Edwards they reinforced the little band of resolute men among the boulders. But this addition to the fighting strength could not move the Boers. They were evidently picked men and their markmanship was deadly. It was at this period and amongst these very rocks that the colonel, two majors, and four other officers of the Light Horse were hit; simply sacrificed in ascertaining the possibilities of the situation. Lord Ava, Colonel Hamilton's orderly officer, was wounded a little higher up. The position of affairs became most critical. If the Boers succeeded in reinforcing and seized the knoll which the Light Horse held, it meant that we should have been driven with cruel loss out of Wagon Hill, and this would have rendered Caesar's Camp untenable. No infantry fire could dislodge the enemy. It was scarcely possible to see them and live. To effect a rush necessitated the passage of 60 yards of open. Major Mackworth, attached to the 60th Rifles, attempted to make the rush with what men he could collect. He fell shot through the head by an explosive bullet, and casualties amongst his men rendered the attempt abortive. Captain Codrington, 11th Hussars, commanding a squadron of the Light Horse, went forward to find cover for his men. If successful he was to signal back. Thirty yards away he fell, and just had strength enough to wave the Light Horse back. Lieutenant Tod, another attached officer of the 60th, with 12 men, made a further attempt to rush the open. He was shot dead three yards from cover, and seven of his men were hit. After this the men could not be brought to face the fire. Firing

Cartoon from *Punch*, 28 March 1900

then slackened, and news was passed round that the whole of the position, Caesar's Camp included, was clear of the enemy with the exception of the few men ensconced on Wagon Hill. It was resolved to wait until dark before attempting to clear them out with the bayonet. This information ultimately proved to be incorrect, but for the time being it was believed and acted upon.

But to return to Wagon Hill West. The mixed troops here were gallantly rallied by Lieutenant Digby Jones, R.E., the only officer present, until they were reinforced by the company of Gordon Highlanders under Major Miller-Wallnutt. Colonel Gore-Browne, of the 60th, also sent two companies to the support of the western post. With these reinforcements it was possible to regain a portion of the plateau and crest-line, and about 10 o'clock the firing slackened considerably. But everyone had to lie as they were, for any movement caused the action to reopen. Hundreds of mounted Boers could be seen moving in the plain to the west. These were kept in check by the 21st Field Battery and the 18th Hussars. The battery was particularly exposed, no fewer than five intrenched hostile guns playing upon it, including a 6in. position gun. But its losses were mainly confined to the gun teams, 11 horses being wounded and four killed. Though the musketry fire slackened towards midday the fire of the enemy's artillery increased. The heavy gun on Bulwana fired over a hundred rounds, dividing its attention between the 53rd Battery and Caesar's Camp, while three very vicious field pieces raked Wagon Hill with common shell or burst shrapnel over the crest-line.

A little after 11 the force on Wagon Hill was reinforced by three companies of the Devonshire Regiment under Colonel Park. They joined the two reserve companies of the 60th Rifles on Wagon Hill proper. Everything went well until about 2 o'clock, when suddenly the mixed troops holding the flimsy sangars on the crest-line of Wagon Hill West, broke their ranks and rushed back to the reverse slope. The Boers had appeared on the crest-line. Luckily it was but a handful of desperate men. If they had been followed by 20 burghers as resolute as themselves the plateau would have been lost a second time. The situation was much the same as the one which had cost us Majuba in the last campaign; the Boers appeared suddenly when not expected, and the men, without officers and practically without non-commissioned officers, broke and fled as soon as the felt hats were level with their feet. Yet out of the eight men who made the brow of the hill only two had nerve enough to continue. Grasping the situation, de Villiers, the commandant, and one other dashed for the gun epaulement. Major Miller-Wallnutt, the only regimental officer there, and a sapper were shot dead at the gun-pit. Fortunately the sappers who, with fixed bayonets, were stationed near the emplacement, stood firm. Lieutenant Digby Jones, who had commanded them with great gallantry since the night attack, led them forward, and shot de Villiers, falling himself a moment later with a rifle bullet through his brain. It was all the work of a moment, but six brave men lay extended on the ground. It is hard to think which were the more valiant, the middle-aged farmers, who, unsupported, had faced a hundred, or the brave boy who had stemmed his men in the stampede, and had sacrificed his own life to save the position. Colonel Hamilton, who was just below when this sudden attack was delivered, at once sent down and ordered up a dismounted squadron of the 18th Hussars. The plateau was then reoccupied.

Our losses by this had been very heavy, and in the majority of cases the wounded were lying where they had fallen. It was impossible to recover them. Lieutenant Denniss, R.E., went on to the crest-line to search for Digby Jones. He likewise was shot dead, and fell beside his brother officer.

The main reason for the Boers' lack of success in storming Ladysmith lay not in a lack of courage, but in the lack of ingrained steadiness of purpose that training and discipline gives to regular troops. Reitz describes his feelings and actions during one of these unsuccessful attacks on Ladysmith: 'Those of us with Isaac escaped annihilation because we were out of the direct line of fire and were able to regain protection before the soldiers had time to turn their attention to us, but we did not go unharmed, for Frank Roos, my tent-mate fell dead among us with a bullet through his heart. . . . We were so bewildered by the suddenness of everything that before we could collect our thoughts it was all over.'[6] In any siege the besiegers have four main ways to achieve success: bombardment, storm, famine and disease. At Ladysmith the Boers were not sufficiently well versed in the methods of regular warfare to press home their obvious advantages in both numbers and armaments, so storm and bombardment failed them. Both sides therefore simply sat down and waited: the British in the hope of relief, the Boers in the rapidly dwindling expectation that famine and disease would do their work for them. After 118 days of siege, on 28 February 1900, Buller finally broke through the Boer cordon and the inhabitants of Ladysmith were finally free to celebrate their long-awaited deliverance.

Notes

1. Reitz, 1950, p. 62.
2. A.J. Crosby, *Diary of the Siege of Ladysmith* (Ladysmith, 1976), p. 11.
3. Ensor, 1980, p. 292.
4. Crosby, 1976, p. 18.
5. Ibid., p. 20.
6. Reitz, 1950, p. 65.

Kimberley

'They say that "war is hell", the "great accursed",
The sin impossible to be forgiven –
Yet I can look beyond it at its worst,
And still find blue in heaven.'

(William Armagh, from 'Is War The Only Thing That Has No Good In It?')

While Kimberley was not as strategically important as Ladysmith, it did have two glittering prizes for the Boers. The first glittered quite literally: Kimberley was the site of the De Beers diamond mines. The second prize was Cecil Rhodes, the arch-imperialist himself. But as with the two other towns, Kimberley was a bauble that the Boers would have done well to have left alone. Unfortunately, the lure of wealth and the chance to humiliate their arch-enemy proved too much of a temptation for even the austere Boers to resist. If one of the main objectives of the Boers was the capture of Rhodes, there must have been numerous occasions during the four-month siege when the garrison commander would have been glad to hand him over to their tender mercies.

The garrison commander, Colonel Robert Kekewich, was an able professional soldier who had used the last few weeks before the siege began on 15 October 1899 to throw a cordon of field fortifications around the town. Kekewich had with him 400 men from his own regiment, the 1st Loyal North Lancashire Regiment, plus a company each of Royal Artillery and Royal Engineers. These regulars were supplemented by 1,500 Natal Mounted Police, and an irregular force of 3,000 men raised and armed by De Beers. Although the latter were a godsend to Kekewich, they also provided the infernally energetic Rhodes with the excuse to interfere in the defence of the town. Rhodes insisted that, as the provider of the greatest number of troops, he should have a correspondingly large say in the conduct of the town's defence. As at Ladysmith, the Boers made no serious attempt to take Kimberley by storm, preferring instead to attempt to reduce the town using artillery. But also as in the case of Ladysmith, *The Times*' correspondent in Kimberley and the editor back in London transformed a rather dull and monotonous four months into an exciting saga of heroism.

KIMBERLEY, OCT. 24.

Major H. S. Turner and 270 men left Kimberley early this morning and marched north to Macfarlane's Farm, where they off-saddled. At 9 o'clock a scattered party of Boers appeared on the right flank. Major Turner at once opened fire and several Boers were seen to fall. The enemy then moved to a sand heap from the shelter of which they maintained a hot fire, which was returned.

At 11 o'clock Major Murray ordered 150 of the Loyal North Lancashire Regiment to entrain and proceed to the help of Major Turner, in support of whom an armoured train had already been sent out. Major Murray himself started at noon, taking with him two guns, two Maxims, and 70 mounted men.

The Boers attempted to advance against Major Murray, and in endeavouring to prevent the movement Major Turner was met with a heavy fire from a dam-wall 600 yards on his left. Suddenly, one of the two guns with the supporting force opened fire on the Boers, who were in an unfavourable position. The Boer artillery responded briskly.

A second armoured train was held in readiness, and at 2 o'clock it was sent forward with additional ammunition.

The Lancashires behaved splendidly and were highly commended by Major Turner.

Commandant Botha and many Boers were killed. The British loss was three killed and 21 wounded. The fight was a brilliant success.

KIMBERLEY, OCT. 23.

Every one is cheerful here. A wedding was celebrated to-day. A relief committee has been formed and liberal subscriptions have already been received. The list is headed by the De Beers Company and by Mr. Rhodes. Many ladies have volunteered their services as nurses. The conduct of all in the camp at Kimberley is excellent. Great enthusiasm has been aroused by the news of the British successes in Natal. An Englishman who has escaped from the Boer camp says that he was submitted to a searching examination on the defences and armaments of Kimberley.

The Boers have ordered the closing of all the liquor bars at Windsorton under a penalty of £600. The magistrate and the district surgeon are prisoners. The Boer commandant said he was glad that the place had submitted quietly. The Landdrost on Wednesday proclaimed martial law. The British magistrate has advised the inhabitants to return to their homes and occupations. Several farmers resident in the neighbourhood have been noticed in the ranks of the Boers.

Writing from Taungs on the 12th inst., Father Rorke says that 600 Boers, with 40 carts and 60 wagons, have formed a laager there and more are expected. All the whites have left except the women, who have taken refuge in the convent. The Boer commandant has promised that they will be protected. The country is completely ravaged between Dryharts and Taungs bridge.

Even after the relief of Kimberley on 15 February, *The Times* persisted in following a simplistic approach to the siege by publishing the 'siege' diary of the Hon. Mrs Rochfort Maguire, a close friend of Cecil Rhodes, who had accompanied him and her husband into Kimberley before the siege had begun.

On Friday, October 13, I arrived in Kimberley, having left Cape Town on the day of the declaration of war, and found the railway and telegraph to the north were both interrupted. On the evening of the 14th communication with the south was also cut off.

THE DEFENDING FORCE

The work of defending the town had for a fortnight before this been proceeding rapidly. A town guard of over 2,000 men, under Colonel Harris's command, had been enrolled. The Kimberley Rifles, consisting of 600 well-trained volunteers under the command of Colonel Finlayson, had been called out, Mr. Rhodes was busy buying horses to the number of about 800 for a new mounted force which was being formed by an amalgamation of the Diamond Fields Horse (a local volunteer force of De Beers workmen chiefly), of the Cape Police (numbers of whom had come in from outlying districts which it was found impossible to hold), and also of a number of raw recruits, making in all about 800 men. This composite regiment was under the command of Major (afterwards Lieutenant-Colonel) Scott-Turner, of the Black Watch. They soon were drilled into shape, and under Colonel Turner's leading inspired great terror amongst our besiegers. The town had been garrisoned since September 20 by 500 men of the Loyal North Lancashire Regiment, some Engineers, and one battery of mountain guns, 7-pounders, under Major (afterwards Lieutenant-Colonel) Chamier, added to which there was a very efficient corps of volunteers under Major May, called the Diamond Fields Artillery, who were also provided with some 7-pounders. The size of our guns left much to be desired; some 15-pounders which were on their way up were too late and remained at De Aar. The whole force was under the command of Lieutenant-Colonel Kekewich, of the Loyal North Lancashires, with Major O'Meara, R.E., as Intelligence Officer.

The defences of Kimberley were about 11 miles in circumference during the first months of the siege and later were somewhat enlarged – the area thus enclosed included the town of Kimberley with the adjoining town of Beaconsfield on the south-east, and on the north the model village of Kenilworth built by the De Beers Company for their *employés*. This village is a real oasis in the desert, for here alone in Kimberley are there avenues of trees along the roads making shady boulevards, and here also are the wonderful fruit gardens and long vine-covered walks created by Mr. Rhodes. Without this green spot to refresh us in our evening walks and rides the four months spent in Kimberley would have been almost unbearable. The town itself is exceedingly unattractive, dry and dusty, no fine buildings, and the houses mostly miserable tin shanties. Some of the houses, however, have very pretty gardens, but owing to a not too plentiful water supply during the siege and to the great drought these poor little gardens had, most of them, almost withered away by the end of two or three months of siege. The town is almost surrounded by a series of "tailing heaps" – *i.e.*, hillocks formed of the refuse earth after the diamond-washing. At the foot of these heaps stretched the huge diamond fields covered with blue ground containing many millions worth of diamonds. On these tailing heaps were placed the sand-bag forts, each manned by a number of the town guard, who proved themselves well able to justify the trust placed in them as defenders of the town. Somewhat outside Kimberley on the south-east is situated the Premier Mine, called after Mr. Rhodes when he was Prime Minister at the Cape. This was our most important fort, as, at an early period in the siege, the Boers cut off our supply of water from the Vaal River to the north and we had to depend entirely on that pumped from the Premier Mine by the De Beers Company. The garrison here, which was a strong one, was under the command of Captain O'Brien, of the Loyal North Lancashire Regiment, who did first-rate work throughout the siege. Here also were some guns under Lieutenant Rynd, R.A.

The sieges of Ladysmith, Mafeking, and Kimberley have been compared, and perhaps the differences between Kimberley and the other two may be pointed out. Ladysmith consisted almost entirely of a military garrison with a small civilian population; Mafeking, though defended largely by a volunteer force, was very well provided with Imperial officers, and most of the women and children had left at the beginning of the siege. At Kimberley the defence, with the exception of the 600 Regular troops, was conducted entirely by citizen soldiers, literally fighting for their hearths and homes, as most of them had their families with them in the town, the siege having come upon them more or less as a surprise.

It is hardly an exaggeration to say that Kimberley is De Beers and De Beers Mr. Rhodes, so huge is the property and wealth of the company and so great the power exercised over it by Mr. Rhodes. Their property consists in Kimberley and surrounding districts of 271,000 acres, on which are situated the De Beers, Kimberley, and Premier Mines. They also possess nearly the whole of two other mines – Bultfontein and Du Toitspan. Their *employés* number about 2,000 white men, who have something like 4,000 women and children depending on them; while in addition to this at the beginning of the siege they had about 10,000 natives in the mine compounds. Of the 2,000 white men nearly every one served in the volunteer forces. The directors of the company also – Colonel Harris, M.L.A., Mr. Oates, M.L.A., Mr. Compton, Mr Ryersbach; and the secretary, Mr. Pickering – did their duty manfully in the trenches and on the forts of the town guard. Almost from the beginning of the siege the mines had to stop working, partly owing to the necessity for economizing our coal supply, partly because the Boers blew up the store of dynamite which had been placed for safety some distance outside the town; so the work at the mines had to be restricted to pumping in order to keep them clear of water, and even this had to be stopped at the beginning of February owing to lack of coal.

THE SUPPLY OF FOOD

Kimberley is the second largest town in Cape Colony, with a population of 50,000. The Europeans and half-castes number about 33,000. The rest are natives of various tribes. As may be imagined, with so many mouths to feed, the food question soon became one of absorbing interest, and it was a matter of wonder to many people how so large a population and such a number of animals, about 6,000 horses, cows, &c., could have been kept alive so long without any fresh supplies coming in. It is owing to a variety of fortunate circumstances that this was possible. For some months previous to the declaration of war the De Beers Company, who appear to have anticipated the possibility of a siege, laid in large supplies of food stuffs, coal, fuel, and other mining requisites. Many of the

Telephonists and
telegraphers getting and
sending news from the
British siege train at
Orange River

townspeople also after the failure of the Bloemfontein Conference laid in private
stocks sufficient to support them for several months. Kimberley of to-day is a
large commercial and distributing centre. Whereas the population immediately
surrounding the mines is only 50,000, the town supplies a large and extensive tract
of country in the Free State, in Griqualand West, and in Bechuanaland, which
probably represents double or treble the population of Kimberley itself. A regular
business is done in foodstuffs by large firms in Kimberley, such as James
Lawrence and Co. and Hill and Paddon, with the villages of Jacobsdal, Petersberg,
Hoofstad, Boshof, Quarrenton, Windsorton, Klipdam, the River Diggings, Barkly
West, Campbell, Schmidts Drift, Griquatown, Douglas, Taungs, Vryburg,
Mafeking, and other places. In addition to this nearly all the food stuffs for the
country west of Kimberley to the border of Great Namaqualand are drawn through
this centre. A further factor to be taken into account is that the new crops of
mealies and Kaffir corn had just been secured by the firms interested in this line.

These supplies, owing to the unsettled state of the Free State, from which they
are largely drawn and where they are often held for the purpose of taking
advantage of other markets, had been rushed into Kimberley. It must be
recollected that both mealies and Kaffir corn (maize and millet) are most useful
food, as they can be used either as food for human beings or animals. The mealies
during the siege were largely used for horses; the Kaffir corn was converted into
meal and sold to the natives. In addition to this was the fact that the new crops of
forage and oats were expected somewhat earlier in the western districts; as a result
the old stocks were cleared out from the colonial towns to business places north.

Then, again, Kimberley railway-station has furnished a considerable supply of stores, stopped in transit. Kimberley is what is known as a transship depôt for the northern system of railways, and this means that there are always a large number of trucks under load here *en route* for the north. These, together with the goods which arrived immediately before the line was cut, came in very opportunely. The railway authorities as soon as the line was cut north of Vryburg ran all goods from that station back to Kimberley. One parcel included 1,000 bags of meal intended for the Transvaal Government. This meal had a very narrow shave on its way back. It arrived by almost the last train that got through from Vryburg. The train itself was rather heavy, and at Border Siding under the very nozzles of the Boer big guns part of it had to be left behind as the engine was unable to pull it up the incline. However, the second part was fortunately got into Kimberley in safety just in time, the engine having been sent back to get it. Several parcels of grain which had been sent to Modder River for Jacobsdal were also brought back. The produce merchants just previously to the declaration of war, finding that large orders were coming in for grain, &c., from places such as Vryburg and Jacobsdal, informed the military authorities of this, and advised them to put a stop to all foodstuffs going out of the town. This advice was acted upon and materially added to our supplies. We were not cut off entirely from supplies of fresh meat from outside till nearly a month after the beginning of the siege – the stocks of the De Beers Company, amounting to about 2,600 head, and others kept the town going for a considerable part of the siege.

MANAGING THE FOOD SUPPLY

In spite of all these stores, the management and regulation of them soon became a very serious question, as, although we hoped for speedy relief, it was always possible that we might have to wait longer than we anticipated. Martial law having been proclaimed soon after our communications were cut off, all power rested in the hands of Colonel Kekewich and his staff, and they proceeded to regulate the price of necessaries, which had begun to go up to an alarming extent. They took over the supplies of tea, coffee, &c., on December 20, regulations as to foodstuffs were issued, and permits were given for weekly supplies in limited quantities per head. On January 3 the meat ration was reduced from $\frac{1}{2}$lb. to $\frac{1}{4}$lb. per *diem* for adults, and the meat was sold under the control of the military authorities in the market buildings. Horseflesh was first served out on January 8, and from that date on it became almost the staple food of the white and coloured population. Towards the end we had a few mules and donkeys thrown in, which were pronounced a great treat; but we never had recourse to dogs or cats. The natives during the last two months of the siege had to subsist almost entirely on a meal diet, and scurvy became terribly prevalent amongst them – in one hospital alone there were 400 cases. On January 19 provisions of all sorts began to run short, and Mr. Rhodes started a soup kitchen for the town. Everybody who wished could give up their meat ration to be converted into soup, and he gave the vegetables from the Kenilworth gardens. The soup was sold at 3d. a pint, and was of inestimable benefit to the public at large, who were beginning to suffer from lack of vegetables, and who also found it almost impossible to procure fuel for cooking operations. It began in a small way, but gradually more and more people brought their rations, and in a very short time the men of the town guard, the mounted force, and even the Regular troops, who had at first rather looked down upon it, clamoured to be allowed to add their rations of horse to this excellent *pot au feu*. It certainly helped to keep at bay the scurvy which had been beginning to appear amongst the white population. The number of people fed daily in this way amounted, by the end of the siege, to about 15,000, while one day, when the shelling was at its worst, about 23,000 were fed. The whole movement was most ably carried out by Dr. Smartt, M.L.A., and Captain Tyson, who distributed soup at the various shelters, very often under heavy shell fire, in the most plucky way. The health of the town was thus, owing to the unceasing efforts of Colonel Kekewich and Mr. Rhodes, fairly good, though, of course, it must be taken into consideration that the siege took place at what is the most unhealthy time of year, a time at which most of the well-to-do people go away with their families for change of air. The heat is very great, the thermometer standing constantly between 80deg. and 95deg. in the shade. Typhoid is always prevalent at this season, and this year was much more so than usual owing to the unavoidable crowding together of the people and to other insanitary conditions. Owing to the lack of milk the infant mortality was also very high. The deaths from different causes averaged about 200 a week during the last part of the siege.

I have endeavoured to show briefly the conditions under which the siege of Kimberley was conducted and to indicate how it was possible for its defenders and people to stand a four months' strain as they did, taking into account the very large population. It must always be remembered that, though, as it turned out, the Boers never did actually attack us, there was always the possibility that they might do so, so that our vigilance could never be relaxed for one moment, added to which it was important to keep them at a distance as much as possible by constant sorties. Our line of defence was of great length, and our defending force of 4,000 could certainly never be accused of being idle. The time allowed for sleep was cut down to a *minimum*, but their health did not suffer; rather it improved from the open-air life.

THE EARLY DAYS OF SIEGE

When the siege first began everybody was very cheerful and happy, thinking it would last at most three or four weeks, and that on the whole it was rather amusing and exciting – a novel experience. The only alarming times in the first few weeks were when parties of Boers were seen hovering about in the distance (who might possibly be going to attack). Then hooters were blown from the different mines as a warning to non-combatants to retire to their houses. These hooters made the most weird and melancholy sound and had a most disastrous effect on the nerves of the people, so they were discontinued in a short time, to the relief of everybody. The whole town was dominated by a conning tower built over the hauling gear of the De Beers Mine. In this tower, which commanded a wide stretch of country, Colonel Kekewich and his officers kept watch day and night, so we had the security of feeling we could never be taken by surprise. At night we had three or four most brilliant search-lights which flashed unceasingly over the surrounding country and inspired some terror in the Boers, who called them "Rhodes's eyes."

The chief reason why we were never attacked was that the enemy believed the town was surrounded by mines, ready to explode and blow them to pieces if they attempted to advance. Meantime, with the hooters stopped and no Boers to be seen (although they were all round us they seldom or never showed themselves), everybody was in good spirits and life went on much as usual. We had siege sports at the different camps, cricket matches, &c., and for most people the chief hardship consisted in not being able to pass beyond the barriers of the town, and in a slight but steady diminution in the supply of the little luxuries of life. Up to the end of October, beyond one or two reconnaissances with the armoured train, and the sound of distant explosions, when the Boers blew up railway culverts and destroyed the dynamite magazine at Dronfied, nothing particular happened.

THE BEGINNING OF THE BOMBARDMENT

On November 4 a letter came in from General Wessels, the Boer commandant, stating that he was going to bombard the town if Colonel Kekewich did not surrender before Monday, the 6th. The contents of the letter were not made public, and we did not know till the end of November the terms of its contents. In one of our sorties a copy of the *Volksstem* was found in a Boer trench, giving the full text of the letter. A translation was published in the *Diamond Fields Advertiser* of November 28. General Wessels, after threatening bombardment, went on to say:–

In case Kimberley declines to surrender, I hereby request your honour to allow all women and children to leave Kimberley, so that they may be placed out of danger, and for this purpose your honour is granted time from noon on Saturday, November 4, 1899, to 6 a.m. on Monday, November 6, 1899. I further give notice that during that time I shall be ready to receive all Afrikander families who wish to remove from Kimberley, and also to offer liberty to depart in safety to all women and children of other nations desirous of leaving.

To the first proposal Colonel Kekewich in his reply returned no answer, and in the view of the British inhabitants, when the fact became known, he was considered to have incurred a grave responsibility by not informing them of the offer made to their women and children. If the offer had been made known I do not think that very many would have availed themselves of it, as at that time they firmly believed the relief column would be in Kimberley in a very short time, but later on in the siege there was a general wish that the offer had been published. Also, the more people that went away, the better it would have been for the town, short of food as we were, in fact they ought to have been encouraged to go. Colonel Kekewich published only the following notice to the Afrikander families:–

Head Commandant Wessels, of the Western Division Burgher Force, O.F.S., having made known to the Commandant, Kimberley, that he is willing to receive into his camp any Afrikanders who are desirous of leaving Kimberley, the Commandant hereby gives notice that any persons accepting this invitation will not be allowed to enter Kimberley on any pretext whatever as long as the siege lasts.

This offer was accepted by a few, but a very few, of the population, most Afrikanders not caring to put themselves in the position of being debarred from re-entering the town, and many also feeling that, by accepting the offer, they would gibbet themselves as Boer sympathizers, which would render their future lives in Kimberley extremely unpleasant. On our refusal to surrender the bombardment commenced, the enemy directing their fire at first on the Premier Mine, then the town itself came in for their attention for the week (Sunday excepted, according to the Boer custom), but luckily they did not at this time bring very heavy guns to bear upon us. People, of course, were considerably alarmed, and it was very unpleasant, but very little damage was done, beyond a native woman being killed in the middle of the town, and two Dutchmen and another man wounded. One or two buildings in the town were hit, and there was a general feeling of insecurity. Our ammunition was getting a little short, so on November 16 the De Beers Company began to manufacture shells, under the direction of their head engineer, Mr. George Labram. These were most successful.

SORTIES AND SUSPENSE

On November 16 we made a sortie, had one killed and seven wounded, and inflicted some loss on the enemy. So far, the town had not run any great risk, but it was felt that at any moment the enemy might place a siege gun in position, which we, with our pop-guns, should be powerless to resist, so a telegram was sent from the principal citizens to the High Commissioner urging that we should speedily be relieved. He replied in a most encouraging way, that the relief of Kimberley should be the first object of the column, and, he hoped, the turning point of the campaign. This was on November 7. After this we remained without any news for a fortnight, till on November 24 it was announced that a relief column had left Orange River on November 21. Our spirits went up with a bound. On the 25th the Kimberley Light Horse and others made a brilliant sortie, capturing 33 prisoners and driving the Boers out of their redoubts with serious loss. Our own losses were six killed and 29 wounded. Our forces were under the command of Lieutenant-Colonel Scott-Turner, and were brilliantly led. On November 28 Colonel Scott-Turner again led an attack on Carter's Ridge, but it was a sad day for Kimberley, for, after having secured our line of trenches by a most gallant rush with about 80 men, Colonel Scott-Turner was killed, and with him 21 others, while 28 were wounded. With their leader gone, the few sound men that remained had to retire, being in an untenable position, exposed to the full blaze of the Boer riflemen, strongly intrenched behind sandbags. In Colonel Scott-Turner the Kimberley garrison sustained an irreparable loss, and the people of the town felt that in losing him they lost their most gallant defender, a man who was always ready to risk his life in order to keep the enemy at a safe distance from their town. He was beloved by his men, and, as organizer of the Kimberley Light Horse, he deserved all praise for his untiring energy, and for the patience with which he drilled what were in many cases absolutely untrained men. Lieutenant-Colonel Peakman was appointed to succeed to the command of the mounted troops, but since our losses at Carter's Ridge it was felt that the storming of Boer positions with a few men and no big reserves to fall back upon was too serious and difficult, as well as useless, a task for the inhabitants of a beleaguered town to attempt, so from this time on our efforts were principally concentrated on keeping clear a sufficient space of ground outside the town for our rapidly-dwindling herd of cattle to feed on in safety. On December 1 we got into touch with the relief column signaller, and on the 4th Lord Methuen reported that he had crossed the Modder River. Then we thought that the relief of Kimberley could only be a matter of a few days, and when, on December 11, we heard a great battle going on beyond the hills of Spytfontein and could see the shells bursting on the ridge, we felt it was only a matter of hours till we welcomed our deliverers. We looked anxiously across the plain, hoping to see the advancing troops.

All we did see, however, was the Boers heliographing to us these words:– "We have smashed up your column." This, though it cast rather a cloud, we did not credit, but so isolated were we that though we thought something had gone wrong, it was not till six days afterwards that we heard the whole truth.

AFTER MAGERSFONTEIN

Now began the second and most dreary portion of the siege. Until then we had always had something outside the town to think about and speculate upon, and hope was always in the ascendant. After this, gloom settled down upon us, as we knew that the Boers, having been given time, were turning Spytfontein into a fortress; in fact, had done so largely after the battle of Modder River, and we felt our troops had small chance of success if they tried to push their way through it instead of coming round on the flat, as we at the time thought they could have done, and as General French eventually did.

Some time before this, Mr. Rhodes had felt that, in view of the uncertain duration of the siege, it was necessary to get rid of as many mouths as possible. This idea had been at first opposed by the military authorities, but they gave way eventually, and he managed to get rid of some 8,000 out of the 10,000 natives in the compounds. This was splendidly managed by Mr. L. Finn, his agent, who, understanding the natives thoroughly, won their confidence and explained the position to them and then led them out of the town in detachments. They started on their way in very good spirits, carrying their belongings, cooking pots, blankets, &c., together with some rations, fully intending, many of them, to return when the war was over. As a rule the Boers allowed them out; in the case of the Basutos and northern tribes nearly always, as they wished to remain on good terms with them, and also, we supposed, they wanted to employ them in digging trenches. In some cases they turned back the Cape Colony Kaffirs, as they said, on account of their friendliness with the English. The behaviour of the natives throughout the siege was very good; they were quiet and orderly and there was little grumbling. In the early part of the siege the Boers pursued a different policy with regard to the natives, as on one occasion, the occupants of the Wesselton compound, between 2,000 and 3,000 having become restive under shell fire, they were sent out of the town, but returned the next day, the Boers having stopped them, telling them "They must go back to their father, Rhodes."

After the battle of the Modder Lord Methuen, who expected to be in Kimberley almost immediately, sent a message to Colonel Kekewich that we would not be able to remain any time, and so practically all non-combatants must leave. A little food would be sent in and the town would be only occupied by its defenders. This idea caused great consternation among the people, who thought it very hard that, after enduring a siege of two months, they should be called upon to leave the town, and go, nobody knew where, at almost a moment's notice. It was strongly felt also that it would be a humiliation for them *vis à vis* of the Boers. Colonel Kekewich stated at a meeting of the town council that the people would have to leave immediately on the entry of Lord Methuen, but all the same numbers of people said they intended refusing to go, the great proportion of them being not at all well off, and having nowhere to go to. At the same time they were too proud to wish to be treated in Cape Town and elsewhere on a refugee basis, and did not enjoy the prospect of exchanging their comfortable houses for, possibly, tents on a beach at Cape Town; so altogether there was a good deal of feeling. A telegram was sent by the principal men in the town setting forth the difficulties of turning out 30,000 people suddenly without provision having been made for them. Affairs were in this state when the battle of Magersfontein took place, and it slowly dawned upon every one that not only was the question of their being turned out over for the present, but that also the date of their relief was exceedingly difficult to fix, and as time went on it seemed to recede more and more into the dim and distant future.

WEARY WEEKS OF WAITING

Now came the most trying part of the siege, and now was it especially that Mr. Rhodes and the De Beers Company came forward with noble generosity to the help of the town, Mr. Rhodes heading and generally originating every movement for the help of the people. Since the beginning of the siege the De Beers Company had settled to continue giving their *employés* full wages, and Mr. Rhodes had also started relief works, by which every able-bodied man willing to work could earn his livelihood. On these works 13,000 men were employed at a cost of £2,000 a week. They were employed largely in roadmaking, and did an immense amount of useful work in this way for the town; in fact a new quarter has been laid out on high ground at Newton, beyond the hospital., with wide roads and proposed boulevards, and Mr. Rhodes hopes that future extensions of the town will be in this direction. At the meeting of the four roads at the top of the hill Mr. Rhodes proposes to erect a monument to those who fell during the siege. There was also a relief committee for aiding refugees from outside and those who were not able to work, by which 650 persons were relieved at a cost of about £100 per week. It was suggested that applications should be made by Kimberley for a portion of the funds being raised in England and elsewhere for the relief of distress caused by the war, but Mr. Rhodes considered that Kimberley was strong enough to bear its own burdens, and this accordingly was done. A fund is now being raised for the widows and orphans of those killed in the defence of the town, which De Beers headed with a first subscription of £10,000. The company also had a cold storage house of 14,000 cubic feet built by Mr. Labram; this was begun and finished in the marvellously short time of nine days. Mr. Labram also built several armoured engines and an armoured train. In January Mr. Rhodes told Mr. Labram that he might make a gun, which for some time past he had been most anxious to do, and in three weeks he had begun and finished a 4.1 gun with carriage and shells complete. This huge gun, made in a besieged town situated in the heart of Africa, without any special apparatus, and at a time when materials of all kinds were running short, is really one of the wonders of the age. It fires with great accuracy at a long range, and caused the greatest consternation amongst the Boers when a shell landed at the intermediate station, where they thought they were in perfect safety out of range. This occurred on January 19, the first time the gun was fired. A letter was found on a Boer prisoner describing his feelings as he sat eating his "sweet mealie pap" and had to run for his life on the arrival of this most unpleasant visitor from Kimberley.

Our Intelligence Department did not succeed in getting much information, so Mr. Rhodes organized a system of native runners and scouts, by which we were enabled not only to receive occasional papers and letters from the outside world, but also learnt what our besiegers were about, where their laagers were, &c. We gathered that there were probably never more than two or three thousand round us at any time, with about six or seven thousand (if as many) more in Spytfontein impeding Lord Methuen's advance, but so mobile are these irregular troops that whenever we made a sortie they collected from all parts in a very short time and made any action on our part very difficult, if not impossible, without great loss of life.

A NEW TERROR

The siege continued to drag on its weary way without much incident for some time; nothing particular happened except that provisions got scarcer and scarcer, and such things as chickens and ducks could only be procured at fabulous prices, and then by great luck. Chickens cost 25s. each, eggs 2s. apiece, and so on. Shelling continued, but in rather a desultory way, when on February 7 the monotony was broken by the arrival of a 6in. Creuzot gun, firing 100lb. shells. This gun opened upon us from Kamfersdam, a high tailing heap which we had not occupied, about 3½ miles from the market-square. The consternation was universal, as, though the enemy had been erecting earthworks on the top of the heap for some time past, the arrival of this new terror was not anticipated by us. It seemed to play all over the town, and hardly a street was safe. It could also be fired very quickly. The chief objects aimed at, however, seemed to be the conning-tower and the sanatorium, where Mr. Rhodes was staying. This horrible firing went on till the following Sunday, doing a great deal of damage among the houses; several people were also killed and wounded. The greatest loss we sustained was on Friday, February 9, when Mr. Labram was killed instantaneously by a shell in his bed-room. His death was a great shock to us all, as, in the exercise of his brilliant talents in our service, he had rendered incalculable service to the town. His funeral was on Saturday evening. In spite of the darkness, the big gun, which up till then had not been fired at night, commenced to fire just as the procession left the hospital, and continued all the evening. Rockets were sent up in the town from Boer sympathizers (of whom there were many) to indicate the time of starting and the route of the procession. The alarm amongst the women and children now became very great. They felt helpless in the dark, and large numbers passed their night in the streets, or in the poor shelters afforded by the railway bridges and culverts, or behind *débris* heaps. There was no shelter to be found in the thinly-built houses against 100lb. shells. It is true a few bomb-proof shelters had been hastily put up, but they were not of sufficient size to accommodate large numbers. Mr. Rhodes, seeing the position was serious, determined to offer the women and children the shelter of the mines. Arrangements were accordingly made, and on Sunday afternoon streams of people could be seen wending their way, some to the De Beers, some to the Kimberley Mine. They were carrying such little comforts as they could, and seemed relieved at this solution of their troubles. Mr. Rhodes, his friends, and staff worked hard till the middle of the night, by which time, without the slightest confusion or difficulty, 2,600 people had been put down the mines, at depths of from 1,200ft. to 1,500ft. Everything was done for their comfort by the De Beers staff, who worked with untiring devotion, supplying them with food and everything they wanted. The people themselves looked upon it as a picnic and were as cheerful as possible, especially when the big gun began to boom again on Monday morning, and they expressed great thankfulness to Mr. Rhodes for having devised this plan for their safety. They remained there quite comfortably till the end of the siege, when they returned to the surface with great joy, after four days of subterranean life, none the worse for their unique experience. There were also many other people in shelters, some in a long tunnel near the entrance of the Kimberley Mine, others in holes dug in *débris* heaps, some again in places built in their own gardens; in short, Kimberley became for the time to a large extent an underground town.

RELIEF AT LAST

And the big gun went on steadily spreading havoc. There were one or two fires, but these were speedily got under. We had been cheered on Saturday, the 10th, by Lord Roberts's announcing that he was going to begin active operations on the following day. On Tuesday night the Boers evacuated Alexandersfontein, which was promptly

One of Lord Roberts'
ammunition columns
en route to relieve
Kimberley

occupied by the Beaconsfield Town Guard, who found quantities of supplies there abandoned by the Boers in their hurry to get away. All Thursday morning the big gun continued to shell us from Kamfersdam, but about 2 p.m. the great news was telephoned round the town from the conning-tower that General French and his Cavalry Division were advancing across the plain towards Alexandersfontein, and we knew that our troubles were over and our 124 days of siege at an end. We could now see the Boers hurrying away from the outskirts of Alexandersfontein, where some of them lingered, carrying their field guns, which they had been firing till the last moment, with them. In the distance great clouds of dust covered the advancing column. Riding out beyond the town we soon found ourselves among the vanguard of our deliverers, and gleaned the first details of the great feat of arms that had just been performed on our behalf. Passing from squadron to squadron, British, Irish, Australian, New Zealander, in turn joined in congratulations to us on their having arrived in time, to themselves on having taken part in General French's great ride.

Kimberley owes much to the foresight, tact, and resolution of Colonel Kekewich, to the genius, breadth of mind, and unwearying and unfailing resourcefulness of Mr. Rhodes, but these would not have sufficed without the stout hearts of the inhabitants themselves. The British population of Kimberley has always been conspicuous in South Africa for energy, independence, and public spirit, and at this crisis of its fate it proved itself well worthy of its reputation. Determined and uncomplaining, the citizens did their duty at their posts, encountered hardships, stimulated by their example their coloured and native brethren, and were fully prepared to endure to the end any sufferings they might be called upon to bear in defence of her Majesty's flag.

The first train of refugees
leaves Kimberley after the
siege

The Hon. Mrs Rochfort Maguire is perhaps unsurprisingly gushing in her praise of
Cecil Rhodes; what is surprising is the fact that *The Times* allowed such an obviously
partisan report to be given such prominence in the paper. This is perhaps explained by
the close links that *The Times* enjoyed with Rhodes himself, as demonstrated during the
'Jameson Affair'. By allowing its reporting to be influenced in this way, *The Times* was
not only guilty of failing in its self-appointed role as guardian of the truth; it had also
committed the major journalistic sin of missing the real story. The real sensation of the
siege of Kimberley was the conflict between Colonel Kekewich and Cecil Rhodes.
From the very start of the siege Rhodes did his best to undermine the authority of
Kekewich, telegraphing Cape Town to say that Kimberley was about to fall after only a
few weeks of siege. Of course, Rhodes did not bother to inform Kekewich of this, and
the first that the unfortunate garrison commander heard of the impending fall of his
command was when a native runner arrived, bearing a telegram from Buller demanding
to know what was going on in the town. Kekewich signalled his superior that the
situation in Kimberley was stable and that the town was in no immediate danger of
capture.

   Having first decided that the town was about to fall, Rhodes now veered through 180
degrees, and proposed that as the town was so secure Kekewich should send over 600
troops to help Baden-Powell in Mafeking. When Kekewich refused, Rhodes became
purple with rage and proceeded to lambast the garrison commander for his supposed
timidity, 'You are afraid of a mere handful of farmers, . . You call yourselves soldiers
of an Empire-making nation. I do believe that you will next take fright at a pair of
broomsticks dressed up in trousers.'[1] Throughout the siege Rhodes was a thorn in the

side of Kekewich, and at one point the strain was so great that Lord Roberts authorized the garrison commander to place Rhodes under arrest. This did not happen, but Rhodes' distorted messages from the besieged town continually affected the whole war effort, as reports of Kimberley's imminent fall caused the relief forces to embark on risky and often damaging courses of action. Such was French's headlong cavalry dash to Kimberley: 'French's instructions were simply to ride like the wind to save Kimberley. How different the instructions would have been if it had not been for Rhodes. French's five thousand men were Britain's only large mobile force in South Africa, a unique instrument for hunting down a mobile enemy and their not-so-mobile siege guns. Instead the five thousand had to expend themselves in a magnificent, but quite unnecessary dash to self-destruction across the veld'.[2]

Rhodes, the author of this act of destruction which quite possibly prolonged the war by months, was allowed to pose as the 'hero of Kimberley'. At the same time, Rhodes was able to arrange the dismissal of Kekewich from his post of garrison commander as soon as the siege was lifted. A few weeks after the siege had ended Rhodes asked, 'Kekewich? Who's he? You don't remember the man who cleans your boots'.[3]

Notes

1. Quoted in Pakenham, 1991, p. 186.
2. Ibid., p. 327.
3. Quoted in Pakenham, p. 327.

Mafeking

'I continue watching with confidence and admiration the patient and resolute defence which is so gallantly maintained under your ever resourceful command' (V.I.R.).

Of all the events of the Second Boer War, the siege of Mafeking is the one that stands out in the minds of the British public; even today Mafeking is a byword for Victorian courage in the face of adversity. The siege lasted for 217 days and made a world-wide reputation for the Mafeking commander, Colonel Robert Stephenson Baden-Powell. Mafeking was threatened by a force of 8,000 men under General Piet Cronje, who had 10 guns, including a Creusot siege gun that became known as 'Long Tom', for use in his attack on the town. The siege of Mafeking gave rise to a number of mysteries, the chief of which is to discover the reason for Baden-Powell being there in the first place. 'Baden-Powell, when ordered to raise two regiments in Bechuanaland and Rhodesia to harass the enemy's rear and flank, marched his force, instead, into Mafeking, a small dusty, tin-roofed town, only eight miles from the Transvaal border, and allowed the Boers to surround him, saying afterwards that he was prepared to "sit tight".'[1] The mystery of Baden-Powell's appearance in Mafeking when he should have been playing the Boers at their own game (as he no doubt would have put it), a game for which his military service had admirably equipped him, set the stage for the war reports that became the newspaper success story of the war. *The Times'* correspondent in Mafeking during the siege was Angus Hamilton. At first Hamilton tried to explain to the British public that Mafeking was not really under siege, but that the Boers were lethargic in the extreme in their prosecution of the attack. However, his editor in London followed the same line as he had with the two other sieges, so that the reports that appeared in *The Times* represented the *Boy's Own* school of journalism, rather than the truth.

MAFEKING, OCT. 25.

To-day is the third day of the bombardment by which Commandant Cronje is attempting to realize his threat of reducing Mafeking to ashes. Up to the present it has been impossible to consider very seriously the attempt of the Boers to besiege Mafeking. The earlier bombardment and the series of events which have occurred during the interval have not augmented the gravity of the situation. The Boer Commandant endeavoured to carry out his word by opening the second bombardment of Mafeking upon the day which he had notified Colonel Baden-Powell. We had been incredulous at the threat of the Boers to send to Pretoria for some siege guns. Monday, therefore, was a day of some anxiety for us, and each was curious to know what result the enemy's fire would produce. Upon this occasion, however, the townsfolk had reckoned without taking into account the intentions of Colonel Baden-Powell, and it was a very pleasant surprise to find that the bombardment of Mafeking by the Boers had been converted into the bombardment of the Boers by Mafeking. At a very early hour, two guns, which had been placed near the reservoir, opened fire upon the enemy's artillery in position at the water springs. The artillery duel which was thus started continued for some hours, and if it did not do much damage to either side it made manifest to the Boers that the defences of Mafeking were not altogether at their mercy. About noon, however, the Boers, who had been observed to place some guns in position upon the south-west side of the town, threw shells at Cannon Kopje. Here again, fortunately, no material damage was done.

Somewhat early in the afternoon, the look-outs reported tremendous activity in the Boer camp. Across the veldt those who cared might have seen the enemy engaged upon some enormous earthwork, which the general consensus of opinion very quickly determined to be the emplacements for the siege guns. They were at least three miles and a-half away from the town, and in a position different to that from which the guns had shelled the kopje in the morning. The frequency with which shells had exploded within the limits of Mafeking had rendered the people somewhat callous of the consequences, and despite an official warning which was issued to the town, a large number of people stood discussing in excited groups the value of this news. However, it was not to be confirmed that afternoon. An hour after noon on the following day the alarm rang out from the market place, the red flag was seen to fly from headquarters, and the inhabitants were warned to take immediate cover. Within a few minutes of the alarm, the proceedings for that day began, and the first shell thrown from the Boer battery burst over our camp. Presently on the distant sky line a tremendous cloud of smoke hurled itself into the air. The very foundations upon which Mafeking rests seemed to quiver, all curiosity was set at rest, and there was no longer any doubt as to the nature of the new ordnance the Boers had with them. With a terrific impact the shell struck some structures near the railway, and the flying fragments of steel spread over the town, burying themselves in buildings, striking the veldt two miles distant, creating a dust, a horrible confusion, and an instant terror throughout the town. In the course of the afternoon, after a rain of seven and nine pound shells, the Boers opened with this gun again, and although no loss of life happily occurred, the missile wrecked part of the Mafeking Hotel. With the curious inconsequence which has marked the Boer proceedings in their investment of Mafeking, the enemy threw no more of these heavier shells during the afternoon, contenting themselves with discharging at odd moments those of lesser calibre.

The two shells which had been fired during the afternoon gave the inhabitants of Mafeking some little ground by which to judge the nature of the bombardment on the morrow. After the cessation of hostilities word was passed round that the two shells which had been launched at Mafeking were a 64lb. howitzer and a 94lb. muzzle-loading siege gun, and that it might be reckoned that these were but the preliminary shots by which to measure the range. Officially it was notified that every precaution must be taken to remain within the bomb-proof shelters which the inhabitants of Mafeking had been advised to construct. It is the presence of these pits which explains the slight loss of life that has occurred during the Boer bombardment of Mafeking. Up to to-day the effect of the terrible hail of shells which has poured into the town has been but a few slight wounds. But there could be no doubt that the more serious fighting was at last to take place, and it seemed to us only natural to expect a general advance upon Mafeking in the morning. The night passed with every man sleeping by his arms and at his post. The women and children had been removed to their laager, the horses were picketed in the river bed, and once again all preparations for defence, and all those measures which had been taken to secure immunity from shell fire were, for the last time, inspected. Firing began very early on Wednesday morning, a gun detachment under Lieutenant Murchison opening with a few shells from our position to the east of the town. When the light had become clear the Boers brought their new siege guns once more into play. We estimated at nightfall that the enemy must have thrown rather more than 200 shells into Mafeking, and if Mafeking be saved for future bombardment its salvation lies in the fact that it is, relatively speaking, little more than a collection of somewhat scattered houses with tin roofs and mud walls. Any other form of building would have been shaken to its foundations by the mere concussion of these bursting shells. Where bricks would have fallen, mud walls simply threw down a cloud of dust. But if Mafeking be still more or less intact, it can congratulate itself upon having withstood a most determined and concentrated shell fire.

After the early morning hours had been whiled away Commandant Cronje made preparations for a general advance upon the town under the protection of his cannon fire. This was the moment which each of us had longed for. As the Boer advance seemed to be concentrated upon the eastern side, I proceeded to the redan at De Kock's corner under Major Goold-Adams, and later on to another a little lower down in the same quarter of the town under Capt. Musson. At Major Goold-Adams's there had been stationed a Maxim detachment, and it was not long before its sharp rat-a-tat-tat was heard speaking to the enemy. The warm reception which was accorded to the Boers from this redan soon began to draw their fire. With Big Ben discharging its 94-pound shells in every quarter of the town, and a 12-pounder from the north-west dropping shrapnel with much discrimination over that quarter, the enemy upon the east side soon followed the example so shown them and discharged shells at the redans along their front. The range was singularly good, and in a very few minutes shells were dropping over and in very close proximity to our two redans. Between the two, and but a little removed from the line of fire, was the building of the Dutch Reformed Church, and several shells intended for the Maxim in Major Goold-Adams's fort found lodgment in its interior. The front of this church had been penetrated in several places by the shells, when the gun was slewed suddenly round upon the hospital and a shell fell in an outhouse attached to the monastery with disastrous effect. When the smoke had cleared away little was left of the building beyond a pile of smoking ruins. Above Captain Musson's redan our untimely visitors constantly burst and scattered, and we began to realize fully the value of the bomb-proof shelters. In a little while, however, the Boers relaxed their shell fire, and beyond maintaining sufficient fire to cover their advance the heavier guns were for the time silent.

With this, the Boers began to open out in extended order upon the east side of the town, advancing on our west to within 900 yards of our defences. At each point the Boer advance was protected by the guns, the heavy artillery to the south-west seeming to be the centre of a circle of armed men, who were advancing slowly upon this gallant little town. At no time did the enemy however, beyond the few upon the west side, come within effective range of our rifles or our Maxims, contenting themselves with taking up positions at 2,000 yards, and dealing out to us prolonged rifle fire with some intermittent shelling. The firing was very rapid, very general, and more or less impotent. We have had two men wounded, while here and there it is believed certain of the enemy received their quietus. Whether we beat them off or whether they lacked the spirit to attack us it is impossible to determine, and it is enough to say that, whatever may have been their intention, Mafeking remains as it was before the first shot was fired. At night, after the attack, Colonel Baden-Powell issued a general order congratulating his forces and the people in Mafeking upon their calmness during the heavy fire to which they had been subjected.

As we are situated at present it is impossible for us to leave our trenches in order to give battle to the enemy, but we are still buoyed up by the hope of being able before long to take in our turn the offensive. In the meantime, most of us live with our rifles in our hands, our bandoliers round our shoulders, existing upon food of the roughest kind, peering over sandbags at the distant position of the Boers, or crouching in the shell-proof trenches as their shells burst overhead. There is much gravity in our isolated position; there is the danger that by good luck more than by skill Mafeking may be reduced, but there is no reason to fear that the determination and courage of the town will give way. Above all else that may be calculated to endure.

OCTOBER 28.

Last night there occurred one of those isolated instances of gallantry by which the British sustain their high reputation. For some days, in fact ever since the Boers secured their siege guns from Pretoria, the enemy has been building a circlet of trenches around Mafeking. At the least distance they are perhaps 2,500 yards, unhappily beyond the reach of our rifle and Maxim fire. We have seen them lounging in their breastworks, we have seen them gathered around their camp fires, and the inability of Mafeking to shake off these unwelcome intruders has been daily a source of irritation. We have not, of course, allowed them to enjoy undisturbed the seclusion of their own earthworks, and, as a continual goad in their side, little expeditions have been despatched to make night fearsome to our besetting foe.

Another of these midnight sorties was undertaken last night, proving in itself to be the most important move on our side since Captain Fitz-Clarence and his men engaged the Boers two weeks ago. The same officer, 55 men of D Squadron Protectorate Regiment, with Lieutenant Murray and 25 men of the Cape Police, were the prime movers in an attempt to rush the first line of earthworks of the Boer position. Shortly after 11 o'clock Captain Fitz-Clarence and his men started on their perilous undertaking. In the faint light of the night we could see their

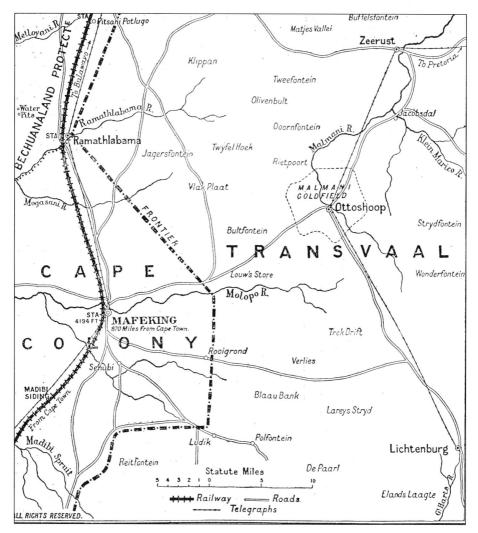

Map showing Mafeking and the surrounding area

figures from our own redans, silently hurrying across the veldt. In the blue haze of the distance a black blur betokened the position of the enemy, and it seemed that at any moment the hoarse challenge of the Boer outpost would give the alarm. The men crept on in slightly extended order, holding themselves in readiness for the supreme moment. Nearer, and yet nearer, they drew to the Boer intrenchments. The silence was intense. The heavy gloom, the wistful noises of the veldt at night, the shadowy patches in the bush, all seemed to heighten the tension of one's nerves. In a little while our men were within a few yards of the enemy; then furtively each fixed his bayonet to his rifle, and as the blades rang home upon their sockets the gallant band raised a ringing cheer. Instantly the Boer position was galvanized into activity, figures showed everywhere, shots rang out, men shouted, horses stampeded, and the confusion which reigned supreme gave to our men one vital moment in which to hurl themselves across the intervening space. Then there was a loud crash, for, as it happened, many of our men were nearer the intrenchments than had been anticipated, and their eager charge had precipitated them upon some sheets of corrugated iron which the Boers had torn from the grand stand of the racecourse for protection from the rain. With our men upon the parapet of the trench, a few rapid volleys were fired into the enemy, who, taken completely by surprise, were altogether demoralized. Those in the first trenches seemed to have been petrified by fright. Where they were, there they remained, stabbed with bayonet, knocked senseless with the rifle's butt, or shot dead. Captain Fitz-Clarence himself, with magnificent gallantry and swordsmanship, killed four of the enemy with his sword, his men plying their bayonets strenuously the while. This was the first trench, and as the fight grew hotter some little memory of their earlier boasts inspired the Boers to make a stand. They fought; they fought well. Their vast superiority in numbers did not enter into their minds, since Commandant Botha told Lieutenant Moncrieff, who had charge of the flag party that arranged for an armistice this morning, that he thought that at least a thousand men had been moved against his position. The long line of front held by the enemy flashed fire from many hundred rifles. Houses in the town caught the bullets, the low rises to the east of the position threw back the echo of the rifle shots. Our men became the centre of a hail of bullets. The Boers fired anywhere and everywhere, seeming content if they could just load their rifles and release the trigger. Many thousands of rounds of ammunition were expended in the confusion of the moment, the enemy not even waiting to see at whom or at what they were aiming.

After the first fury had been expended, our men charged at the bayonet point right across the line of trenches. It was in this charge that the Boers lost most heavily. So soon as the squadron reached the extremity of the Boer position they retreated independently, their movement covered by the flanking fire of the Cape Police, which added still further to the perplexities of the enemy. The galling fire of the Cape Police disturbed them for some time longer than was required in the actual retirement of the force.

The Boers had been completely unnerved by the onslaught of the Protectorate men, and a feature of the hours which elapsed between the final withdrawal of our force from the scene of conflict and the advent of dawn was the heavy firing of the enemy, who still continued discharging useless volleys into space. The loss to us in this encounter had been six killed, ten wounded, and two of our men taken prisoners, but the gravity of the loss which the enemy sustained can be most surely measured by the fact that until a late hour this afternoon they could not find the spirit to resume the bombardment. It is said in camp here that some two hundred Boers will have reason to remember the charge of the Protectorate Regiment.

OCTOBER 31.

In the small hours of Monday morning, when the cold mists of the African night were still down upon the horizon, the Boers made a desperate attack upon a fort manned by a detachment of the Frontier Police.

Sunday night the look-out from Cannon Kopje saw a body of 800 Boers making their way to a point somewhat nearer the town that had hitherto been their custom, and some little expectation was felt that the enemy might attack the following morning. The Boers to the south-west of the town had by no means despised the claims of Cannon Kopje upon their attentions, and to every three shells which had been thrown into the town during the siege one other at least had been fired at Cannon Kopje. It had gradually come to be considered that Cannon Kopje was a point against which the Boers would sooner or later direct an attack. Since its capture was necessary to the successful execution of any general movement against the town, the detachment of police who formed the garrison at Cannon Kopje upon this day performed a most brilliant service for the town by their determined and gallant stand. Perhaps in war more than in anything else chance is a more decisive factor than we like to consider, and had it not been for the diversion of the Boer forces upon Cannon Kopje and their subsequent repulse Mafeking itself might have been invaded by the enemy. The reduction of this post was, however, of vital concern to Commandant Cronje, since it had been his intention to bombard the south-eastern portion of the town from its ramparts, carrying Mafeking with a large force which he had assembled in the night in the adjacent valley of the Molopo River. The look-out from Cannon Kopje had already reported to Colonel Walford that there was unusual activity in the Boer camp, and the fatigues for the night had barely been dismissed when a passing shell from the Boers opened the action. During the night, and about the close of Sunday, the enemy had shifted men and artillery to positions from where they completely covered the area of the fort. At least a third of the forces before Mafeking had been concentrated upon Cannon Kopje. Against a mere gun emplacement and a mere handful of men shell fire from four guns was directed, and the services of 800 men utilized. In the extreme west there was Big Ben and a 7-pounder. In the extreme east there was a 12-pounder. Within a circle from these two points and within effective range a 7-pounder and quick-firing Nordenfelt had been stationed. The big gun threw seven shells only during the attack upon the kopje, but at any moment that the enemy's shell fire lapsed the Boers opened with their Mausers. Their rifle fire stretched from the two extremities of their flanks, and enfiladed the interior trenches of the kopje.

Nothing perhaps in the history of their operations along this frontier was so calculated to prove successful as the Boer counter attack upon Colonel Walford. It would seem morally impossible that 44 men could withstand the unceasing shower of shells and hail of bullets which dropped in Cannon Kopje. Had our men wavered they might well have been excused; had they fallen back upon the town their movement would have been in order. But they stopped at their posts, the mark for every Boer rifle, the objective of the enemy's shell, until so great had been their execution upon the enemy that the Boers themselves proclaimed an armistice under the protection of their Red Cross flag. When this was decreed one-fourth of the detachment in the kopje were out of action; but, on the other hand, not 400 yards away, we could see the Boer ambulance picking up their dead and wounded. It has been stated that they lost 100 men, and that a further 50 were seriously wounded; but it is exceedingly difficult to compute the losses which we

may have possibly inflicted upon them. Though we saw two wagonloads pass
from their firing line to their laagar, I am inclined to doubt if we killed more than
47 of the enemy. Still, in the face of such a hail of bullet and shell, that is a
wonderful achievement, since to every shot which we fired there were at least 400
barrels emptied at our marksmen. Such was the unfortunate construction of
Cannon Kopje that it was not possible for the men to use their loopholes, and it
was necessary for each to stand to his feet and to expose himself above the
breastwork as he fired. We fired by six, we fired independently, and whenever it
was possible the Maxims were turned on, but it remains almost a mystery how we
could prevail against the Boer numbers. It was easy enough to hold them in check,
since the first well directed volley made them fall back some few yards, but the
heavy shell fire would sooner or later have told its tale. It had already claimed the
majority of those who were hit, since if the shell itself did not burst within the area
of the fort it splintered upon stone, thereby adding a fresh danger to the position of
those who were crouching behind the parapet for shelter.

Cannon Kopje, in itself a mere cluster of stones, is a terrible lesson, and also a
magnificent example of gallant conduct in the field. Captain the Hon. D. Marsham
was killed, and Captain Charles Alexander Kerr Pechell died in the course of the
morning from wounds received. Colonel Walford and Colonel Baden-Powell have
each expressed their high appreciation of the conduct of the men; and if, as befits
their rank, the example of the officers was admirable, it was unhesitatingly
followed by the men under them. Captain Marsham was struck by a rifle bullet in
turning to render some assistance to a wounded comrade. As he attempted to do
this a rifle bullet passed through his chest, and a moment later he was dead just as
a second bullet passed through his shoulder. It was as fine a death as any soldier
could perhaps have chosen, and it had the crowning mercy of being instantaneous.
Captain Pechell was busying himself in directing the rifle fire from the fort, and
thereby directly drew the attention of the enemy. He, with a detachment of six
men, ranged up from time to time, and picked off the enemy with well aimed
volleys. They had taken up their position behind the eastern arm of the kopje,
engaging a body of the enemy, whose flank fire enfiladed our position. The first
shell which came at these men fell short, but the second and the third, bursting
together, scattered the outer covering of the breastwork. Pechell ordered his men
to retire from the direct line of the shell fire, when just as they were shifting their
position a shell struck the stone parapet, and burst among them. Private Burrows
was killed at once, just as he had been admiring the shot from a comrade.
Sergeant-Major Upton and Captain Pechell received some terrible injuries, poor
Pechell being wounded from the thigh to the shoulder. By the death of Captain
Marsham and Captain Pechell, her Majesty loses two officers of exceptional
promise and soldierly qualifications.

The casualties for this action alone were eight killed and three wounded – four
being killed upon the spot, and four dying of their wounds within 12 hours of the
action. Captain Marsham, Sergeant-Major Curnihan, Private Burrows, and Private
Martin were killed in the fort; Captain Pechell, Sergeant-Major Upton, Private
Nicholas, and Private Lloyd died from wounds; Sergeant-Major Butler, Corporal
Cooke and Private Newton were the survivors and are progressing satisfactorily.

NOVEMBER 5.

The garrison here has paid its farewell duties to those gallant men who were killed at Cannon Kopje. Their interment took place at 6 o'clock in the evening of the day upon which they lost their lives (October 30). By the orders of the Colonel, those who were desirous of so doing were permitted to follow the remains of the men to the grave, and, although there was no little danger, a large proportion of the town attended their final obsequies.

With the solemn notes of the Last Call in our ears, we retraced our steps to the various trenches and earthworks, which for the moment were our shelters, little imagining that within a few hours those of us who were correspondents would follow the body of one from amongst ourselves once more upon this road. The following night Lieutenant Murchison, who was in charge of the guns, accidentally shot with his revolver, Mr. E. G. Parslow, correspondent of the London *Chronicle*. The horror of such a mistake still hangs over us, and is not in any way diminished by the fact that the officer, who had already distinguished himself by his career, is now awaiting the verdict of a field Court-martial. Mr. Parslow had endeared himself to everybody by the genial sympathy which he extended to those who were themselves in trouble, and he had won the admiration of many by the calmness with which he conducted himself under the heaviest fire.

Up to the present we have some good cause to believe that when the Boers are particularly silent something ominous portends. Towards the close of this week we had observed the enemy moving their big guns to fresh emplacements, and although we explained their inactivity with a happy optimism which attributed the silence of their artillery to lack of ammunition, we were nevertheless prepared to receive another messenger from the Boer camp. When he came it was to intimate through a letter from Commandant Cronje that a most determined onslaught on the town would take place upon the Monday, and that it would be wiser for us to surrender at once. The messenger was bowed out with that cold and dignified courtesy which is so characteristic of our commanding officer. It was soon seen that the Boers had procured, as they affirmed, some further artillery supplies, since the noiseless one-pound Nordenfelt began to harass the eastern and western fronts. The aim was excellent and the range effective, and although no one was actually hurt, there were a few minor casualties and a good many buildings penetrated by the steel-capped shell.

It has become quite impossible to expect the Boers to make any judicious selection from the reserves of artillery in Pretoria, with which to assail the mud walled-houses of Mafeking. It would appear that they have yet to learn the first principles of artillery attack, although it would seem that the slight damage which has hitherto been done in Mafeking has not at present revealed to them the futility of their procedure. Ever since the siege began now we have been accustomed to shells coming from all quarters. The Boers have made no attempt to concentrate their fire upon one spot until they had effectually silenced its defence. Now, however, the big gun, which stood alone in its isolated glory, has been shifted, and it would seem from the nature of the Boer emplacements that Monday may witness an attempt upon the part of the Boers to consolidate their artillery. In the meantime, however, we have again drawn their attention to the Red Cross flag, against which with cruel persistence they still direct their heavier metal. With the pleasures of the general bombardment already arranged for Monday, the 6th, we did not expect a determined attempt to blow up Mafeking with a load of dynamite. Nevertheless, between 6 and 7 on Saturday night the town was shaken to the uttermost depths of its foundations by a tremendous explosion. A ruddy glare which covered the sky led us at first to believe that a powder magazine had blown up, and it was not until the following morning that we found out that the Boers had endeavoured to push into Mafeking along the railway two trolley loads of dynamite. The concussion of this explosion, which was two miles off, broke several windows, shook buildings, and threw a few people to the ground, and had it not been that it prematurely exploded the official opinion here prefers to believe that Mafeking would have been in ruins.

Colonel Baden-Powell sympathizes as much as his official position will permit him with the inhabitants of Mafeking in their unfortunate predicament, and since the Boers wished to preserve Sunday as a day of rest, the Colonel encourages the people to indulge in as much simple pleasure upon this day as is possible. To-day week the band of the Bechuanaland Rifles played in the Market-square. They repeated their performance to-day, while to this innocuous pastime has been added a firework display for the evening's attraction and as a means of perpetuating the historical "Fifth".

NOV. 7 (by Native Runner to Kuruman).
Only this morning the western outposts under command of Major Godley made a reconnaissance of the Boer laager upon that front. The men of C Squadron under Captain Vernon, the Bechuanaland Rifles under Captain Cowan, and three guns under Lieutenant Daniels were engaged in the movement, which was completely successful. The previous night, after the men had turned in, when the glow of the camp fires had died out, a headquarters orderly brought the command that the men were to form up at 2.30 to make an attack at dawn upon the enemy's position. C Squadron has up to the present not enjoyed so great a share of the fighting as has fallen to A, B, and D Squadrons, and, although C Squadron contains a larger number of time-expired men than any other in the regiment, since hostilities commenced these troops have not been blooded.

At a quarter to 2 we turned out. Great-coats had been left behind, men slinging their water-bottles and bandoliers across their shoulders. Each had 50 rounds, although here and there others more fortunate than the rest had secured some few extra. We were to meet at the base of the hill which rose a few hundred yards across the veldt from Major Godley, and from there we were to march to our position. Night hung upon us heavily. The sky was dark, and everything seemed to point to the wisdom of choosing such a night. We stepped out briskly, yet trod as lightly as possible.

The sole objective of the night attack was to effect a reconnaissance of the enemy's camp upon the west side of the town. The guns were to throw a few shells, the men were to fire a few volleys, and then the whole force would regain their own trenches as quickly as possible. In respect to the constantly increasing force surrounding Mafeking almost the one means of temporarily checking their advance which remains to us is through the medium of these daybreak sorties. Information had been brought into headquarters that the Boers were massing upon the east side of the town, the small laager on the west being temporarily evacuated. The opportunity which was thus afforded of both surprising and annoying the enemy was very welcome, and the night dash was entered into with infinite zest. So soon as the guns had discharged their first shell our men began to fire by volleys, but the sortie had not progressed very far when the activity in the Boer lines showed that they were preparing to repel a force much larger than the mere sniping party which was actually before them. In the uncertain light of rising morn a body of 600 Boers could be seen riding from the main laager upon the western front to the support of the minor camp. We have hitherto thought the Boers timid at close quarters, but in this case there was every sign of haste and eagerness on the part of the reinforcements to arrive upon the scene of action. We could see them dismounting as they came up and run to the laager, some of them firing as they ran, others of them forming into detached parties and firing from isolated positions. After volleying for some minutes our men fulfilled the object of their morning excursion and were preparing to retire by troops, when, owing to the presence of the reinforcements, firing became general. Our rifles replied to their rifles, our two seven-pounders replied to their guns, but beyond this nothing was permitted to interfere with the successful completion of our work and the fitting execution of the Colonel's orders. It mattered very little to us how fiercely the enemy's Nordenfeldts spat out defiance or what their rifles said, for we fell back steadily, the different troops doubling 50, 100, and 150 yards each time. The fire as the various troops took up the retirement became very hot, the enemy cheerfully Mausering into space. For some hours after our men had gained the security of their own trenches the enemy maintained a heavy fire upon the several outposts along the western front. During the retirement of C Squadron Major Godley had ordered Captain Cowan to occupy Fort Eyre, a rifle trench, with a detachment of Bechuanaland Mounted Rifles, so that he might check any signs of advance which the enemy might display. In consequence of this, added to a mistake upon the part of some Boers that had brought about 300 of them to within 800 yards of the trench, Major Godley, Captain Cowan, Lieutenant Feltham, and the B.M.R. experienced the most severe fire which has at present been received from the Boers since operations began. The enemy made a determined onslaught upon Major Godley, but fortunately lacking the courage to charge the trench, after some few hours' rifle firing, they incontinently withdrew. These little fights are all the outposts have to do, and the success with which they have been conducted has been sufficient to check the enemy and to cause him to reflect upon the relative value of the means at our command.

It is true that from the start of the siege Baden-Powell insisted on censoring the despatches of the correspondents, but it is also true that the correspondents could have evaded his censorship if they had really wanted to. Most of the correspondents were able to ride in and out of Mafeking almost at will during the greater part of the siege. Despite penning the report that appeared above Hamilton wrote privately that, 'There has been no battle round Mafeking . . . A few slight skirmishes upon our part, and much proud boasting upon the part of the Boers, is the limit of mutual operations which have centred around Mafeking. We are waiting and, in the interval preparing. That is all which can be said.'[2] During the siege Hamilton observed the true state of affairs in Mafeking, but was reluctant to report it because his editor did not regard the truth as sufficiently exciting to induce the reading public to buy *The Times*. Hamilton thus cobbled together reports that implied that life in Mafeking was far more adventurous and arduous than it really was.

MAFEKING, JAN. 3.

The New Year has brought to Mafeking and the garrison that is beleaguered within its walls no signs of the fulfilment of the prophecy that relief would come by the end of December. Indeed, the closing year of the 19th century was ushered in with the boom of cannon and the fire of small arms, and in a style generally which does not differ from any one of the many days during which the siege and bombardment have lasted. There was no cessation of hostilities similar to that which characterized Christmas Day; firing began at an early hour in the morning from the enemy's artillery, and did not terminate until the evening gun gave a few hours' peace to the town. For quite a fortnight there has been no such heavy fire, and it would seem that for our especial edification the authorities in Pretoria had sent to the commandant of the Boer forces that are investing us a New Year's gift of three wagon-loads of ammunition. A new gun was also despatched to them, and, its position being constantly shifted, its fire has since played upon every quarter of the town. For the moment we had attached no great importance to this new weapon, but after the first few rounds it was discovered to be employing what are called combustible bombs. These new shells do not usually explode, seeming to discharge a chemical liquid which ignites upon contact with the air. They are also filled with lumps of sulphur, and so severe might be the damage from this new agency of destruction which the Boers have turned against Mafeking that the most stringent orders have been issued for any one finding these shells to see that they are immediately buried. At present, beyond a few unimportant blazes in the gardens of the town, no damage has been caused, while in the meantime our situation here has in no way altered.

THE INHUMANITY OF THE BOERS

It would appear that our resistance is beginning to exasperate the enemy, driving him to a pitch in which he is determined to respect neither the Convention of Geneva nor the promptings of humanity. Again, despite the innumerable warnings which he has received, for two days in succession has he made the hospital and the women's laager the sole object of his attentions. Yesterday the shells fell sufficiently wide of these two places to justify the broad-minded in giving to his artillery officers the benefit of the doubt; but to-day it is impossible to find any extenuating circumstances whatever in his favour, and your Correspondent very much regrets to have to state that through the shelling of the women's laager many children's lives have been sacrificed, many women mutilated. From time to time, every effort has been made to give to the gentler sex the most perfect immunity, but it would seem as though we can no longer consider as safe these poor innocent and helpless non-combatants. The children of some of the most respected and most loyal townspeople have been killed in this manner, just as they were romping within the trenches which encircle their retreat. For two hours this morning the quick-firing guns of the enemy fired into the laager, creating scenes of panic and consternation which it is not fitting to describe. These actions upon the part of the Boers, as Colonel Baden-Powell has repeatedly pointed out to them, make it almost impossible for us to regard our foe as other than one which is inspired with the emotions of a degraded people and the crude cruelty and vindictive animosity of savages. Just now, when the press of our feelings is beyond confinement, there is nothing but a universal wish that we may speedily be relieved and so enabled to enjoy the initiative against the Boers. When that moment comes it must not be forgotten that we have suffered bitterly, and in a way which must be taken as excusing any excesses which may occur.

A NATIVE CHIEF DEPOSED

During the time which has elapsed since Christmas the only other event has been the deposition of Wessels, the chief of the Baralongs. At a *kotla* of the tribe, to which the councillors and petty chiefs were bidden by the Imperial authorities, Colonel Baden-Powell and the Civil Commissioner, Mr. Bell, notified the tribe of their decision. The deposed chief, a man of no parts whatever, but one who unfortunately reveals all the vices of civilization, has been put upon sick leave, the reins of government being placed in the hands of his two chief councillors. Wessels has been instigating his tribe to refuse to work for the military authorities here, and through his instrumentality it has become difficult to obtain native labour and native runners. With the change which has been adopted and which has been given the sanction of the *kotla*, it is hoped that matters may progress more smoothly and the tribe itself increase in prosperity. It was an interesting meeting, and one which recalled the early days of Africa, when the authority of the great White Queen was not a power paramount in the council chambers of the tribes. Wessels, unwilling and assuming an air of injured dignity, filled his place in the *kotla* for the last time; around him there were the chiefs of the tribe, his blood relatives, and his councillors. Their attire was a weird mixture of effete savagery and of the civilization of the sort which is picked up from living in touch with white Africa and missionary societies. Many black legs were clothed in trousers, many black shoulders wore coats. Here and there, as relics of the past, there was the ostrich feather in the hat, the fly whisk, composed of the hairs from the tail of an animal, the iron or bone skin-scraper with which to remove the perspiration of the body. A few wore shoes upon naked feet, a few others sported watch-chains and spoke English. At the back of the enclosure there was a native guard who shouldered Martinis or elephant guns, Sniders or sporting rifles. A few of these were garmented with skins of animals upon the naked body. After a stately and not altogether friendly greeting to the two white men who had ordered the assembly to meet, the reasons which had brought about the contemplated change in the head of the tribe were stated in English and then translated by the interpreter. The old chief snorted with disgust and endeavoured to coerce his people to reject the demands made upon them. But they had been made before a body of men who were capable of realizing the worthlessness of their chief, and who, under the protection of the Imperial delegates, did not mind endorsing the suggestions and expressing their opinions. The younger and more turbulent, who recognized in the failings of the chief follies dear to their own hearts, were inclined to express sympathy for the man who was so soon to be compelled to relinquish the sweets of office. They spoke at once in an angry chatter and confused chortle of sounds, which, if eloquent, were wholly insufficient. The chief then threw himself back upon his chair, spat somewhat contemptuously, and finally acquiesced in the decision, obtaining some small consolation from the fact that his official allowance would not be discontinued. Then the *kotla* ended, and the indunas rose up and left, standing together in animated groups around the palisades, for the discussion of the scene in which they had just taken part. Then, as the decision spread throughout the tribe, children and women, young and old, banded together to watch these final indabas.

A NATIVE DANCE

The scene had been solemn enough beneath the *kotla* tree, but outside the natural instinct of these children of the veldt soon asserted itself, and they began to dance. They formed into small groups of about 40, to the sound of hand-clapping, a not unmusical intoning, and much jumping and stamping of feet. It would seem that they were dancing an old war dance which had degenerated into one symbolical of love and happiness. Around the joyous groups the old crones circulated, clapping their withered hands, shrieking delight in cracked voices, and generally encouraging the festivity. The dance was curious, and appeared to catch echoes of many lands. There was a diffident maiden, anxious to be loved, but bashful, modest in her manner and in her gestures, until she saw the man that could thrill her; then she glowed, and her steps were animated, buoyant, and caressing. A smile irradiated her face, while a slight, almost imperceptible, movement pulsed through her body. Behind her were her companions, the same age as herself, who imitated her with feverish sympathy, instinctively reproducing her moods of body and of mind. The vibration that stole through the bodies of the dancers increased gradually as the potency of their feelings grew steadily stronger. The air became heavy with noise, thick with a veritable tumult, as the dancers jumped more wildly. As they glided their actions seemed always to be marked with the same regularity, with the same regard to rhythm, and with an innate conception of grace. As they rose to the pinnacle of their happiness, when their countenances were suffused with love and tenderness, they infused into their emotions an appearance of sadness. It was as though a cloud had suddenly fallen upon them, revealing that they had been flouted. Then there stole upon them the incarnation of sorrow, in which, finding themselves alone, uncared for, unconsidered, they resolved, in a burst of artificial tears, to have done with giddiness, and to take up with the delights of placid domesticity. Then the dance terminated, she, who had by her graceful contortions and sympathetic bearing moved her audience to laughter and tears first, being considered the victorious. Thus did these simple natives celebrate the new era.

THE DEFENDER OF MAFEKING

As your Correspondent returned from the staadt, the man who had instigated this important change in the tribe was lying in his easy chair beneath the roof of the verandah of the headquarters office. Colonel Baden-Powell is young, as men go in the Army, with a keen appreciation of the possibilities of his career. His countenance is keen, his stature short, his features sharp and smooth. He is eminently a man of determination, with great physical endurance and capacity, and extraordinary reticence. His reserve is unbending, and one would say, quoting a phrase of Mr. Pinero's, that fever would be the only heat which would permeate his body. He does not go about freely, since he is tied to his office through the multitudinous cares of his command, and he is chiefly happy when he can snatch the time to escape upon one of those nocturnal silent expeditions, which alone calm and assuage the perpetual excitement of his present existence. Outwardly, he maintains an impenetrable screen of self-control, observing with a cynical smile the foibles and caprices of those around him. He seems ever bracing himself to be on guard against a moment in which he should be swept by some unnatural and spontaneous enthusiasm, in which by a word, by an expression of face, by a movement, or in the turn of a phrase, he should betray the rigours of the self-control under which he lives. Every passing townsman regards him with curiosity not unmixed with awe. Every servant in the hotel watches him, and he, as a consequence, seldom speaks without a preternatural deliberation and an air of incisive finality. He seems to close every argument with a snap, as though the steel manacles of his ambition had check-mated the emotions of the man in the instincts of the officer. He weighs each remark before he utters it, and suggests by his manner, as by his words, that he has considered the different effects it might conceivably have on any mind as the expression of his own mind. As an officer, he has given to Mafeking a complete and magnificent security, to the construction of which he has brought a very practical knowledge of the conditions of Boer warfare, of the Boers themselves, and of the strategic value of the adjacent areas. His espionage excursions to the Boer lines have gained him an intimate and accurate idea of the value of the opposing forces and a mass of *data* by which he can immediately counteract the enemy's attack. He loves the night, and after his return from the hollows in the veldt, where he has kept so many anxious vigils, he lies awake hour after hour upon his camp mattress in the verandah, tracing out, in his mind, the various means and agencies by which he can forestall their move, which, unknown to them, he had personally watched. He is a silent man. In the noisy day he yearns for the noiseless night, in which he can slip into the vistas of the veldt, an unobtrusive spectator of the mystic communion of tree with tree, of

Colonel Baden-Powell

twilight with darkness, of land with water, of early morn with fading night, with the music of the journeying winds to speak to him and to lull his thoughts. As he makes his way across our lines the watchful sentry strains his eyes a little more to keep the figure of the colonel before him, until the undulations of the veldt conceal his progress. He goes in the privacy of the night, when it is no longer a season of moonlight, when, although the stars are full, the night is dim. The breezes of the veldt are warm and gentle, impregnated with the fresh fragrances of the Molopo, although, as he walks with rapid, almost running, footsteps, leaving the black blur of the town for the arid and stony areas to the west, a new wind meets him, a wind that is clear and keen and dry, the wind of the wastes that wanders for ever over the monotonous sands of the desert. He goes on, never faltering, bending for a moment behind a clump of rocks, screening himself next behind some bushes, crawling upon his hands and knees. His head is low, his eyes gaze straight upon the camp of the enemy; in a little, he moves again, his inspection is over, and he either changes to a fresh point or startles some dozing sentry as he slips back into town.

JANUARY 16.
Since my last letter news has reached Mafeking of the departure from England for the seat of war of Field-Marshal Lord Roberts, with Major-General Lord Kitchener as his chief staff officer. The tidings has been received here by the inhabitants, as apart from the garrison, as confirming the gravity of the general situation. We would hope, of course, that so sombre a view may prove to be

mistaken, and that up to the present there has been nothing at which to cavil in the conduct of the campaign; but, despite the uncertainty of the news, there can be no doubt that it has in one way had a cheering effect upon the garrison, since there is no one here who thinks that, with such a warrior at the head of affairs, England can do aught but achieve an immediate supremacy. We are inclined to believe that Lord Roberts will bear in mind the position of Mafeking and despatch a column immediately to our relief.

"SNIPING" AND CATTLE RAIDING

This week has seen the return to Mafeking of a gun which accompanied Cronje when he moved south, but what this implies we cannot tell, and although it has since taken part daily in the bombardment of the town it has not secured to the enemy any great advantage. The result of one day's shelling, however, was unfortunate, since, in conjunction with a five-pounder, the Boers shelled the Cape Police fort at Ellis's Corner. Since the siege began sharpshooters have been in the habit of going regularly to this fort, which is in reality merely a trench with a mud wall, roofless house at either end, for the purpose of sniping the outlying trenches of the enemy. At one end of Ellis's Corner, beneath the tarpaulin, which has been spread across the four walls of the hut, is the Maxim position, while the building at the other is more or less open to the sky and used as a coign of advantage from which to fire. This Cape Police post is the most advanced of any upon the eastern front of the town. Trenches have been made so that a safe passage can be secured between the town and the fort, while a trench running at right angles with the position leads to the Kaffir church and to another sniping point in the river bed. From the fort itself one can obtain an excellent view of the enemy's advanced earthwork, the range being some 1,200 yards. It is therefore an interesting place to visit, and one eminently adapted to the somewhat exciting pastime of sniping. Such sniping, however, as this is in no way so dangerous as is the case when one is situated in the most outlying of our positions. In these cases the snipers take up their posts during the night in trenches which have been dug within 700 yards of the enemy and maintain during the day a steady fire upon the position against which they have been pitted. Along the eastern front of the town there are numerous posts which are in occupation by snipers, and from which it is impossible to move during the day. Occasionally these advanced trenches are shelled, and this is taken as a compliment to the accuracy of their fire, since the Boers have by now learnt that it is inadvisable to dress their guns when within reach of our snipers. Recently these men were instructed to direct their attention to the emplacement of the big gun, and so hot was the fire that was poured upon Big Ben that the enemy were found on the following morning to have raised the parapet of their emplacement, while a few days after it was found that they were preparing to withdraw the gun to a position in which it could not be reached by our fire.

Black and white alike take part in sniping, but to the native here the siege has brought the means and opportunity of indulging in a pastime of quite a different character. If sniping be the rule by day, cattle raiding by night gives to the natives some profitable employment. During last night the Baralongs secured by a successful raid some 24 head of cattle, and in the course of last week another raiding detachment looted some 18 oxen. The native enjoys himself when he is able to participate in some cattle raiding excursion to the enemy's lines, and, although the local tribe may not have proved of much value as a unit of defence, their success at lifting the Boer cattle confers upon them a unique value in the garrison. We were deploring the poorness of the cattle which remained at our disposal only a few days ago, but the rich capture which these natives have made has given us a welcome change from bone and skin to juicy beef. These night excursions are eagerly anticipated by the tribe, and almost daily is the consent of the colonel sought in relation to such an object. During the day the natives who have been deputed to take part in the raid approach as near to the grazing cattle as discretion permits, marking down when twilight appears the position of those beasts that can be most readily detached from the mob. Then, when darkness is complete they creep up, divested of their clothes, crawling upon hands and knees, until they have completely surrounded their prey. Then quietly, and as rapidly as circumstances will allow them, each man "gets a move on" his particular beast, so that in a very short space of time some ten or 20 cattle are unconsciously leaving the main herd. When the raiders have drawn out of ear-shot of the Boer lines, they urge on their captures, running behind them, and on either side of them, but without making any noise whatsoever. As they reach their staadt, their approach having been watched by detached bodies of natives, who, lying concealed in the veldt, had taken up positions by which to secure the safe return of their friends, the tribes go forth to welcome them, and when the prizes have been inspected and report duly made to the colonel, they celebrate the event with no little feasting and dancing. Upon the following day merriment reigns supreme, and for the time the siege is forgotten.

MAFEKING BEFORE AND AFTER SIEGE

JANUARY 20.

Yesterday we completed the first 100 days of our siege, and when we look back beyond the weeks of our investment into those earlier days it is difficult to realize the trials and difficulties which we have undergone and to believe that the period which has elapsed has witnessed the inauguration of a new era for South Africa. In those early days when we first came here Mafeking was a flourishing commercial centre, contented with its position, proud of its supremacy over other towns, and now, perhaps, if outwardly it be much the same, its future is impressed with only the faint echo of its former greatness. The town itself has not suffered very much; here and there its area has been more confined for purposes of defence, while the streets and buildings bear witness to the effects of the bombardment. Houses are shattered, gaping holes in the walls of buildings, furrows in the roads, broken trees, wrecked telegraph poles, and that general appearance of destruction which marks the path of a cyclone are the outward and visible signs of the enemy's fire.

We shall leave in Mafeking a population somewhat subdued and harassed with anxiety for their future, since the public and private losses will require the work of many anxious years before any restoration of the fallen fortunes can be effected. The pity of it is that all this distress might have been so easily avoided, and would have been, had the authorities in Cape Town and at home taken any heed of the very pressing messages which were despatched daily to them; but it was decreed that Mafeking should shift for itself for so long as it was able, and then – surrender. This, however, did not meet the approval of Colonel Baden-Powell, with the result that we are still fighting and still holding our own. We have even achieved some little place in the sieges of the world, and our present record has already surpassed many of the more prominent sieges. We have not yet equalled the siege of Azoth, which Herodotus tells us lasted for 29 years, nor come within appreciable measure of the siege of Troy. But there is not much consolation to be gained from contemplating the position which we may eventually take up in the records of famous sieges, and, truth to tell, there is such glorious uncertainty about the date of our relief that it is perhaps possible that we may surpass the longest of historic sieges. At one time we confidently anticipated that the siege would be over in ten days. This, however, was in the days of our youth; since then we have learned wisdom, and eagerly seize opportunities of snapping up any unconsidered trifles in the way of bets which lay odds upon our being "out of the wood" in another month. Events are moving so slowly below that it does not seem as though we shall be relieved by the end of February. The relief column, which a month ago appeared almost daily in "Orders," now seems to have passed out of existence, although there is little reason to doubt that, at some very remote date, the troops may make their appearance here.

SIEGE PRICES AND SUPPLIES

We have now begun to prepare for an indefinite sojourn in Mafeking, and almost all food-stuffs beyond a few luxuries have been taken over by the military authorities. Although we have enough food to last several months, this precaution is necessary, as when the siege is raised many weeks must elapse before supplies can come in. The garrison has been put upon a scale of reduced rations – $\frac{1}{2}$lb. of bread, $\frac{1}{2}$lb. of meat per day. The reductions in bread took place in the early part of the year, while the orders in relation to the meat supply were issued during this week. Matches and milk are prohibited from public sale, and the latest order prevents the shops from opening. All supplies of biscuits, tea, and sugar – preserves also – have been commandeered. It is, perhaps, difficult to define precisely what in the present circumstances are luxuries, but, lest there should be any doubt upon the point, the price of every variety of comestible has been inflated to an abnormal value. The shopkeepers and the hotel proprietors, and indeed anybody who can find any possible excuse for doing so, have trebled the price of their goods, pleading that the inflation is due to the siege. In many instances there is no reason which justifies such an action, but each merchant in his turn puts the blame upon some one else. Accordingly, meal and flour have jumped from 27s. per bag to 50s.; potatoes, where they exist at all, are £2 per cwt.; fowls are 7s. 6d. each; and eggs 12s. per dozen. Milk and vegetables can no longer be obtained, and rice has taken the place of the latter upon the menus. These figures mark the rise in the more important food-stuffs as sold across the counter, but the hotels have, in sympathy, followed the example, they upon their part attributing it to the increase which the wholesale merchants have decreed. A peg of whisky is 1s. 6d., dop brandy 1s., gin 1s., large stout is 4s., small beer 2s. In ordinary times whisky retails at 5s. per bottle. This rate has now advanced to 18s. per bottle and 80s. per case. Dop, which is usually 1s. 4d., is now 12s. per bottle; the difference upon beer is almost 200 per cent., and inferior cigarettes are now 18s. per 100. Upon an inquiry among the publicans here your Correspondent was informed that the chief reason for the increase in their prices was to hinder the local soldiery from becoming intoxicated, but this sudden regard for the moral welfare of the garrison on the part of the saloon keepers is oddly at variance with their earlier practices, and is in reality the flimsy pretext by which they seek to condone an almost unwarrantable act. Hitherto the constantly recurring evils arising from the sale of drink to soldiers and others performing military duties have been openly encouraged by the hotel proprietors, who, although they now profess a fine appreciation for the moral obligations attached to their trade when prices are high and profits great, took no very serious steps at the outset to allay what was becoming a very serious menace to the community. Moreover, the hotels have demanded from such people as war correspondents and others brought here through business connected with the siege rates which are far in advance of the ordinary tariffs, with equally preposterous demands for native servants and horse-feed. Indeed, whatever Mafeking may lose through the absence of business with the Transvaal, many will receive ample compensation from the high prices by which those who are able are endeavouring to recoup themselves, and in a way which it is not possible to consider other than extortionate. Stores of all kinds are, however, rapidly giving out, and it would not have been possible for Mafeking to have sustained the siege so long had not the Government contractor, upon his own initiative, laid in far greater stocks of provisions than were provided for by his contract, and in this respect every credit should be given to the commercial foresight and sagacity by which these arrangements were inspired. For everything which is in daily want, in fact for the bare necessities of life upon the existing scale of reduced rations, Mafeking now depends upon the stores and bonded warehouse which represent the local branch of the contracting firm, Messrs. Julius Weil and Co. In their hands lies the issuing of the daily allowances of bread and meat to the garrison, of the forage for the horses, of the feeding of the natives. There have, of course, been numerous complaints, but one is inclined to regard the spirit which inspires them, when we are oppressed by the siege and upon short commons, as more extraordinary than the cause at which exception is taken. Upon the whole it is generally allowed that such arrangements as were made by the contractor have been eminently satisfactory, and when the time comes to give honour to whom honour is due, notice should be taken of the important *rôle* which this firm has fulfilled during the siege of Mafeking.

Hamilton in this piece also contributed to the growing myth of Baden-Powell, 'The Defender of Mafeking'. Baden-Powell was undoubtedly the journalistic find of the siege: a true British eccentric, enthusiastic and indefatigable, a singer of comic songs, a soldier of consummate coolness who organized the defence of the town with verve and imagination. But there was also a dark side to this 'Victorian hero': faced with the problem of feeding the Europeans within the town, Baden-Powell elected to starve the natives who were trapped in Mafeking. Baden-Powell hoped that the natives would simply decamp rather than starve; however, he also knew full well that the Boers were unlikely simply to let the natives go. Thus faced with the choice between eventual starvation and the prospect of immediate death at the hands of the Boers, the bulk of the native population simply sat down and waited for death. To give Hamilton some credit, he at least tried to report what was happening to the natives, but again his reports were considered unsuitable and the treatment of the natives went unreported. The main complaint of the Europeans was that tinned butter had replaced the fresh variety; at the same time Baden-Powell was executing natives caught stealing food.[3] The plight of the natives is vividly caught in this quotation from Emerson Neilly of the *Pall Mall Gazette*, 'I saw them fall down on the veldt and lie where they had fallen, too weak to go on their way . . . words could not portray the scene of misery; five or six hundred human frameworks of both sexes and all ages, from tender infant upwards . . . standing in lines, awaiting turn to crawl painfully up to the soup kitchen where the food was distributed. Having obtained the horse soup, fancy them tottering off a few yards and sitting down to wolf up the life fastening mass. . . . They fed like outcast curs. They went farther than the mongrel . . . Day after day I heard outside my door continuous thumping sounds. They were caused by the living skeletons who, having eaten all that was outside the bones smashed them up with stones and devoured what marrow they could find. They looked for bones on the dust heaps, on the roads, everywhere.'[4] Unfortunately, this piece did not appear in the *Pall Mall Gazette*, but in a book Neilly wrote some years after the war was over.

The siege of Mafeking thus became one of the most powerful and enduring of Victorian myths. The news of the relief of Mafeking in May 1900 after 217 days of siege set off an orgy of hysterial celebration throughout Great Britain. Perhaps if the British people had been aware of the atrocities that had been committed in their name in Mafeking it might have been a different story. However, newspapers like *The Times* decided to prevent the public from learning the truth. According to Phillip Knightly the siege of Mafeking and the legend of Baden-Powell, 'represents one of the most serious failures on the part of the war correspondents in South Africa'.[5] Certainly one must agree with this sentiment, but we should also include the editors of the various newspapers, such as George Earle Buckle of *The Times*, in any condemnation of the newspaper coverage of these events.

Notes

1. Knightly, 1975, p. 69.
2. Quoted in B. Gardener, *Mafeking. A Victorian Legend* (London, 1966), p. 86.
3 Ibid., p. 112.
4. Quoted in Knightly, 1975, p. 71.
5. Ibid., p. 69.

Victory at Paardeberg

'What 'e does not know o' war,
  Gen'ral Bobs,
You can arst the shop next door –
  can't they, Bobs?
Oh 'e's little but 'e's wise,
  'E's a terror for 'is size,
An'-'e-does-not-advertise
  Do yer, Bobs?'

(Rudyard Kipling, 'Bobs', 1898)

The advancing British columns finally lifted the siege of the three beleaguered South African towns. To do this they followed the plan that had arrived in South Africa with Lord Roberts and Lord Kitchener. Roberts and Kitchener had at their disposal some 40,000 men, which included a whole cavalry division. Roberts's plan called for the wholesale reorganization of the forces in South Africa: unsuccessful commanders were replaced and the whole structure of the British force was changed. This included Kitchener's infamous centralization of the transport system that caused utter confusion at regimental level, but the overall effect of the arrival of Roberts and Kitchener was to lift the morale of the troops and to kindle a new enthusiasm and energy in the campaign. Roberts's plan called for the assembly of an army corps on the Modder River that would drive northwards along the flank of Piet Cronje's commandos based around Magersfontein, and subsequently invade the two Boer republics with an overwhelming force. Roberts began his advance in February 1900 and the British 'steamroller' moved inexorably forward, but all was not well. In Natal, Buller's attempt to relieve Ladysmith had ground to a halt with another reverse at Vaal Krantz. In defence of Buller it must be said that he had a much harder task than Roberts. Buller had only 30,000 men to deal with a force of 25,000 Boers, an enemy that was also heavily entrenched in a series of natural fortifications.[1]

Lord Roberts and staff on
the great march –
ascending the north bank
of the Zand River

CHIEVELEY CAMP, FEB. 13.

After General Warren's retirement across Trichardt's Drift on the night of January 25 the only position we retained on the north bank of the river was Krantz Kloof, the line of kopjes occupied by General Lyttelton's Brigade. The rest of the force went into camp between Spearman's Farm and Springfield, where they had a week's rest and had extra rations served out to them. This time it was not long before there were signs that we were going to make another attempt. On January 30 and 31 the Engineers were busy making a road along the southern side of Zwart's Kop. Zwart's Kop is a solitary wooded hill, flat-topped, about two miles to the east of Mount Alice, where the 4.7in. naval guns were mounted. Zwart's Kop stands some distance in advance of the line of hills of which Mount Alice is the westernmost and highest, and between the two lies a valley almost tropical in its fertility, and thickly wooded. Along this valley wound the Engineers' road, mounting slowly until it came to the last hundred yards, the steepest part of the whole hill. Two naval officers – Lieutenants Ogilvy and James – had inspected the place and were of opinion that guns could be pulled up this part with ropes. The road, therefore, made a sharp turn and went perfectly straight up the steep part. A tackle was rigged to two trees on the top, and during the night of February 1 and the following day six naval 12-pounders and two 15-pounder field guns were hauled up by men. The first gun, a naval 12-pounder, which was being pulled up in the dark, was overturned by a rock, but this was the only accident and the rest came up safely. On the afternoon of the 2nd the 4th Mountain Battery was sent up and, so steep was the hill, several mules lost their footing and rolled down.

The top of Zwart's Kop is flat and open, save only for a thick fringe of trees along the northern edge, which effectually masked the guns. At either end of Zwart's Kop the river, which here takes an extraordinarily tortuous course, runs close along the foot of the hill, but between the two a long tongue of land runs out almost to the foot of Brakfontein, the name given to the ridge running eastward from Spion Kop along the other side of the Tugela valley. Opposite Zwart's Kop Brakfontein practically comes to an end in a sharp knife-like spur called Vaal Krantz, very bare and rocky, with a few trees on it, running very straight almost due south, over a mile in length, and terminating in a round, steep kopje close to the river and dominating the flat ground all round it. Round Vaal Krantz turned the whole of the operations of February 5, 6, and 7. To the immediate east of Vaal Krantz lies flat ground much intersected by dongas sloping gradually up on the north-east to the plateau which runs from behind Brakfontein nearly the whole way to Ladysmith and on the east up to Doorn Kloof, the highest hill in the neighbourhood and most irregular in shape, whose sides are a mass of sharp peaks, deep gullies, wooded kloofs, and big dongas. When we first attacked Vaal Krantz, Doorn Kloof was not strongly held by the enemy, though they had an elaborate line of trenches on the lower slopes of it guarding Schiet Drift. During the later stages of the fighting the Boer position was an almost complete semicircle from Spion Kop on the right to Doorn Kloof on the left, with only one small break in it, the gap between Brakfontein and Doorn Kloof through which the Ladysmith road runs. Even this, being much cut up by dongas, was always held in considerable force by Boer riflemen. This great semicircle, nearly ten miles across, completely overlapped our position, where we had a front not more than four miles long.

On Sunday, February 4, the troops struck camp. General Clery's Division marched to the valley behind Zwart's Kop and General Warren's to Potgeiter's. In the evening General Wynne's Brigade crossed over the drift followed by six field batteries, and relieved General Lyttelton, whose brigade was to make the attack on the right on the following day. The plan of battle was as follows. In the morning General Wynne's Brigade was to advance from Krantz Kloof (the kopjes where he had relieved Lyttelton) and make a demonstration in front of Brakfontein, supported by all the field guns; the latter were then to retire, battery by battery, and, recrossing the river by a pontoon bridge in front of Zwart's Kop, come into action on the tongue of land in front of that hill and assist the main attack which was to cross the river by another pontoon further east and advance upon the southern spur of Vaal Krantz. It was to assist this attack that the guns had been mounted on Zwart's Kop.

Monday morning dawned fine, but very hazy. As the haze cleared away the army on the plain below Mount Alice appeared like some great beast slowly awakening and stretching out its limbs. From the main body, bivouacked below Zwart's Kop, long sinuous arms of infantry, artillery and wagons stretched slowly eastward, winding along between the river and the foot of the hill; whilst from Krantz Kloof long lines in extended order began the advance upon Brakfontein. Their advance was slow, and it was not till 7 o'clock that the field batteries advanced and took up a position in the middle of the open ground between Krantz

Kloof and Brakfontein. Then the howitzer battery on Brakfontein opened, quickly followed by the 4.7in. naval guns, one of which had been moved a mile to the eastward of Mount Alice, and in a few minutes a heavy bombardment was in progress. Very slowly General Wynne's Brigade, the York and Lancaster Regiment leading, supported by the South Lancashire Regiment, advanced in widely-extended order, and several hours elapsed during which the Boers did not reply to our artillery and only maintained a desultory musketry fire upon the advancing infantry from a farmhouse and donga on their right front. At 10 the first battery limbered up and withdrew, keeping to the north bank of the river till it crossed by the pontoon bridge north of Zwart's Kop. The rest followed at the rate of about one every half-hour, and by 1 o'clock the last had retired. But long before this the enemy, thinking perhaps that the attack was really repulsed, had opened a very heavy and well-directed shell fire upon the batteries with every available gun, the most telling fire coming from Spion Kop. Our guns were under quite as heavy a shell fire as were Colonel Long's batteries at Colenso, though here they were not, as on that occasion, under a deadly musketry fire as well. The gunners worked their guns splendidly, though they were utterly unable to silence the far heavier guns that were firing down upon them. The casualties were not heavy considering the severity of the fire, for the Boer shells do not seem to burst with much power. Colonel Montgomery was wounded by shrapnel. The 78th Battery, which was the last to leave, suffered most heavily. At 1 o'clock, the object of the demonstration having been achieved, General Wynne's Brigade, which had come within about a mile of the Brakfontein position, received the order to retire. Hardly had the first line faced about when a perfect storm of fire arose from the trenches in which the Boers had hitherto not shown the faintest sign of their presence. Fortunately, the range was a long one or the casualties would have been far heavier, but the York and Lancaster Regiment were pursued for nearly a mile with musketry and were shelled until they got under cover of Krantz Kloof. Their casualties numbered 23, which is heavy considering the range.

As the fire on the left slackened that on the right increased in volume. All the morning a continuous stream of horse, foot, and wagons had been pouring eastward, and now lay only very slightly concealed at the foot of the wooded re-entrants of the northern face of Zwart's Kop. It had been pretty generally considered that the one possible flaw in the plan of battle was the bridging and crossing of the river. As it turned out, however, this was carried out with scarcely any loss. The spot chosen was to the north-east of Zwart's Kop, close under it, and about 1,200 yards from Vaal Krantz. The Engineers were under musketry and Maxim fire from the broken ground at the foot of Doorn Kloof as they were making the bridge, but the high banks gave them shelter, and they lost only eight wounded. By 12 o'clock the bridge was finished, the gunners on Zwart's Kop had unmasked their guns by felling the trees that hid them, the 5in. garrison guns on a small kopje to the west of Zwart's Kop had opened fire, and the main attack had begun. After two hours' bombardment General Lyttelton commenced his attack. The Durham Light Infantry were the first to cross, supported by the Rifle Brigade. Under cover of the high bank they advanced nearly half-way to Vaal Krantz, but there the shelter came to an end, and they were forced to extend across the open.

They immediately came under a rifle fire which, though not so heavy as we have usually gone through in attacking fortified positions, was quite as searching. It came from the kopje in front and it also came from Monger's Farm on their right flank, and from the broken ground to their right rear. To meet it the attack spread out like a fan, and, though the main body still advanced straight toward Vaal Krantz, a part were forced to turn aside, and, after crossing a very open bit of ground, took possession of the farmhouse. Meanwhile all the artillery that could be moved had come into action on the right, and the concentrated fire of 70 guns at comparatively short range was poured into Vaal Krantz. Notwithstanding this terrific fire, however, many Boers remained on the hill, and could be seen dodging about among the rocks, and when at last the Durhams fixed bayonets and charged up the hill nearly 50 of the enemy fled precipitately down the other side. Our men rushed across the hill firing into them as they fled and killed about 20. Ten or 15 had been killed by shell fire, and five or six prisoners were taken, together with about 20 ponies. Our first attack was a brilliant success; it remained to be seen whether it could be followed up.

Of the enemy, who remained on the hill till our men reached it, more than half were armed natives – of what tribe it is impossible to say, though probably they were Basutos from the conquered territory. They were undoubtedly fighting. One of them, slightly wounded, remained in the trench when the Durhams reached it. They were about to bayonet him, when Lieutenant Lambton, perceiving that he was wounded, ordered his men to spare him. This was done, and the native promptly picked up his rifle and shot Lieutenant Lambton through the wrist. This is not the first time that armed natives have been seen with the Boers. During the fight on Spion Kop they were seen on the hill, and at Colenso they came across the river after the fight was over in order to pick up what they could in the way of loot.

There is no doubt that the enemy were not in the least prepared for our main attack. The prisoners themselves admitted as much, and to this was due the comparative slightness of our loss. The total casualties in the Durham L. I. for the day were only 35 including, unfortunately, two officers killed.

In a very short time, however, the Boers were making every preparation to prevent our further advance. Even before the kopje was taken a gun had come round the back of Brakfontein, run the gauntlet of all the naval 12-pounders on Zwart's Kop, and disappeared into one of the big dongas on Doorn Kloof. It was a plucky ride on the part of the gunners, for they were within easy shot of the long-range guns and the last shell enveloped them in dust; but they got safely through. On the far side of Vaal Krantz a steadily increasing rattle of musketry very soon drove us off the eastern face of the hill altogether. The western face was under a less severe fire from a large donga running from the angle where Vaal Krantz and Brakfontein meet to the river. By the evening of the 5th General Lyttelton held about half a mile of Vaal Krantz, his men being all on the western side of the hill, taking what shelter they could amongst the trees and rocks. It was now becoming increasingly evident that the strategic value of Vaal Krantz for turning the Brakfontein position had been over-estimated. Between General Lyttelton and the nearest of the Brakfontein trenches lay half a mile of bare knife-edged hill, commanded on one side by any amount of broken ground culminating in a line of kopjes, and on the other by an unbroken line of trenches stretching away to the eastward. Besides this he was already being considerably harassed by guns the enemy had mounted in the deep kloofs of Doorn Kloof, invisible to our artillery.

During the night the enemy mounted a 100-pounder gun on the very top of Doorn Kloof. This gun, probably a 6-in. Creuzot, was mounted on some sort of a disappearing carriage. When it fired its muzzle could be seen quite distinctly against the skyline for 12 seconds before it disappeared. As it took our shells 18 seconds to reach the place, it did not make a very good mark. Till well on in the afternoon there was nothing but an artillery duel, in which, so well had the Boers placed their guns, we were unable to silence a single one of them. At 4 o'clock there was a sudden burst of musketry at the far end of Vaal Krantz. At the same moment the Boers began to shell the kopjes heavily. They were making a desperate attempt to retake the hill, and had already driven back the first line. For a few minutes it looked critical. Then half a battalion of the 60th Rifles advanced in support with fixed bayonets, and under a heavy rifle and shell fire the attack failed as quickly as it had begun. The whole affair lasted only about half an hour. That day the pontoon, by which the field guns had crossed the river the day before, were taken up and thrown across just below Vaal Krantz, and after dark General Hildyard's Brigade relieved General Lyttelton's.

That night and the following morning the kopjes were shelled again, and more heavily than before, and it was obvious on the 7th that, unless the enemy were attacked in their present positions, Vaal Krantz would be untenable. We found ourselves in what was in reality a defile bounded by Spion Kop on one side and Doorn Kloof on the other, both well-nigh impregnable mountains. Merely to get through meant an assault on Brakfontein, an extremely strong intrenched position impossible to turn, and the cost of such attacks we had learnt at Colenso; but there is not the slightest doubt that, had General Buller ordered it, it would have been promptly and successfully carried out. To establish lines of communication through the valley would have entailed the taking of at least Doorn Kloof as well, and Doorn Kloof, a vast pile of kopjes rising one above the other, was the ideal fighting ground of the Boer. The strength of the Boers on our right flank was the new factor in the case that had arisen during the three days' fighting, and we were now in the unpleasant position of being ourselves outflanked by the enemy we had been attempting to outflank. It was this that had wrought the deadlock of the last two days, and at the end of them, finding our efforts to clear away the obstruction with our artillery absolutely fruitless, there was nothing left but to retire. At 9 o'clock on the night of the 7th General Hildyard's Brigade received the order to retire across the river. The pontoons were taken up and all night a continuous stream of wagons passed up the hill on their way back to Spearman's Camp. In the morning the mounted troops and infantry followed, pursued by an occasional shell from the Boer 100-pounder. That night the guns on Zwart's Kop were lowered and marched to Springfield, escorted by General Warren's Division. All attempt at crossing by the Upper Tugela was abandoned and in three days most of the force was camped at Chieveley.

Kit inspection before forcing the
Modder, 12 February 1900

Despite this setback the British advance continued, and Roberts ordered General
French to move forward at top speed to relieve Kimberley once an opportunity
presented itself. The British forces totally deceived Cronje, who, once he realized that
the British had left their base camp, thought that they were headed for the town of
Fauresmith. Instead the British, with French's cavalry in the lead, raced to the Modder
River and established a bridgehead on the far side of the river. Cronje realized with
growing horror that British infantry as well as cavalry were moving around his flank.
At the Modder River a scene of incredible activity was taking place, as the British
forces streamed forward to outflank the Boers.

MODDER RIVER, FEB. 10.

The drift is the centre of the life of Modder River. Now, while the troops are
concentrating here in their tens of thousands, every night bringing its three or
four battalions more, it is the scene of restless activity from before dawn till long
past sunset. All day long squadrons of cavalry horses come down to water, horses
of all kinds, from the high-withered, sloping-quartered pony of the country to the
great giants of the Household Cavalry; all day long in endless lines the ten-muled
wagons jolt and creak across the shallows, and the hurrying mounted orderly
splashes past them.

The drift is 300 yards wide – perhaps more – and the bleak, black rocks, with
their flat backs a foot or so above the water at lowest tides, spread themselves to
the sun for three-quarters of the distance. In between them grow rushes and a
white-flowered spray of water-weed; seven foot reeds, too, here and there. All
over the rocks the kivikes run and flutter in hundreds, little brown and white

sandpipers with absurdly long legs, hardly moving to avoid one as one comes
upon them; a few yards up stream you may often see a solitary crane, quite the
most awkward walker, almost the most graceful flier, of all winged things; but
neither he nor the hawks that can be found in pairs all over the veldt dare to come
now near the drift itself.

A few yards down stream is the low temporary railway, spanning the river on
heaps of grey boulders, and ascending on either side through the cuttings of the
banks to the level of the permanent rails, by a gradient unknown to the
calculations of English engineers. Here, with a garrulous cock crow or an insistent
whistle, the trains go night and day, and overhead the strong men of the army are
lifting the wrecked bridge on new piers to its old place. The dynamite used so
lavishly by the Boers has done curiously little harm to the material. Only the
concrete blocks of the piers have been shattered, the damage penetrating in a
latent form far within the broken surface of the piers. These are being repaired by
natural stones quarried a mile or two up the river, where the fire was hottest at the
beginning of the battle, and are being hewn into shape on the banks, the ceaseless
clicking of the mason's hammer adding another to the many noises of the place.

But, of all sounds, the incessant clatter of hoofs is that which is always
uppermost, marked now and again by a jarring clash, as some horse misses his
step in a crevice and regains his footing with a plunge. The birds in the primrose-
scented bebel-thorn trees, on the tongue of land that comes down between the
"Twee rivier" to Watersmeet, are cheery little whistlers, but very little more, and
one has to be sitting beneath them to hear the thin notes at all. Here and there a rat
runs for cover, or a tortoise flaps his paddles at the mud-edge, hardly
distinguishable at ten yards from the mud he moves in.

In flood time the water comes over the rocks with a long droning roar that
warns one a quarter of a mile away that the pontoon is the only means of getting
over. Theocritus remarked upon the sinewy lines of water overrunning stones.
Here they are giant's muscles indeed, and a foot of such water will sweep off his
feet the steadiest horse. And there is another danger. Flood water is here so muddy
that the underlying rocks are invisible with even a three-inch coat of water. It is
better to go round. A boat has been swept down stream from Jacobsdal and has
landed with the bottom torn out of her on the very middle of the late causeway;
weed and branches of willow form a dense, and soon an unsavoury, zariba, until
the deepening stream throws them over the bar and they go spinning down to
Koodoesberg. The Modder River rises some three inches more than the Riet
during an ordinary flood, and the angry swirl round the point of land leading into
the stagnancy of the back eddy on the northern bank of the Riet is worth watching.
Here, indeed, is a limbo of useless orts. Just under the khaki walls of the row of
rooms called out of civility the Island Hotel, jagged and spattered with shrapnel
and rifle bullets, this curious mass of flotsam heaves during a flood, bits of wood,
boxes, dead animals, heaps of river weed, scraps of flannel or khaki, half a bundle
of oat-hay floated down from God knows where, half a broken scull and the seat of
a boat, a cap – all that ever went down rivers collects and heaves in a mass tangled
about with lengths of water-grass, a sargasso that moves heavily down stream with
the slackening tide, and lodges itself in the crannies and clefts of the drift.

The garrison artillery saving
the Modder River Bridge

The Modder, 60 yards from Watersmeet, is crossed by a pont. We should call it a ferry in England, if we gave any name at all to the water-logged raft with its wire rope leash. Few rivers are so crossable as the Modder. Two railway bridges, four pontoons, one pont, and two drifts afford wide choice. As if these were not enough, the foundations of a road bridge, built upon piers of railway sleepers and rails, have been laid near the Guards' dam a mile up. But the centre of interest is still the drift. Any man with an hour to spare comes and fishes, comes and washes – strictly against orders – comes and lies lazily under the willows and the thorn trees. A few Kaffirs with their women folk in electric blue and Indian red-printed cotton gowns group themselves round their watering-place, sometimes singing a hymn tune in harmony, either without words or with words that should not be translated to a missionary, always of the long-drawn evangelical type that appeals so strongly to the native taste.

The general rides across, perhaps still a little stiff from the wound, followed by two or three of the Staff with little red tabs at the throat like goldfinches, and even a casual "resident" stiffens as he passes, so deeply imbued with militarism is this little African imitation of Maidenhead.

All day long from the drift the railway sidings diverge and lengthen slowly, as the rails are borne to their place, each by 15 natives calling out "huh-ya-hee!" as each step is taken. One siding in particular is worth notice. It runs from the drift · east by south, along the river bank 40 yards from the Boer trenches, and as a siding it has long become remarkable. Surely a siding a mile long is sufficient for the needs of even this camp; but at the end of the mile an accumulating heap of sleepers, rails, and fish-plates betrays the birth of the much-talked-of railway to Bloemfontein.

Half-way along this siding stands a camp of marquees and tents of a class somewhat better than that of the ordinary regimental tent. Round this camp go the flying sentries night and day armed with a bayonet only, and within the largest marquee the general we had just seen is closeted with Lord Roberts.

Here on the spot, to us tired with the monotony of the day that never differs from the last, too much accustomed to the boom and drone of our 4.7in. shells even to watch the explosion on the purple violet hills of Magersfontein to the north, to us the place has perhaps little of the interest that will attach to it in future as a battleground, as a camp, and as the starting-place of the great expedition. The evening and the morning alone to us make the day. The weaver birds in their scarlet and velvet-black robes, like little doctors of divinity, hustle and hop among the willows, and the vertical flutter up and the despairing whine of the kohran, who never moves or sings his ascending note – six tones in perfect chromatic scale – after the sun is risen, comes across from the worn and dusty veldt and the morning rises over Jacobsdal. The cranes croak and the peckers knock among the willows as the sun sets. To those who have never seen an African sunset it is difficult to speak of it without seeming preposterous. To say that the reflection in the eastern sky would often provide in England a notable sunset is but the bare truth, and it would be difficult to find a better place from which to watch the never-failing glories of the evening than the drift at Modder River.

Up to the last moment the river keeps its steel-blue tinge, running among the blackening grasses and rocks of the ford, while overhead the sky stretches and sweeps its barbaric splendour, set off by the sharply-etched black girders of the broken high-level bridge; then, as the colour mounts and darkens into crimson, the water, surrendering in one short minute, flows into the west a moving waste of blood, and the silhouette of the water-wheel on the south bank, with its broken and shrapnel-pierced vans, dominates the scene of black and red.

But, whether in the evening or the morning, whether in the heat of the day or the semi-darkness of the moonlight just tinged with blue, whether in the brown twilight of the tingling dust-storm or the shimmering haze of the noon-day, the wagons creak and blunder for ever through the drift.

As Roberts's forces consolidated their position around the Modder River, dozens of small actions took place as the Boers frantically sought to stem the tide of the British advance. But the Boer activity was in vain. Cronje had moved far too slowly, and his whole force was in serious danger of encirclement, as they fled from their defensive position around Magersfontein. For once the British had managed both to anticipate their enemy's moves and to move swiftly enough to take advantage of his weekness.

CLOSING IN ROUND PAARDEBERG

The battle began soon after daybreak with a heavy rifle fire, opened by the Boers from the river bed upon the mounted infantry while still at their breakfast. After some fairly severe fighting the mounted infantry succeeded in driving back the Boers and clearing the river bed for about a quarter of a mile above Paardeberg Drift. Meanwhile, at the sound of the firing, the Sixth Division – after first marching a short distance in the direction of Paardeberg Drift till in the growing daylight Lord Kitchener perceived that the enemy's main position was not there, but at Wolveskraal – was marched down into the plain, Colonel Stephenson's Brigade being on the right and General Knox's on the left. Colonel Stephenson, with the Welsh and Essex, marched right across the plain, past Cronje's laager, and then deployed opposite the river at the bend below Koodoosrand Drift, leaving the Yorks on the right of Knox's Brigade, which had deployed right across the middle of the plain. The Highland Brigade, at the same time, marched down into the plain from the Klipkraal road, and extended on the left of Knox's Brigade, the Argylls being on the right, the Black Watch in the centre, and the Seaforths on the left. The Highland Light Infantry had been left at Klip Drift on the lines of communication. The whole line rapidly advanced across a perfectly smooth plain, offering even less cover than the ground across which Lord Methuen advanced at Modder River. While the infantry advanced the 76th and 81st Batteries, with one naval gun, and the 65th Howitzer Battery, which had just arrived with the Ninth Division, posted themselves on a slight rise about 2,000 yards south-south-east of the laager and 1,600 yards from the nearest point of the river. The naval gun, owing to some accident in the mechanism, was unable to fire; but the others did great execution on the laager, setting the wagons on fire in several places. During the day three loud explosions were heard in the burning laager, due probably to the setting on fire of ammunition wagons. The laager became practically untenable, and the Boers made very little attempt to use their guns except the Vickers-Maxims, which they used freely in the afternoon.

About 9 o'clock General Smith-Dorrien's Brigade, except the Cornwall Light Infantry, which was kept in reserve, crossed the Paardeberg Drift and fought their way nearly a mile up the north bank among the bushes. Finding it impossible to get any further up the bank at that point, the brigade made a curve at some distance to the north-east, so as to get above the lower bend, which was tremendously strongly held, and extended, the Shropshires on the right, the Canadians in the centre, and the Gordons on the left, but considerably advanced to the north-east, rather separated from the others. The Shropshires and Canadians advanced by a series of short rushes in the most gallant style, the Canadians especially showing a magnificent and almost reckless courage. These two battalions and the 82nd Battery, which Colvile had sent in support, did great execution among the Boers in a stretch of the river bank above the bend, where they were able to some extent to enfilade them. At about 11 o'clock French's horse artillery planted itself on the rising ground north of the laager and shelled the laager and the river bed. Some of their shells went a little too far, and at one time their shrapnel was falling unpleasantly freely into the fighting line of the Highland Brigade. As the morning went on our troops pressed steadily forward across the open ground, in spite of a terribly hot fire kept up by the Boers and in spite of unexampled fatigue and privation gone through during the last few days of marching. Towards midday the mounted infantry, who had occupied a kopje south of Koodoosrand Drift, crossed the river and advanced some distance along the north bank under a very heavy fire. It was here that Colonel Hannay is believed to have been killed early in the afternoon. Soon after 1 o'clock the Welsh and Essex rushed the river bank below the point crossed by the mounted infantry, and, after crossing, worked their way down among the bushes on both sides and in the river bed. The work done by both of these regiments was splendid, and both suffered very heavily. In one of the rushes made by the Welsh towards the end of the afternoon 24 out of a party of 25 who attempted to storm the laager were killed or wounded. About the same time the Thirteenth and the Highland Brigades, whose brigadiers were both wounded, General Knox through the shoulder and General MacDonald through the foot, made a most determined attempt to get down to the river, the Highlanders being reinforced by half of the Cornwalls. At about 2 o'clock Knox's Brigade and the Yorks got down to the river bank just above the bend, while three companies of the Seaforths and three companies of the Black Watch crossed the river below. The bend itself was so strongly held that the rest of the Highland Brigade were unable to get within 400 yards of it. Though our troops held the river bank both above and below this bend, the Boers maintained their position in it till nightfall, when they withdrew to the laager. The Canadians and Shropshires, by 3 o'clock, found themselves unable to advance any further. At 3.30, Colvile sent three and a half companies of the Cornwalls to support them. Passing through the Canadians and Shropshires, and picking up a certain number of them, the Cornwalls advanced to within 800 yards of the Boer position and then made a charge which, with the advance of the Welsh on the other flank, may be considered the most striking performance of the day. No troops could have carried a charge home against such a position, and it in nowise detracts from the gallantry of their performance that the Cornwalls, after the fall of Colonel Aldous, failed to get more than 400 yards further.

Kitchener's Hill was the scene of some rather purposeless operations. Early in the morning Kelly-Kenny posted three companies of the Gloucesters on the hill, which was unoccupied. Afterwards these were recalled to strengthen the fighting line, and a small party of Kitchener's Horse was sent up. About 4 o'clock most of these were watering their horses and cooking a meal in Osfontein Farm, when their horses were stampeded and they themselves surprised by some Boers coming from the south; 30 men and four officers, out of 45, were captured.

A SOLDIER'S BATTLE

When once the battle had begun, it was almost entirely a soldier's and regimental officer's battle. And the way the soldiers fought reflects the greatest credit on them. Exhausted by a week's marching and fighting, many of them without food or drink since the previous afternoon, their steadiness and courage could hardly be surpassed. Perhaps the most reckless bravery was shown by the Welsh, the Cornwalls, and the Canadians; but all the regiments behaved splendidly, and it would be invidious to distinguish specially any single one. The heaviness of the casualty list, over 1,100, and the evenness with which the casualties were distributed bear witness to the bravery displayed equally by every battalion of the two divisions engaged. One cause of the heaviness of the casualty list was the extreme thirstiness of the men, who, when they got near the river bank, could not be prevented from rushing down to the bed of the river and drinking regardless of the fire poured into them. By nightfall we held the whole river on both sides except a stretch of about a mile on each side of the laager, into which Cronje's whole force is now cooped up, and from which it cannot possibly escape unless relieved by a very large force. His position is in a way very defensible, being, in fact, one enormous shelter trench, with numerous short cross-trenches, and a supply of water running through it. It would be difficult to take it by storm without a very heavy loss; but any attempt to escape from it would mean that the Boers would have to attempt to cross open ground enclosed, for a complete circle, by a vastly superior force.

The only question that may be asked about the battle of February 18 is whether it was really necessary and whether the object of surrounding Cronje might not have been attained just as well by occupying all the high ground we now hold, so as to surround the Boers, and then gradually pushing our way up from Paardeberg and Koodoosrand Drifts. Looking back, one feels inclined to think that this course would have been better, but at the time it probably did not seem quite certain whether Cronje might not get his men away unless seriously damaged by fighting. And no doubt Lord Kitchener entertained some hope that the whole force might have been captured that day, and that Cronje's transport and provisions might be utilized for pushing on the advance to Bloemfontein. If there had been time to arrange the battle after a previous study of the ground, the attack would probably not have been so strongly pressed in the middle of the position. But the battle developed very suddenly and unexpectedly, and it would have been very difficult to withdraw any of the battalions when once they had advanced in extended order within the zone of a dangerous fire. In such cases retirement is almost more dangerous than advance. One may reckon it to the good that the Boers undoubtedly lost heavily in both men and horses, and that the loss of the latter would render them practically helpless, even if not invested.

On Monday Lord Roberts and his staff arrived, followed by General Tucker's Division. Cronje asked for 24 hours' armistice to bury his dead, which was refused as it was feared he would only use the opportunity to strengthen his position. Owing to some misunderstanding of the Dutch phrases in which Cronje's reply was couched, Lord Roberts first believed that Cronje intended to surrender; but that stubborn warrior had no such intention, and replied contemptuously to the suggestion that he should come out of his camp and surrender personally to some senior officer. Since the 19th the enclosing circle has been steadily drawn closer. The laager and river bed have been shelled daily, while Smith-Dorrien, astride of the river to the west of the laager, and Chermside, succeeding Stephenson to the east, have been steadily pushing their way along. The Cornwalls, helped by the Engineers in constructing trenches, have in the last two nights pushed their way to within a few hundred yards of the Boer laager. Kitchener's Hill, which the Boers captured on Sunday and occupied by a force of over 500 men, was taken on Wednesday by a combined operation of the artillery batteries, on the rise opposite

General Tucker's
artillery engaging the
enemy across the Zand
River

the laager, and Broadwood's cavalry. The Boers who held it escaped to the north-east, and, after being hunted all round the plains from one detachment to another like driven game, got away with the loss of some prisoners and about 30 casualties. On Friday a party of about 500 Boers, mainly belonging to the Winburg and Heidelberg commandos, who had come straight from Ladysmith, made a very determined attempt to drive the Yorkshires off the kopje. But the Yorkshires held their own and, being later supported by the Scottish Borderers and Buffs, drove off the enemy, 87 of whom, having had their horses shot, surrendered to the Buffs after keeping up a sniping fight for two or three hours. Numerous other parties of Boers have been hovering round our positions lately and have had skirmishes with our outposts, usually losing more heavily than our men. The investment of Cronje is not only useful in drawing off Boers from Ladysmith and Colesberg, but it gives rest to our forces, especially to our horses, which, owing to want of forage, are in a very poor condition. Many of them are quite useless.

One can only hope that the War Office authorities realize fully how absolutely our Army in South Africa is dependent on its cavalry and mounted infantry, and how absolutely helpless those forces are without horses. The necessity for making up the constant drain in horses is even more necessary than that for replenishing the casualties made in the ranks of our men. At the present moment a horse is worth more than a man; and no surer proof could be given of the incompetence of the War Office than if a sudden outbreak of horse sickness, or the fatigues of a march on Bloemfontein found us without horses. The Boer supply of horses is strictly limited; but we have absolutely unlimited supplies to draw on from all the world over. Our present success is entirely due to the rapid movements of French's Division, which the infantry admirably supported, but without which the infantry would have been perfectly useless.

Roberts had succeeded in bringing Cronje to bay with the bulk of his forces, and was now preparing to deliver the *coup de grâce* in the most spectacular British victory of the war. But we must not forget Buller ploughing his lonely furrow in Natal. At last, despite the many obstacles that faced him, Buller was about to achieve his objective of raising the siege of Ladysmith.

BULLER'S ADVANCE TOWARDS LADYSMITH

(From our special correspondent)
Colenso Camp, Feb. 27 (by telegraph to Cape Town).
Very little time was lost after our retirement from Springfield before we were again advancing. By February 11 the whole force, with the exception of Colonel Burn-Murdoch's Cavalry Brigade and the York and Lancaster Regiment and Lancashire Fusiliers, left at Springfield, was once more at Chieveley. The first intimation of our next move was given on the 10th, when General Buller reconnoitred Hussar Hill, six miles north-east of Chieveley, with the Mounted Infantry Brigade.

Hussar Hill, so called because a Cossack post of Hussars had been cut up there soon after the battle of Colenso, is the point where the open veldt, in which we have hitherto always moved, ends and the bush country begins. In front lies the thickly-wooded valley of the Gomba Spruit, a small stream running eastward from Hlangwane Hill, and to the south lies the equally bushy Blaauwkrantz Valley. The bush consists chiefly of stunted mimosa and is intersected by innumerable dongas, so, though it forms excellent cover for troops, their advance is necessarily very slow. The point reconnoitred by General Buller was the left of the vast Colenso position. Since the battle of Colenso the Boers had considerably extended their fortifications on the south side of the river, and a practically continuous line of intrenchments now ran eastwards from Hlangwane Hill along the north side of the Gomba Valley. They terminated on Green Hill, a steep kopje, barren of trees, nearly three miles from Hlangwane. East of Green Hill rose Monte Cristo, a great range of hills, nearly 1,000ft. high, running in a north-westerly direction to the Tugela, and extending far away to the south-east. The Boers' position is, in fact, a spur of the Monte Cristo range. The reconnaissance having ascertained this returned to camp. It was not considered necessary to hold Hussar Hill, as it was not a strong position.

On the 14th tents were struck, baggage packed, and we moved out towards the hill, leaving General Hart's Brigade to guard the camp. Lord Dundonald took the hill, which he found weakly held. The Boers were evidently in the habit of occupying it, and, when they found it attacked, came across in considerable numbers from Hlangwane to defend it. They were too late, however, for the South African Light Horse and the Celts Battery were already on the top. There was a

A British field telephonist at work, February 1900

sharp fight for about half an hour, when the Irish Fusiliers and a field battery came up, and the Boers were driven back. That practically ended the fighting for the day. The Irish Fusiliers met with very slight resistance as they advanced eastwards, securing the low hills, known as Moord Kraal, which form the southern side of the Gomba Valley. General Lyttelton's Division, composed of his own brigade, under Colonel Norcott, the Rifle Brigade, and General Hildyard's, making a detour through the Blaauwkrantz Valley, occupied the eastern extremity of Moord Kraal, which gave us a front of about two miles.

On the following day, which was excessively hot, little was done, except that a very strong battery of heavy guns, including two 5in. garrison guns, two 4.7in. and four 12-pounder naval guns, and the howitzer battery, were brought into position on Hussar Hill. Behind Green Hill the Boers had one large calibre gun and probably two smaller ones, and a desultory artillery duel continued all day. On the 16th General Hildyard's Brigade reconnoitred the slopes of Cingolo, one of the hills in the Monte Cristo range. The conformation of the hills takes something the shape of an irregularly-formed letter T, the base being Hlangwane and Green Hill, the cross stroke to the northward being Monte Cristo Hill, and that to the southward being Cingolo. The two latter hills are divided by a deep nek. The fighting of the next two days was exceedingly hard to follow in detail. Both sides were practically invisible in the dense bush, and, as the only intrenched position the Boers had was Green Hill, which was not attacked till the afternoon of the second day, the relative position of the opposing forces was often difficult to discover. Our ultimate object was Green Hill, which was to be achieved by the capture of the heights commanding it, and the first day's operations were confined to the taking of Cingolo.

We had three brigades engaged. On the left, General Barton's advanced under good cover towards Green Hill and kept up a heavy fire upon it all day. On the right, General Hildyard's, with Colonel Norcott's in support, advanced up the nek between Cingolo and Monte Cristo. After crossing the Gomba the Queen's was detached and sent with the composite regiment of mounted infantry on a flanking movement to climb the hill at the far end, nearly two miles away. The march through the thick bushes was a long and trying one, but it was accomplished very successfully, and at 12 o'clock they were seen crossing a little bare space on the very top. This movement took the enemy completely by surprise. The hill was weakly held, and before reinforcements could come up the mounted infantry was sweeping along and driving what few Boers there were from ridge to ridge. Meanwhile, the rest of General Hildyard's and Colonel Norcott's brigades had reached the nek. Judging from the intensity of the fire, there must have been a considerable number of the enemy, but, though they were very often at close range, our casualties were very slight, owing to the thickness of the cover. In the evening the Queen's descended into the nek, and all the men bivouacked there for the night.

Next day the same manoeuvre had to be repeated. At dawn General Hildyard's Brigade and the mounted infantry brigade marched through the nek and climbed the eastern side of Monte Cristo. The hill was higher and steeper than Cingolo, and was far more strongly held. Profiting by their experience of the day before, the Boers were in considerable force on the hill, and they came a good way down to meet the advance. The actual ascent took six hours, and the Queen's and the West Yorkshire Regiment, who led it, fought almost every yard of the way. The Boers had no trenches and fell back slowly as our men advanced. Two mounted infantry guarded the flanks, and when they had nearly reached the top, and the Boers began to retire, the Natal Carbineers did a very smart piece of work. Seeing the Boers making for a crossing of the river to the north, they galloped off and, taking up a position between it and the retiring enemy, headed them back so that they had to pass under the fire of the Queen's. On the other side of the hill the attack had changed front on the left and Colonel Norcott's Brigade was advancing along the side of Monte Cristo towards the nek between that mountain and Green Hill. Their advance was slow, for they were encountering a heavy fire from Green Hill and also from some trenches on the western side of Monte Cristo. On their left were the Scots Fusiliers and beyond them were the Irish Fusiliers. The two latter regiments were to attack straight up Green Hill, which had been heavily bombarded since dawn. At 12 o'clock General Hildyard's leading companies appeared on the skyline, and, as if the Boers knew exactly where to expect them and had their guns ready trained, they instantly came under a heavy shell fire, chiefly shrapnel and Maxim-Nordenfelt. From where we were watching it looked terribly accurate, and, only seeing their movements very indistinctly in the bushes, it seemed as if their advance was checked. For over an hour it lasted, and all our guns were unable to find the range of the two or three Boer guns that were doing the mischief. Then suddenly the fire slackened and we became aware that the whole line was pushing rapidly forward. In a very few minutes the Fusiliers were rushing up the bare face of Green Hill. They gained the top with scarcely a shot fired. A few shrapnel burst over them, and then, save for a few shots far forward on the right and an occasional shot from the batteries far behind, all firing ceased. What had happened was this. Unperceived by us, and probably also by the Boers on Green Hill, General Hildyard had pushed very rapidly along Monte Cristo and had appeared, still on the top of the hill, threatening their right rear. Before the main attack could reach them they fled incontinently, leaving everything behind. The Rifle Brigade, who, with three companies of the Durham Light Infantry, formed the firing line of Colonel Norcott's attack, were considerably in advance of the left. They passed rapidly through the nek and the hollow beyond where the Boers had made their laager. When they saw half a mile beyond them a body of mounted men, two or three thousand strong, manoeuvring apparently in troops and squadrons, they thought it was Lord Dundonald's Brigade, and forbore to fire. They only realized when it was too late that it was the main body of Boers whose retirement had been checked for a moment. Then guns were brought up, and a few who had made a stand in a farm half a mile beyond were quickly driven out. Our success was complete.

Seeing us in possession of Green Hill, the Boers evacuated Hlangwane, and their first and strongest line of defence south of the Tugela was in our hands. They had a large camp at the back of Hlangwane and another very scattered one behind Green Hill. These we were free to examine. There were not many tents, and it looked as if most of the Boers bivouacked under trees or, if they were near trenches, in exceedingly well-made bombproof shelters. The trenches themselves were marvellous. There must have been several miles of them, cut or blasted in many cases out of the solid rock, often as much as 6ft. deep so that it was difficult to know how they could fire out of them. They mostly had sandbags in front, and a carefully screened way in or out. It is not to be wondered at that our shell fire does little damage when the Boers are in their trenches. In the camp a considerable amount of ammunition was found, including, I regret to state, a quantity of expanding bullets of various patterns, including Dum Dums, soft-nosed, and split bullets. The Boers did not appear to be short of food. A great many oxen had been slaughtered, and a quantity of biltong was found hanging to dry in the sun. Besides this there were sacks full of bread, potatoes, onions, and tea. The Boer's personal effects were limited in most cases to a blanket, a saddle, and a Bible, which he did not apparently take into battle with him. That night the troops bivouacked on the position they had taken.

The following day Hlangwane was occupied, but no advance northward was made. A small force of Boers recrossed the river and occupied a wooded hill above the wooden bridge by which they usually passed to and from Hlangwane. They were not attacked, and, after keeping up a desultory rifle fire all day, they retired in the evening. That evening two companies of the Composite Rifles Battalion entered Colenso and found it, and the kopjes beyond, evacuated, except for a few snipers. The Fort Wylie group of kopjes formed the right of the Boer position, and our occupation of Hlangwane rendered it untenable. That day the heavy guns were moved forward to Green Hill. The following day, February 20, General Hart, leaving the Border Regiment to guard Chieveley, occupied Colenso with the rest of his brigade, and Colonel Thorneycroft, crossing the river with some of his men, reconnoitred the kopjes beyond. They found them only weakly held and all the guns gone. Colonel Norcott advanced to the Tugela and occupied the south bank, from the point where Monte Cristo touches the river to Colenso. On the other side the Boers could be seen in small numbers digging trenches, but they did not show anything approaching to the same vigour as they had shown during the first days of our arrival at Spearman's Hill. In fact, their tactics appeared to be those of a rearguard action.

Cronje, having been forced to draw his troops into a laager, was surrounded by the much superior British forces, and it was only a matter of time before he had to surrender.

PAARDEBERG, MARCH 3.

From the reports of scouts and deserters and from such observation as is possible from a balloon, supplemented by the stories of prisoners and careful inspection of the laager, this account of the last stand of the great Boer general is compiled. Written within four days of the surrender, and on the spot, it cannot, perhaps, be claimed that accuracy in details has been always secured, but the following is substantially a true history of the internal history of that brief resistance.

On Sunday, February 18, Cronje realized that the trap in which he found himself had no outlet. With the instinctive knowledge of an able general, he recognized that not a kopje ringing the even plain that gently shelved down to the river bed in which he found himself was without its hidden complement of troops, and that the escape of any considerable force even by night was, without outside relief, an impossibility. He was in possession of perhaps a mile of the river bed on either side of the Wolveskraal Drift, with the 19th Brigade of the English troops intrenched and sapping up towards him from the west and General Tucker's division slowly encroaching from the east.

To the south he was exposed to continual bombardment from the field guns massed on Gun Hill at a range of hardly more than a mile; from the north he received the shell of the naval guns and another battery of howitzers. It is said that he deliberately retreated into the river in order to try again the tactics that might, if vigorously persevered in, have beaten off Lord Methuen's column at Modder River; that he expected a general advance from all sides, and relied with some reason upon having ample men, rifles, and ammunition to man the line of trenches which he hastily threw up. But the more probable solution of his having entered this *cul de sac* is simply that he had no option. To retreat further was impossible, and defence for even three days was equally out of the question except in a position where water could be obtained. It is difficult to say what expectation of relief he had. Heliographic communication from one of the hills of the Petrusberg range, 20 miles to the south-west, undoubtedly reached him, as that communication was resumed after our occupation of the laager, but no signalling apparatus was found there after the surrender and the value of a one-sided conversation by heliograph is very small. His stores were terribly deficient in everything but ammunition; wagons containing provisions had been outspanned and abandoned during the retreat to help those containing munitions of war, and the actual supply of food was not more than sufficient to last a week. The presence of a few women and children added to his difficulties, and with the gravest misgivings he ordered Monday, February 19, to be spent in preparing a system of trenches that deserves more than a passing mention.

Reference to the map will show the general disposition of the earthworks, but the skill with which they were constructed as defences against both rifle and shell fire is worthy of the highest praise. All except those of the outer lines of pickets were made so narrow and deep that it seems as though they were in many cases entered from one end rather than the top, as any such ingress must even in a week's time have considerably widened the neck of the excavation. At the top they are, perhaps, 18in. wide, at the bottom about 3ft., and by crouching down the most complete protection is afforded from bursting shell.

Every natural protection, such as the ramifications of the dongas which eat into the banks on both sides of the river, has been utilized, though the bombardment from both sides compelled them to abandon their first hasty breastworks cut into the actual top of the bank, which is here from about 50 to 100 yards from the river itself, and 30ft. in height.

For the first time here the "T" trenches, of which much has been said during the present campaign, were used. Frankly, they do not seem to present the least advantage over the ordinary shapes except that in an exposed angle they may provide additional protection against an enfilading fire.

The Red House – a kind of dak-bungalow which is found near every drift in South Africa – was used as Cronje's headquarters. Here his wife slept, though during the daytime she joined the women in the carefully-made shelter constructed for them. Albrecht probably remained in the northern intrenchments with the guns, though the ammunition for the Krupp guns ran out on Tuesday. Speaking of his experiences in the trenches, he says that one of our lyddite shells burst within five yards of him, covering him with dirt and leaving a foul taste in his mouth, but otherwise not affecting him, even to the extent of knocking him down.

It is extraordinary that so few should have attempted to escape. Burnham, the well-known American scout, who for several nights crept up to the very trenches on either side of the river under cover of the scanty scrub, reports the "spoor" of only three or four deserters a night, of whom quite half must have been secured by our outposts and sentries.

Tuesday, the 20th, was marked by the severest bombardment of the entire investment, and a Boer doctor describes the position as awful. Nothing could be done but crouch in the trenches and wait till dusk prevented further attack, while wagon after wagon in the laager caught fire and burnt away into a heap of scrap iron amid a pile of wood ashes. The desolation produced was fearful, and it soon became impossible to make any reply. The losses inflicted upon the horses were

Cronje's men at Modder River
waiting to be assigned to tents
in the British prison camp

the turning-point of the siege. So enormous a proportion (estimated by some at 75 per cent. of the total number present) of the horses, for which no protection could be made, were lost that any dash for freedom by night was impossible, and the condition of the laager rapidly became so foul that that alone, apart from the want of food, would have compelled an early surrender. There was no opportunity of getting rid of the vast number of dead animals; burial was impossible, and the low state of the river prevented them from sending them down stream for several days; all they could do was to drag them to leeward of their camp. Meanwhile decomposition set in, and the absolute need of clean air caused a serious rebellion in the camp, most of the 4,000 men demanding that surrender should be made at once. When on Sunday, the 25th, the flood brought down past our lines an unending series of dead animals that cannot have been less than 1,500 or 2,000, the desperate straits of the enemy were apparent indeed.

More to get rid of this plague than for the ostensible reason, General Cronje sent in asking for a day's armistice to bury his dead. Lord Roberts, suspecting that the delay was asked for merely to give time for the relieving force of Boers to come up, refused it, offering in turn to send doctors in to look after the sick and wounded. This offer, though subsequently accepted in a modified form, was refused, and Cronje, criticizing our Field-Marshal's attitude as "inhuman," closed his letter with the words, "Under the circumstances I have no other choice." By this the Boer commander merely meant that he had no option but to continue the struggle, but the mistake of an interpreter led to its being regarded as an offer of surrender. An answer framed on this misunderstanding led to an indignant refusal by Cronje, who announced his intention of holding out till we should take the position by storm.

As a matter of fact a day's grace was given the besieged force, and the active bombardment only began again after the triple assault of small bodies of Boers, amounting in all to perhaps 4,000, on Wednesday and Thursday from the Kameelfontein, Osfontein, and Poplar Farm directions.

Hopelessness now settled down upon the imprisoned Boers, and among the arguments used to lessen Cronje's authority was that he had wilfully suppressed Lord Roberts's offer of safe-conduct to the women and children before the bombardment was begun. Hunger and nausea worked upon the despairing Boers, and all that could be put forward was used to compel Cronje to yield. For one whole day the struggle went on, and then a compromise was arrived at. If no help should have come by Wednesday morning, the 28th, the place should be surrendered, but Cronje, pointing out the abundance of rifles and ammunition, absolutely refused to surrender on the anniversary of Majuba-hill.

From that moment the Boers scarcely obeyed orders. A sharp division between the Transvaalers and the Orange Free State Boers ensued, and the only bond of sympathy that united them, besides their common adversity, was a long-hidden hatred of the Germans in their ranks. Albrecht, who had worked for them faithfully and well, whose orders had been hitherto implicitly obeyed, and to whom indeed the credit of nearly the whole of the successful opposition to the relief column is due, was openly accused of incompetence and even disloyalty. He, in turn, took no pains to conceal his opinion of the fighting powers of the Boers when on equal terms with the enemy, and the breach was complete. Until sunrise on the 27th the state of affairs among the Boers was pitiful. Apart from the ever-increasing hunger, despair of relief, and unhealthiness of the position, mutual recriminations destroyed the last consolation of adversity, good-fellowship, and Cronje sat aloof, silent and unapproachable.

The events of the early morning of the 27th can best be told from outside.

Brigadier-General MacDonald sent from his bed a note to Lord Roberts reminding him that Tuesday was the anniversary of that disaster which, we all remembered, he had by example, order, and threat himself done his best to avert, even while the panic had been at its height; Sir Henry Colvile submitted a suggested attack backed by the same unanswerable plea. For a moment Lord Roberts demurred to the plan; it seemed likely to cost too heavily, but the insistence of Canada broke down his reluctance, and the men of the oldest colony were sent out in the small hours of Tuesday morning to redeem the blot on the name of the mother-country.

From the existing trench, some 700 yards long, on the northern bank held jointly by the Gordons and the Canadians, the latter were ordered to advance in two lines – each, of course, in extended order – 30 yards apart, the first with bayonets fixed, the second reinforced by 50 Royal Engineers under Colonel Kincaid and Captain Boileau.

In dead silence and covered by a darkness only faintly illuminated by the merest rim of the dying moon, "with the old moon in her lap," the three companies of Canadians moved on over the bush-strewn ground. For over

"BRAVO, BOBS!"

Cartoon from *Punch*, 28 February 1900

Cronje's chief
commandants after the
surrender at Paardeberg

400 yards the noiseless advance continued, and when within 80 yards of the Boer
trench the trampling of the scrub betrayed the movement. Instantly the outer
trench of the Boers burst into fire, which was kept up almost without intermission
from five minutes to 3 o'clock to ten minutes past the hour. Under this fire the
courage and discipline of the Canadians proved themselves. Flinging themselves
on the ground they kept up an incessant fire on the trenches, guided only by the
flashes of their enemy's rifles, and the Boers admit that they quickly reduced
them to the necessity of lifting their rifles over their heads to the edge of the
earthwork and pulling their triggers at random. Behind this line the Engineers did
magnificent work; careless of danger the trench was dug from the inner edge of
the bank to the crest, and then for 50 or 60 yards out through the scrub. The
Canadians retired three yards to this protection and waited for dawn, confident in
their new position, which had entered the protected angle of the Boer position,
and commanded alike the rifle pits of the banks and the trefoil-shaped
embrasures on the north.

Cronje saw that matters were indeed desperate. Many Boers threw up their
hands and dashed unarmed across the intervening space; others waved white flags
and exposed themselves carelessly on their intrenchments, but not a shot was
fired. Colonel Otter and Colonel Kincaid held a hasty consultation, which was
disturbed by the sight of Sir Henry Colvile, General of the Ninth Division, quietly
riding down within 500 yards of the northern Boer trenches to bring the news that
even while the last few shots were being fired a horseman was hurrying in with a
white flag and Cronje's unconditional surrender, to take effect at sunrise.

Lord Roberts and staff
cheering the Queen on the
occupation of Pretoria

Of the three Canadian companies the foremost, and that which suffered most, was the French company, under Major Pelletier.

Meanwhile, a few formal preliminaries were being arranged at headquarters, and General Pretyman went out with a small escort to meet the Boer commander and his secretary.

Lord Roberts, in the plainest of khaki, without a badge of rank except his Kandahar sword, awaited the arrival of his distinguished prisoner.

"Commandant Cronje," was the brief introduction as the Boer swung himself off his white pony and, curtly answering the Field Marshal's salute, shook hands. "I am glad to see you, I am glad to meet so brave a man," was Lord Roberts's brief welcome, and a formal surrender followed, the conversation being interpreted by Cronje's secretary.

The general, a man of few words, sat deeply sunken in his chair with his hands in the pockets of his overcoat, and sullenly regarded the scene. Every consideration was paid him, but until the last was seen of his bulky form driving away to Modder River in the closed carriage which had been provided for him, his set, hardened face only suggested that the bitterest hour of his life was being barely endured by the man whose pluck, whose capacity, and whose straightforwardness we his enemies are the first to admit.

With the surrender of Cronje and the relief of Ladysmith and Kimberley, the war seemed to be on the verge of ending, 'We knew that the siege of Ladysmith would have to be raised, and now came the news, while we were halted here, that Kimberley had

Portal of the fort at Johannesburg, occupied by the Cheshire Regiment

also been relieved, and that General Cronje had been captured at Paardeberg with four thousand men, so that the whole universe seemed to be toppling about our ears. From the way in which the commandos were hurrying past, it looked that morning as if the Boer cause was going to pieces before our eyes, and it would have taken a bold man to prophesy that the war had still more than two long years to run.'[2]

Reitz was correct in assuming that most people would think that the war was all but over. On 13 March Roberts marched into Bloemfontein. The change in the British position was dramatic: Ladysmith and Kimberley had been relieved, the Orange Free State occupied and the Boers had been evicted from Cape Colony. On 17 May the siege of Mafeking was lifted; at the same time the much maligned Buller was quashing the last remnants of regular Boer resistance in Natal. During May and June of 1900, Roberts led his troops into the Transvaal, capturing first Johannesburg (31 May) then Pretoria (5 June), capital of the republic. All regular Boer resistance collapsed when Roberts and Buller joined forces at the town of Vlakfontein on 5 June 1900. In September 1900 the Transvaal was formally annexed to the British Empire.

Notes

1. Pakenham, 1991, pp. 317–18.
2. Reitz, 1950, p. 89.

Guerilla Warfare

'My father confirmed what Mr. Smuts had told us of the military position, and he said that guerilla war was better suited to the genius of the Boer people than regular field operations' (Denys Reitz, *Commando*).

Reitz's father was undoubtedly correct in his summation of the Boers' martial virtues. Lord Roberts left South Africa in December 1900 convinced that the war was almost over. He was to be proved wrong, as the Boers, moving into a field of warfare that was undoubtedly more to their liking, discovered two commanders who could harness their national talent for irregular warfare. These two men were Christiaan De Wet and Johan De La Rey (known as Delarey to the British at the time). Before looking at the coverage of the guerilla campaign it is important to note that, somewhat typically, *The Times*, in line with what could be called newspaper tradition, began to relegate coverage of the war in South Africa to a position of lesser importance in the paper: quite simply the Boer War was not as newsworthy as it had been. In June 1900 The Boxer Rebellion began in China, and this exotic tale of violence and barbarous people, coupled with the Victorian obsession with the heroism and stoicism of sieges, pushed the Boer War from its position at the forefront of the British public's consciousness. To be fair to *The Times*, the swift moving conditions of guerilla warfare were much more difficult to report on, but nevertheless it is difficult to escape the conclusion that *The Times* was just a little bored with South Africa.

Well before Roberts's departure in December 1900, the Boers had shown their intention to keep up the fight; British forces wherever they found themselves were in danger of sudden attack and could never afford to let their vigilance slip.

RUSTENBURG, AUGUST.

During the first days of July, we, the garrison of Rustenburg – 80 of us with a gun – found ourselves in a trap. With a certain amount of recklessness, patrols of inadequate strength had been allowed to scour the country collecting surrendered arms, gathering too much confidence as day after day went by without their experiencing any opposition. Arms they collected by the score, but such arms! – blunderbusses, elephant guns, muzzle-loaders and flintlocks of every description, but few Mausers or Martinis. And so it was that, after General Baden-Powell with his column had marched on towards Pretoria, we, a mere post, holding the important town of Rustenburg on the line of communications, suddenly found ourselves threatened by armed Boers, who, like Roderick Dhu's warriors, seemed to spring from the rocks. On the night of July 4, a somewhat alarming despatch ordered the evacuation of Rustenburg – all stores to be abandoned if necessary. As soon as darkness set in, confusion reigned; ox-wagon succeeding ox-wagon, half-laden, crowded the roads to the westward, hastening as fast as patient oxen could crawl back towards Zeerust, 70 miles away. Throughout the night of the 4th, on the 5th, and for half of the 6th, we marched, while oxen fell dead in their yokes; then we received a fresh despatch; it appears that there had been a false alarm, and so we countermarched; on the 6th, two squadrons of Australians, which we had met and swept back in the ebb-tide of our retreat, were ordered to press on, in the hope of their being able to regain the precious ground, and, above all Rustenburg.

In the meanwhile, 120 men, under Major Hanbury-Tracy, a young officer of the Blues, had been sent back by Baden-Powell to Rustenburg, and the general was himself hastening to his support. It appears that the most conflicting reports had been furnished by our intelligence department. The British troops at Pretoria had lost all touch with the enemy; the most alarming information continued to reach General Baden-Powell during July 4 and 5. Contradictory orders followed one another in rapid succession and, on the 7th, between dawn and sunset, Colonel Plumer's brigade received eight distinctly conflicting commands. The responsibility for this mismanagement must rest to a great extent with the headquarter staff at Pretoria. It certainly is difficult to understand why it should have been necessary to withdraw all protection from the western line of communications. A promised reinforcement of 2,000 men had not left Mafeking by the second week of July.

Though two squadrons of Australians were hastening from the westward and General Baden-Powell, with his entire force, was returning from Commando Nek, a position some 18 miles from Pretoria, to which he had penetrated by July 4, the position of Major Hanbury-Tracy was decidedly precarious. By the 6th 300 of the enemy had surrounded the gaol and adjacent heights occupied by his 120 men and demanded his surrender. To an order from Lord Roberts directing him to evacuate Rustenburg, Major Hanbury-Tracy had replied:– "I consider a retirement would be most impolite and I propose holding out." It is unnecessary to say that his reply to the enemy was of no less determined a character. On the 7th, in the early morning, the Dutch opened fire upon the British force, and a 37 millimètre Maxim gun was also brought to bear upon the garrison of the gaol. Fifteen men of the British South Africa Police, under Lieutenant Bateson, held a kopje in the vicinity, though for some hours they were subjected to an exceedingly hot fire. By 11 a.m. the two squadrons of Australians with a 12-pounder had approached to within a mile or two of the town, and, hearing firing, immediately dashed forward. While one squadron streamed across the open plain to the south of Rustenburg, the other clattered through the town, and, working to the eastward, enveloped the Boer right flank. At 400 yards the Bushmen dismounted and poured in their fire upon the

"HOOP-LA!"

JOEY (to the Premier Equestrian). "NOW 'S YOUR TIME, GUV'NOR!"

"The War is practically over. The British flag is by this time flying at Pretoria."—Times, May 31.

Cartoon from *Punch*, 6 June 1900

now retreating enemy, and by the time that their field-piece had come into action and had sent one screaming shell after the flying Dutchmen Rustenburg was saved. Many Boers in the town who had already made submission had rearmed themselves to fight Hanbury-Tracy; on the approach of the Bushmen these quickly disappeared, juggling their rifles out of sight. A few, however, were taken. The losses of the Australians were insignificant, more especially, strange to say, in the squadron which galloped across the open plain; several of their horses were shot, two men were killed, and an officer and two men were wounded. Though wounded in two places, Captain McKattie led his men, who followed up the retreating Boers, of whom he himself captured two with his own hand. On July 9 the general re-entered Rustenburg, and during the next week or so this important position was strongly reinforced.

The mountains around Rustenburg form a part of the Magaliesberg range. To approach the town from the westward either Magato's or Oliphant's Nek must be crossed. By the 10th the Boers had seized Oliphant's Nek, but, racing for Magato's Pass, we arrived there first on the 11th. East of Rustenburg the

Magaliesberg sweeps round to the northward and again crosses the Pretoria road. Some passes in that neighbourhood, the best known of which is Commando Nek, fell into the enemy's hands on the 11th; thus, by the 12th, General Baden-Powell was completely cut off from Pretoria, this success of the enemy being emphasized by another of the many humiliating surrenders of our troops which have periodically occurred during this campaign. In the meantime our western line of communications was by no means free from menace; nor did it appear improbable by the third week in July that the defender of Mafeking might have to submit to a second siege – this time with worthier opponents, men who had fought at Spion Kop and Wagon Hill.

If, in his first occupation of Rustenburg, General Baden-Powell had appeared to ignore the possibilities of an attack, he made up for his previous carelessness when, in the second week of July, he found himself confronted with the possibility of an investment; the 75 millimètre gun, a piece of artillery whose cumbersome mounting places it in the category of guns of position, was hauled to the top of a precipitous kopje. The Boers have taught us during this campaign that where there's a will there's a way to move heavy ordnance; in this instance, 20 mules and many men made a way. From this lofty site our gun frowned circumspectly upon Rustenburg plain, stretching to the eastward and northward in smiling contrast to the sombre heights of the Magaliesberg. Besides placing the 75 millimètre gun in position, bombproofs were constructed, troops were disposed for the defence of the town, and arrangements were made for the rationing of the forces. General Baden-Powell well maintained his reputation for forgetting nothing.

The rapid evacuation of Rustenburg on July 4 had not been without its effects, and the 300 Boers established at Oliphant's Nek, during the first week of July, had increased to over 1,000 by the 15th, while the Boer general was putting forth all his energies to render his position impregnable. During the latter part of the month the enemy continually showed himself upon our line of communications to the westward, and skirmishes took place between our patrols and the Boers.

On July 20 the General received information that Lord Methuen, with 6,000 troops working from Krugersdorp, had succeeded in occupying Hekpoort and that it was his intention to attack the enemy at Oliphant's Nek from the south-west. General Baden-Powell was directed to move on the 21st to positions commanding the north-eastern exit of the pass and so to bar the escape of the Boers. Colonel Plumer, in furtherance of this plan, held a force of 300 men with four guns in readiness to move out at dawn at the first sound of Lord Methuen's cannon. It has been explained that, to the eastward, the country was open, hence any concealment of Colonel Plumer's operations was an impossibility; added to this, our intelligence department had given information, on the previous day, of commandos threatening our front and flank from the east and north-west. The General, in consequence, apprehensive of the safety of Rustenburg, insisted on a considerable force being retained in position to guard the town; and, as a result of this, one of our most mobile corps in South Africa was debarred from assisting Colonel Plumer in his attempt to perform the office of terrier to Lord Methuen as ferret. Owing to contrary winds and intervening features of ground the action fought by Lord Methuen, which had been commenced at 8 a.m. to the westward of the pass, was not announced by the sound of his cannon to the officers at Rustenburg until 11.25, by which time the force from Krugersdorp had succeeded in working its way into the nek.

Previous to this the main body of the enemy, estimated at 1,000, had contrived to slip round Lord Methuen's left and was well on its way to Potchefstroom. To catch the remaining 400 Dutchmen, Colonel Plumer should have been already in position at 11 a.m.; but, unfortunately, owing to the causes referred to above, he was still at Rustenburg and had some seven miles to march. The Protectorate and Rhodesia regiments started at once, but they reached the outlet to the pass only in time to see the enemy streaming away to the south-east; fire was opened upon the retiring columns by the Canadian Artillery, but the range was too great for it to be effective. The failure of this scheme was a great disappointment to Baden-Powell's force, but worse was to follow. At 5 p.m., after Colonel Plumer had returned to camp, the officer on the look-out observed a string of wagons moving eastwards – the Boers had again tricked the British. On their retirement in the morning they had left, concealed in a kloof, some 90 wagons, hoping that they might escape observation; their hopes were realized, and the whole convoy was saved to the enemy, who succeeded, during the night of the 21st, in joining hands with the commandos holding Wolhuter's Kop and Commando Nek.

During the night of the 22nd Lord Methuen, who was encamped at Oliphant's Pass with some 7,000 men, received information that General Delarey was actively employed in the south and had succeeded in destroying the railway line between Krugersdorp and Potchefstroom. At 4 a.m. on the 23rd, accordingly, Lord Methuen struck his camp and moved back to Krugersdorp; thus all his plans for the following up of the enemy and for the clearing of General Baden-Powell's lines of communications had to be postponed. In the meantime a fresh misfortune had overtaken our column. Lord Methuen's despatches, received by General Baden-Powell on the 20th, were brought in by two cyclists, who reported that on their way from the westward a Boer laager had been seen by them some 25 miles away on the Zeerust road. As the General was expecting a convoy of wagons from Mafeking, he directed a patrol of between 200 and 300 men to leave Magato's Nek on the afternoon of the 21st to reconnoitre and, if possible, capture the Boers, whose laager had so nearly proved a pitfall to the cyclists. During the morning of Sunday, the 22nd, a succession of messages reached Rustenburg from Colonel Airey, who commanded the patrol in question. These messages conveyed the impression that, with reinforcements, the capture of the Boers who were threatening our convoy could be effected. A section of the Canadian Artillery, two squadrons of police, and two squadrons of the Protectorate Regiment were accordingly despatched forthwith; while from Magato's Pass 200 more Australians, under Colonel Sir A. Lushington, moved at a trot to join Colonel Airey's Bushmen and Queenslanders. Unfortunately, Colonel Airey's messages were quite misleading, and the facts were as follows:– On Saturday night, the cyclists, acting as guides to Colonel Airey's patrol, were fired upon by a Boer picket; they succeeded, however, in regaining the main party uninjured. In consequence of this occurrence the Australians were extended across the road, and so they camped for the night. Before dawn on Sunday Colonel Airey, having made a detour to the northward, again struck the Zeerust road at that point where it dips into the hollow formed by the Koester river. The enemy, who occupied the high ground on either flank, after allowing the advance guard to cross the river, opened fire upon the patrol. The Australians, dismounting, sought such cover as was available; but so exposed were their horses to the murderous volleys of the Boers that in a short time more than 200 were lost. The first reinforcement to arrive on the scene was the party from Magato's Nek under Colonel Lushington. That officer, either ignorant of the true state of affairs or anticipating from Colonel Airey's morning despatch an easy capture of the Boers, did not at first appear to grasp the nature of the action required of him. It was Father Hartmann, the Roman Catholic pastor to the forces, who first discovered the misfortune which had overtaken the patrol. In riding towards the sound of firing he first came upon dead horses in great numbers; he then saw the Australians huddled together in a hut, from the roof of which a white flag, composed of five handkerchiefs knotted together, was flying. Finding his party completely surrounded, Colonel Airey, after consulting with his second-in-command, had decided to surrender. A message was, accordingly, sent to some men, who, under Major Vial, had become separated from the patrol, but that officer flatly refused to lay down his arms. In the meantime the Boers made no attempt to take over prisoners; whether they recoiled from the awkward task of disarming the Australians while a certain portion of the force was still showing fight, or whether the handkerchiefs doing duty as a white flag were too soiled for their colour to be recognized, will never be known, for, before the enemy could make up his mind to consummate his success, the Protectorate Regiment, under Captain FitzClarence, had galloped to the spot. Captain FitzClarence, taking in the situation at a glance, after ordering a detachment to move to the southward, so menacing the rear of the Boers, opened fire upon their flanks, causing them to retire at once.

The sun went down that night upon the forgotten five handkerchiefs, and the first glance of dawn embraced this symbol of surrender. Father Hartmann, for whose valour throughout the campaign with the Rhodesian Field Force no praise can be too high, was the first to observe that the shameful flag was still fluttering aloft. With the intention of tearing it down he climbed to the roof, only to be beaten in the race for a memento by the native servant of an officer.

Our loss in this unfortunate affair was one officer and five men killed and 10 wounded, while quite 200 horses were killed or captured. The Boers left two dead upon the field.

The story of a bayonet charge in connexion with the surrender, which went the round of camp and which even appeared in the newspapers, was the product of some imaginative brain; bayonets appear to serve as pinions on which imagination soars, for in this campaign they have led to many extraordinary fictions; a not less remarkable instance than the above being the night sortie from Mafeking, in which no single Boer was killed, though the most blood-curdling details of hand-to-hand slaughter were vouched for by the garrison.

By the 23rd General Baden-Powell's position at Rustenburg was, if anything, worse than before the arrival of Lord Methuen. He had certainly gained possession of Oliphant's Nek, but his western line of communications was effectually cut, his scanty supply of rations was still further reduced by the transfer of five wagon-loads of provisions to Lord Methuen, and the enemy had been encouraged by his successes. For most of our reverses the blame must rest with our Intelligence Department, whose information was throughout defective. Had it not been for Miss Back, a young lady residing at Woodstock, who most gallantly rode through the Boer lines at considerable risk to herself to give warning to our officers, there is little doubt but that the disaster of Sunday, the 22nd, would have had more far-reaching results. As an instance of the blunders into which the department fell it may be remarked that, while Delarey was destroying the line between Potchefstroom and Krugersdorp, he was emphatically declared to be 20 miles to the north-west of Rustenburg. From the 23rd Rustenburg remained in a state of siege, all communications with the outside world being effectually severed. No incident is worth recording until the month of August.

The approach of General Carrington from the west and of General Ian Hamilton from the east now threaten to extinguish the individuality of the little column which, under Colonel Plumer, has penetrated to the interior of the Transvaal, after suffering hardships to which those of other troops in this campaign must be reckoned insignificant. Fights have been fought and reverses sustained, but the existence of the force has been more than justified. That the foes encountered by it were throughout of the same quality as those who for so long held in check the British Army it would be unseemly to maintain; yet certain correspondents have, without sufficient reason, accused the Boers of cowardice, forgetful that, in degrading the enemies of Great Britain, they have hardly exalted the prowess of her arms.

When Colonel Plumer's column was brigaded with that of General Baden-Powell after Mafeking's relief it was already cast into the outskirts of the penumbra. Now that heavy divisions of the vast British army of occupation are approaching, it becomes finally veiled in the deeper shadows of the eclipse.

It quickly became apparent that these incidents were not the work of isolated die-hards, but the concerted actions of a well thought out guerilla campaign. Buller's pacification drive soon ran into trouble.

VAAL STATION, JULY 16.

The method first adopted for securing our communications did not prove a success. The enemy had collected in considerable strength in two laagers – one to the north of Greylingstad, the other 15 or 20 miles to the north-east of it. The former force occupied the attention of our two forces at Vlakfontein and Greylingstad, the other had the long stretch of railway between Greylingstad and Standerton, undefended save for half a battalion of the 60th Rifles at Vaal Station without guns, at its mercy. Consequently, the line was cut for the first time on the 7th. On the night of July 8 the railway was again cut and a bridge 15 miles from Greylingstad blown up. By a strange irony General Buller, who had some days previously wired that communication was complete to Johannesburg and was now on his return from Pretoria, had to wait 24 hours at Greylingstad before he could get through. A construction train sent out from Standerton was fired on and forced to retire, and the Devon Regiment and a squadron of the South African Light Horse had to be sent out from Standerton, but it was now obvious that the force thus disposed could not successfully guard the line. On the 11th General Clery was recalled to Greylingstad, and the next day he formed a flying column and marched northward. The column consisted of two and a half battalions of the Light Brigade (the Rifle Brigade remaining at Greylingstad with a 5in. gun and half the 60th being still at Vaal Station), 500 of Thorneycroft's Mounted Infantry and Strathcona's Horse, two sections of the Chestnut Battery, the 63rd Battery, R.F.A., two howitzers, and one 5in. gun.

It could never have been hoped that a column so constituted could administer a severe blow to the enemy, the paucity of mounted troops and long-range guns in its composition making this impossible. It was probably sent merely to divert the enemy's attention from the railway, and in this, as long as it was out, it succeeded. The first day's march was to Vidpoort, six miles north of Greylingstad. The enemy were found in small numbers on some ridges beyond, and were driven in a running skirmish, in which the horse battery and the Colt gun battery took part, about six miles to the north-eastward, over ground which, though by no means mountainous, was considerably more hilly than most of this great tableland and was covered with rocky ridges, which gave excellent cover to the enemy. The column had halted at Vidpoort, and the mounted infantry, who were too weak to act independently, returned to camp. Next day the enemy were found in much greater force holding the same ridges that they had been driven off the day before. Strathcona's Horse became engaged on a long ridge about two miles from camp. On the right the enemy had brought up a high velocity gun and a Maxim-Vickers, and speedily drove in the advanced squadrons. On the left they began to press Strathcona's, and would probably have driven them off the hill, but two Colt guns were brought up, and under a heavy fire at a range of about 800 yards drove back the advancing Boers. The way in which these guns were handled and their practice were both admirable. Their work was completed by the Chestnut Battery, and the Boers retreated just as the infantry came up. Lord Dundonald followed them up and engaged them again four miles to the eastward. The Chestnut Battery, the Colt guns, and Strathcona's Maxim-Vickers opened fire at a range of 1,700 yards and drove them from their position, though at that short range two of the gunners were wounded by rifle fire. The Boers had four guns in position further behind and opened fire on the ridge as soon as their men retired, but as it was late in the afternoon we did not again follow up, and the force returned to camp. After their first retirement the Boers brought their four guns round into the open on our flank at a distance of between 5,000 and 6,000 yards. The 63rd Battery was using shrapnel with the new fuse, which enables them to burst it up to 5,900 yards. They promptly opened on the Boer guns and burst a shell almost on the top of one of them. After that the Boer guns only fired a couple of shells and then retired. It was one of the few occasions when the Boer field guns have been silenced by our own. The next day was more or less a repetition of the previous one. The Boers were again in considerable force on the ridges from which they had been driven the day before, and held a position far too large for the mounted infantry to attempt to attack, though behind it we could see through the smoke of the grass fires a Boer convoy of 16 wagons moving rapidly away. The mounted infantry had to remain inactive waiting for the infantry; and by the time the head of the column had arrived, both Boers and convoy had disappeared through the smoke. Next day the column turned southward and returned to the railway near Vaal Station.

The Boers concentrated their efforts on supply and communication lines, and the name of Christiaan De Wet soon came to the attention of the British military and public at large.

PRETORIA, JUNE 20.
"The strength of an army lies in its communications." In a previous article I gave the reasons for the apparent weakness of our line of communication in the Orange River Colony. But, although it was anticipated that De Wet would cause trouble, we were hardly prepared for his wholesale successes during the early days of June. As a matter of fact, when he was in front of Heilbron he mustered a following of barely 1,000 men. This was augmented by a desperate band of ruffians who had been driven out from Thaba Nehu in front of Rundle's advance. And it is probable if De Wet had not been successful in his attack upon the Heilbron convoy that his successes would have terminated much earlier than they did. The history of the loss of this convoy is so unfortunate, and marks such an important phase in the military operations, that it is worthy of special mention. The convoy was under the command of Captain Corballis, A.S.C., and started for Heilbron with 55 wagons, carrying foodstuffs for the Highland Brigade, a quantity of warm clothing, and ammunition for all arms. Its escort consisted of 60 details belonging to the Highland Brigade marching from Kroonstad, under the command of Lieutenant Mowbray. It was understood that when the convoy left the railway communication at Vredefort Road that an escort would be detached from Heilbron to meet it half-way. On June 1 the escort was increased by 100 further details under Captain Johnson, Seaforth Highlanders, and Lieutenant Lang, Highland Light Infantry. Here the first of a series of deplorable mistakes occurred. The convoy received conflicting orders. By one authority it received orders to "move on Heilbron." Then the staff officer at railhead advised the officer commanding to wait. A further authority gave the information that the escort had already started to meet the convoy. In consideration of these conflicting instructions the convoy laagered on June 2 north of Rhenoster. It will be seen that at this period a large and very important convoy was adrift on the line of communication, and that there was no one in authority to direct it with confidence. The enemy were known to be in the vicinity, yet the convoy was only provided with a scratch escort formed from details from various corps, and though the enemy were known to be in possession of artillery it was allowed to start with simply an infantry guard. It so happened that by the luck of war a force of 1,000 men – drafts waiting to join their regiments at the front – were assembled at railhead. Otherwise there was no force within reach to which the convoy could look for aid in the event of the enemy menacing its progress. On June 1 a colonial conductor had been despatched to search for some loose oxen. This man was absent from the convoy for a period which was out of all

keeping with the requirements of his quest. From remarks which subsequently escaped De Wet, in the hearing of the prisoners, and from the undoubted precise knowledge which the Boer commandant had of the strength and movements of the convoy, a grave suspicion is attached to the actions of this conductor.

Corballis determined to move on the night of June 2. At 1.30 a.m. the convoy was four miles beyond Steyn's farm. The convoy was supposed to be moving with its infantry escort detached half a mile on either flank. It is regrettable, but it is no less a fact, that during the night march the infantry officers so far neglected their duty that part of the escort were asleep on the wagons. This I give as an incident to show how in some cases the trust given for the safety of the army in the field was kept. It is only fair to the men in the fighting line that this should be made public. The convoy moved on steadily throughout the morning. At 2 p.m. oxen were seen on its right flank. This was the first indication of the presence of the enemy. These oxen undoubtedly belonged to De Wet's laager. As the road to Heilbron passed over a low ridge commanded by two kopjes, and suspicion being already aroused, the convoy was laagered and devices considered as to the best means of securing aid. A Kaffir was detached with a note to Heilbron. This man, meeting another Kaffir, who informed him of the presence of the enemy, returned without accomplishing his mission. Captain Johnson then conducted a reconnaissance with an orderly. He apparently simply despatched the trooper a short way and then returned to the laager to report failure. Conductor Webster was then sent to Vredefort Road. He returned on June 4 at 8 a.m. with a message from Major Haig, K.O.S.B., commanding the details at the railhead. The message ran, "Started with 600 men; got to within four miles of your camp." At 9 a.m. a flag of truce was sent in by De Wet with the following curt message:- "I have twelve hundred men and five guns. Surrender at once." At this juncture Captain Johnson, being the senior combatant officer, took over the command. He sent Lieutenant Lang to get terms from the Boer commandant. Not unnaturally, seeing that the convoy lay in the hollow of his hand, De Wet refused to negotiate, but insisted upon unconditional surrender. After a short parley, Johnson capitulated under the condition that the details of the force and convoy were to be prisoners of war and to retain their kit-bags and personal effects. It appears that Major Haig with his relief column of 600 men had come to within two miles of the laager, but had returned without making a junction as he had heard that the unprotected railhead was threatened. This portion of the history will not be clear until the Court of inquiry has sifted the evidence, which at present is conflicting. But the bare facts remain that an inadequately protected convoy marched through a country known to be in the occupation of the enemy, and that a relief column turned back when it was within a short march of the trouble. It is probably untrue that De Wet had only the force with him named in his formal summons to surrender, but it is certain that the news of the capture of this convoy played an important part upon the whole operations of the campaign. It brought scores of waverers to De Wet, and it certainly influenced Botha in the negotiations which took place immediately after the surrender of Pretoria.

The following history of an officer who was captured with this convoy, and ultimately escaped, is interesting in that it shows the feeling existing in the Orange River Colony with regard to the war. The prisoners were taken south-east, whence

De Wet left them to conduct his raid against Roodeval Bridge. They were then taken north-east to Vrede. The Boers seemed absolutely sick and weary of the campaign. They were only held together by the personal influence of De Wet and the terrorism of Theron, who had joined the Free State commando with his outlaws. Many deserted along the road. Even Field Cornets came up to inquire about passes to return to their farms. Smythe deserted with his following of 160 men. Those that remained were anxious to hear about Lord Roberts's proclamations, which had been carefully kept from them by the officials. All that they had seen had been "bogus" copies, which gave a complexion diametrically opposed to the real terms offered. When informed of the true tenor of the proclamations they openly admitted that they would desert as opportunity presented itself.

De Wet was so short of men that he could only spare an escort of 20 men to guard the prisoners. On June 9, when they had reached Woodside, the sound of General Buller's guns was distinctly audible. In fact, some of the prisoners were taken under escort to view the sight of 1,500 Free Staters holding Botha's Pass against the attack, real or feigned, of Buller's men. The Boers seemed demoralized, and whenever they heard firing collected in groups and sang psalms to keep up their spirits. The chief of the police passed the convoy that day going west with what remained of the treasury of the late Orange Free State. The headquarters of the Free State force appeared to be Frankfort. The late President is a nomad, without influence and without following. He spends his time wandering from farm to farm. On June 10 the officer who relates these facts nearly induced the commandant in command of the convoy and prisoners to desert his cause and to go over with the whole party and the wagons to General Buller's lines. Unfortunately on the following morning the heart was taken out of him by the arrival of a strong commando of Transvaalers, who were bringing guns from Standerton. As the officer could not induce the other prisoner officers to overpower the weak escort and to break away he determined to make the attempt himself. He therefore bought two horses from one of his guards and, taking one of his conductors as guide, slipped away across the convoy in the direction of Buller. Three roads to escape lay open to him. East to Buller, south to Rundle, or west to Vereeniging. He chose the latter. The journey was not without incident. The first was pathetic. He passed 450 of Spragge's Imperial Yeomanry, incredible as it may seem, guarded by eight armed men. Fifteen miles from Vrede he met a Boer convoy for the front of ten wagons, in the custody of one armed burgher. Having spent the whole of one day in a cave in the bed of the Valseh river, he arrived, without further incident, to tell the story just given, which reflects so little to the credit of British arms in South Africa.

DE WET'S RAIDS ON COMMUNICATIONS

JUNE 22.
The satisfaction of being in the possession of the enemy's capital was rudely broken on June 6 by the news that Commandant De Wet, our old enemy in the

Free State, had captured a convoy and set himself to destroy the communications which the Railway Company R.E. had repaired with such labour. His movements have been so rapid, and so shrouded in mystery, that it is impossible to give more than a brief diary of the events as they succeeded each other. On June 4, as has already been shown, De Wet effected the capture of a convoy in the vicinity of Vredefort Road. This convoy was carrying stores and ammunition to the Highland Brigade then at Heilbron. The Highland Brigade was in an extreme state as regards supplies, and for six days had subsisted upon quarter rations. General Methuen, who had moved out from Kroonstad, was at Lindley. On June 5 De Wet, with a detached party, demolished Roodeval Bridge. On the following day another force of Boers so threatened Vredefort Road that Major Haig, K.O.S.B., who was there with a miscellaneous force of about 1,000 details, was forced to take up a defensive position south of the railway station. There was some sharp rifle fire, but Haig maintained his position, ultimately falling back upon Vredefort Road, when the Boers desisted from their attempt. On June 7 General Methuen arrived at Heilbron from Lindley. De Wet thereupon demolished the line at Vredefort Weg and moved south to join Commandant Nell, who had undertaken a raid against the military post at Rhenoster. This raid had been a complete success. The post was held by a battalion of Derbyshire Militia. Nell surrounded the position and, to his surprise, was unchallenged by the outposts. He placed his artillery in position and waited for the moon to rise. He then attacked in the moonlight, with the result that the whole post surrendered in the morning. On Friday, June 8, general movements were set on foot to check the trouble on the communications. Lord Kitchener came down from Pretoria and a flying column, consisting of the Shropshire L.I., the South Wales Borderers, two guns of the 74th Battery, and four guns of the 87th Field Battery, marched south from Vereeniging. It is uncertain where De Wet had his headquarters on June 9, but part of his force was watching the Heilbron–Vredefort Road. Methuen, advancing west from Heilbron, was able to engage this force and utterly scatter it, taking 23 prisoners. On the following day the flying column from Vereeniging and Methuen's column concentrated at Vredefort Road. The latter force consisted of 1,400 Mounted Infantry, mostly Imperial Yeomanry, 5th Northumberland Fusiliers, Loyal North Lancashire Fusiliers, Munster Fusiliers, and the Northamptonshire Regiment. They also had the 38th and 39th Batteries R.F.A. and half a battalion 42nd Highlanders. There was a small skirmish between the Mounted Infantry and the Boer rearguard outside Vredefort Road. On the following day Methuen marched south to clear the line. The Vereeniging flying column took the west of the line, the main force the right. The enemy were engaged on both sides of the line at long ranges. They scattered east and west, leaving a laager of empty wagons. The British force halted for the night at Rietvlei. On June 12 news was received that Kroonstad, garrisoned by a single battalion of Argyll and Sutherland Militia, had fallen. Methuen, therefore, continued his march south, but on learning that the news about Kroonstad was false he turned east. On Wednesday there was little news, but on the following day (June 14) the Boers again appeared on the railway. The construction train, under the personal supervision of Lieutenant-Colonel Girouard, had arrived to repair the damage which the Boers had done. The men were working at night when they were suddenly fired into. The rifles of the construction party had, unfortunately, been left in the rear train. In the actual working train there were only nine rifles available. The men turned out pluckily with these and answered the enemy's fire with such good effect that they kept them at bay. By a merciful chance 150 Mounted Infantry, with two guns, were within earshot. They arrived on the scene at 3.45 a.m., and one round from a field piece was sufficient to scare away the attacking Boers. The morning revealed how narrow the escape had been. A dead Boer and patches of blood-stain were found within 20 yards of the construction train, the coaches of which were riddled with bullets. It is also interesting to note that Lord Kitchener and his staff were bivouacked a few hundred yards from the scene of the conflict. The enemy succeeded in carrying away 40 of the construction workers as prisoners. In the morning the Boers were still in the vicinity. The Mounted Infantry, with one gun, pursued, and the enemy, as is their custom when on these raids, scattered to the four winds. During the next three days the relief forces were encamped in the vicinity of Rhenoster, it being reported that De Wet had withdrawn towards Frankfort. There was no further menace to the line north of Kroonstad; but a small raiding party, presumed to have fallen back from before Rundle, appeared in front of the Zand River. The post at this important bridge was sufficient to repel the enemy, and they retired after having done some temporary damage to the telegraph line. On June 18 Methuen moved from Rhenoster back upon Heilbron. In the meantime all due precautions are being made to prevent a serious recurrence of De Wet's enterprise. Strong posts with artillery have been established all along the line well within support of each other and a military train carrying field and automatic guns passes up and down the line at all hours. Having satisfied himself that all was in order, the chief of the staff returned to Pretoria on June 18. On June 21 a train ran through from Pretoria to Bloemfontein without a break.

The incidents of this fortnight's upheaval on the line are many. At one of the stations a party of officer's servants and details were stranded. They could only muster nine rifles between them, and they had not 15 rounds of ammunition apiece. A party of 15 mounted Boers was seen approaching. The men turned out to repel attack, when the Boers quietly rode in and surrendered as prisoners of war. At Vredefort Road three weeks' mails for the army at the front had been detrained to be forwarded by convoy. These fell into De Wet's hands, and he ruthlessly burnt them after he had extracted all that was of value. The commandant himself apologized to one of his prisoners for this ungracious act. He said it was a mistake, but this did not deter him from opening a parcel containing cigarettes and offering them to his prisoner guests.

De Wet's activities encouraged other Boer commanders to continue to resist the British. Louis Botha, one of the most successful of the Boer commanders in the regular warfare of the first part of the war, also made the transition from regular military commander to guerilla leader without any real problems, and he was soon carrying out a series of defensive actions and hit and run raids against superior British forces east of Pretoria.

New South Wales
Lancers bringing Boer
prisoners into Pretoria

PRETORIA, JUNE 17.

There were many who believed that with the occupation of the capital of the
Transvaal by Lord Roberts that active hostilities would cease. Unfortunately
this has not proved to be the case, for on the very evening of the occupation De
Wet placed himself across the communications in the Free State, and from then up
to the date of this letter we have practically been isolated from all direct
communication with the south. A single wire has been working spasmodically
from the western frontier, otherwise little or no news would have filtered through.
In a previous letter I pointed out that when Lord Roberts withdrew General
Hamilton's Division from the right flank after the occupation of Heilbron he
undertook a great risk – a risk which left De Wet master of the situation between
Lindley and Heilbron, and which practically invited him to tamper with our
communications. It must not be thought that this risk was not realized. It was an
unavoidable weak spot in the scheme which enabled Lord Roberts to hurl an army
corps across the Vaal before Botha had time to rally his forces from the
demoralization of rapid retreat. There is no doubt that General Hamilton should
not have fought the rearguard action outside Lindley if time could have been
spared for him to do otherwise. Under ordinary circumstances De Wet should
have been thoroughly hounded out of the positions of his own choosing before
Lindley was evacuated. But this could not be. There was only one course open to
the Field-Marshal, and that was to follow up the advantage which his rapid
movement from the south had already given him. He realized that De Wet would
touch his communications sooner or later. The risk lay in the Free State general

coming astride of the railway before the vital blow upon the capital had been struck. This is why there was no halt upon the Vaal, why the cavalry and Hamilton's divisions were fighting at Roodepoort on half rations. Once we were in possession of the Rand and Pretoria any attack upon our southern railway communication came too late to have any permanent effect upon the issue of the campaign. Johannesburg and the capital supplied the army with a month's food. Once established there two alternative lines of communication were within reach. Two brigades were sufficient to hold the towns, and consequently the rest of the army was set free to move in such direction as the Field-Marshal considered fit. But if De Wet had closed in a week earlier than he did; if he had established himself at Rhenoster when we were upon the Vaal, the result would have been very different. It would then have been necessary to detach a strong force south to re-establish communication. This would have left only a weakened force with which to strike against the capital, a force to which Botha, armed with news of De Wet's success, might have shown a very different front. It was a great risk, which none but a great man would have undertaken. De Wet's movements were calculated to the hour, and as Lord Roberts had calculated the Free State general made his effort too late. We can now view the situation with equanimity.

While Louis Botha on June 4 was endeavouring to check the British advance at Six Mile Spruit the greatest consternation prevailed in Pretoria. There was no discipline at the front, and it seemed that all cohesion had left the commandos. The town itself was in a state of chaos. But the individuality of the Commandant-General appears to be great. When he arrived in the evening he collected the scattered commandos and withdrew them in some order to Eerste Fabricken. Here during June 6 and 7 the officials of the Republics discussed the advisability of continuing the struggle. When the last trains had left Pretoria, the Republican cause certainly had not been encouraging, and upon the first few days succeeding the occupation the majority of the burgher military leaders seemed disinclined to continue the war. Not that their military system completely collapsed. While these deliberations were taking place Botha had seized and put into a state of defence the long range of hills known as Pienaar's Poort, from the railway cutting of that name which passes through them, and the British troops which were moving out to the east of Pretoria were constantly exposed to long-range shell fire. But from the reports which came in concerning the conditions of affairs in the Boer lines it seemed that the general feeling leaned towards some arrangements which might lead to peace. All confidence was gone. Except among the most ignorant and fanatical of the burghers all reliance in President Kruger and his constitution had vanished when he had left his capital after plundering the banks. The President left on Monday, May 29, and he took with him two and a half millions in specie. But this was not all. The ordinary State officials, whose arrears of salary had been allowed to accumulate under the plea that the war was engrossing all attention, were paid by the President in a paper money specially issued. Cheques were issued and dated after the hour specified for the closing of the banks to the public. Thus, when the "seat" of government moved, the ordinary educated officials of Pretoria and the Transvaal, other than those closely connected with "the Royal family of Pretoria," found that the enemy was at their gate and that their President, who had led them into their trouble, and to whom they not unnaturally turned in the moment of despair, had vanished like "a thief in the night." Not metaphorically, but actually. He had stolen their money and left them with bare signatures, the only value of which will be the few pence which they may fetch as curiosities. From the day that the President swept clean the public coffers of Pretoria, abandoned the city and left its defrauded inhabitants to their fate, the cause of the Republic was lost. How far Louis Botha was cognisant of the movements and actions of the State officials it is impossible to say upon present information. But we have during the last month had constant proofs of his inability to infuse his own fighting spirit into the hearts of his men. Even his great personal influence could not rebuff the shock caused by the President's flight. And then, when, on the day preceding the occupation, the State Attorney followed his chief into flight, taking with him the final sweepings of the wealth of the Republic, the people of Pretoria "held up their hands" and surrendered. Five thousand stand of Mausers were handed in to the Provost-Marshal during the first ten days of the British occupation of Pretoria.

But an untoward influence was suddenly brought to bear upon the negotiations, for negotiations were now proceeding – that is to say, emissaries were passing between Lord Roberts and Commandant Botha. The news that De Wet had placed himself in command of our communications probably reached Botha on Saturday, June 9. For on the preceding day he had shown even some eagerness to treat, but on the day following his whole attitude changed and he sent an answer to the Field-Marshal couched in language studied to convey the impression of haughty indifference.

Now, although Lord Roberts was quite prepared to receive any overtures which might represent the unanimous wish and feelings of the burghers of the Transvaal, he had no intention of leaving Botha to gather strength and confidence in the commanding position which he occupied at Pienaar's Poort. The chain of hills which form the position define a front of about 25 miles. This is difficult to trace on the map, as the hills on the ordnance survey sheets are indifferently marked. But, roughly, the Boer position was an unbroken chain of kopjes extending from Krokodil Spruit on the north to Rhenosterfontein-Riet Vlei on the south. In the use of the defining adjective "unbroken" it is meant that the irregularities which existed in the range were such that a force could not make use of them without finding the enemy in position within short range. To the east of Pretoria you shake off the hilly country, and a more or less undulating plain stretches away until it is rudely broken by the cliff face of Pienaar's Poort. Half-way between Pienaar's Poort and the capital the small hills of Koedoespoort and Hartebeestepoort break the plain. But their existence is immaterial to the present history, as the enemy did not hold them to any extent. The actual approach to Pienaar's Poort, as seen from Hartebeestepoort, bears a great resemblance to that great gate of the Himalayas – the entrance to the Khaibar Pass from the Jamrud plain. The actual poort through which the railway passes is crowned on either hand by cliffs which seem to rise sheer from the plain like the portals of the Indian pass. But, of course, the Transvaal hills are on a much smaller scale. The poort may be said to have been the centre of Botha's position, and it certainly had the appearance of being impregnable. On Friday, June 8, Ian Hamilton's divisional headquarters were at

Garsfontein, about eight miles south-east of Pretoria. These headquarters consisted of Bruce Hamilton's Brigade (General Smith Dorrien's having been detached to the south for duty in the line of communications), de Lisle's M.I., and Gordon's and Broadwood's Cavalry Brigades. General Pole-Carew's Division was at Hartebeestepoort. Henry's M.I. held the spur of hills which, running north of Pretoria, connects with Pienaar's Poort, while General French, with the remainder of the cavalry and Hutton's M.I., was at Haartebeestefontein, eight miles north-east of Pretoria, and north of the connecting spurs occupied by Henry. Pretoria itself was garrisoned by Maxwell's Brigade. On Saturday, June 9, Lord Roberts commenced the movement by which he intended to dislodge Botha from his position on Pienaar's Poort. The cavalry were ordered to attempt both flanks of the position. In the event of this movement not proving sufficient to cause the enemy to fall back, the infantry were to advance and feel their way for an opening possible of assault. The country towards the left of the position seemed the most promising, and General Hamilton had orders to move to his immediate front from Garsfontein in the event of Broadwood and Gordon making headway. It will be seen that the Field-Marshal, when he moved against Pienaar's Poort, was undertaking the most comprehensive operation which he had had under his personal direction since Paardeberg. It was evident that, if the enemy showed any tenacity of purpose to hold their position, it would take several days before it would be possible to turn either of the flanks sufficiently to be able to assault the main positions with a certainty of success. And just at this moment the army was so circumstanced that it could not afford to undertake an operation and not succeed. On June 9 Hamilton's cavalry moved out on the left, the 2nd Cavalry Brigade towards Rhenosterfontein, and the 3rd Brigade away again to the extreme right. They worked the Boer left with some success. It seemed that Botha had not anticipated so wide an enveloping movement, and on the night of June 9 Broadwood at least was in position to strike for some kopjes which practically commanded Elands River Station. But, unfortunately, orders arrived that night directing the cavalry on the right to halt on the following day. The reason of this suspension of the original plan was that negotiations, which seemed likely to terminate in a personal interview between Lord Roberts and Commandant Botha, were proceeding. It may be that the Boer general was only trifling with the object of gaining time, or it may be that the despatches received from De Wet decided him, but he brusquely repudiated his expressed intention of a meeting. In the meantime he had, during the halt on Sunday, taken advantage of Broadwood's inactivity to occupy the very hills which the 2nd Brigade would have secured on Sunday morning if it had not been detained. Botha had evidently realized the jeopardy in which his flank was placed during the negotiations, and had reinforced from his centre. This move on his part was the cause of all the cavalry fighting on the Boer left on Monday, June 10, the narrative of which comes within the province of *The Times* Correspondent who was present during Hamilton's action on the left during June 10, 11, and 12.

The movement of French on the extreme right of the Boer position furnished another surprise to Botha. But it was a surprise from which he recovered with rapidity, and, realizing that French was again bent upon rolling up his right, he reinforced with all his available strength, entrusting the counter move to Delarey and Grobler, his two most trusted lieutenants. French, whose command through casualties to the horses was now considerably reduced and, including Hutton's Mounted Infantry, did not exceed 1,800 men, pushed on on Saturday and crossed the first of the three spruits in front of him at Kameel Drift. The country was an impossible one for cavalry, and few cavalry leaders would have continued. On Monday night they were at Kameel Drift, across the Pienaar River. It was then that they came into close contact with the enemy. Porter's Brigade was on the left in the vicinity of Krokodil Spruit, Dickson on the right. Speaking of a cavalry brigade at this period means a few hundred mounted men and an underhorsed battery. As Porter advanced small parties of Boers were seen galloping across his front to the left. The enemy were evidently attempting to outflank an outflanking attack. A machine-gun was detached to cover the left and to deter the small groups of enemy from reinforcing those already across the front, when suddenly a heavy Mauser fire broke out from the direct front. It had been well reserved and the range was short. But it was not disastrous, neither had it the effect for which it had evidently been reserved. General Porter conceived that he would be able to hold a low smooth kopje on his left front, and he dashed for this. He was able to secure the position, while "O" Battery, R.H.A., from a smart trot came into action in the open against the rifle fire, which had been augmented by field artillery. This was another instance of the supreme discipline of this branch of the service. This battery remained in action all day in the open, exposed to a galling rifle fire. It kept down the latter with shrapnel and subdued the artillery fire. The cavalry bivouacked for the night on the positions which they held. They had by this time, as far as the existing situation was concerned, ceased to be cavalry, for they were spread out along the summit of the hills, and only maintained their position by the use of the carbine. It was a situation which few cavalry leaders would care to have faced out, especially on the Monday, when Botha, drawing from his centre, reinforced Delarey until he had at least 3,000 men and 12 guns, including one large calibre French howitzer. One is almost inclined to think that General French would have been justified in withdrawing the cavalry. It was evident that the Boer commander realized the weakness of this flank attack and was endeavouring to surround the force. In fact, Lieutenant Brinton, who was sent back on Tuesday night with a verbal message to the Field-Marshal, found the enemy in occupation of one of the drifts in rear of the division. He himself succeeded in getting through, but his escort have been missing since. Lieutenant Brinton was able to rejoin on the following morning with the orders that "the cavalry were, if possible, to maintain their position, but were not to undertake any severe risks."

But on Tuesday night the Boers in front of the cavalry division fell back parallel with their centre and left as it retired before Hamilton, and the situation was relieved. On Tuesday evening they had bombarded the positions, which the cavalry held, with great vigour and had withdrawn under the cover of this fire. It will be remembered that they had followed similar tactics when they had evacuated their positions in front of Generals Rundle and Chermside at Dewetsdorp. The casualties in the Cavalry Division had been 20 wounded, including Major Hathaway, R.A.M.C., and one killed. The proportion was absurd in comparison with the amount of ammunition which the enemy expended. But the men were much extended, often 30 and 40 yards apart. Consequently the Boer gunners had few targets. In any other formation it would have been impossible to have withstood the artillery bombardment. But the severity of the fighting can be realized from the fact that the horse batteries on Wednesday had only a few rounds remaining. The division pushed on and bivouacked for the night at Tweefontein. On the following day it came upon the tail of the Boer retreat upon Elands River. It was impossible to go further. The cavalry is utterly spent; squadrons now parade 40 and 45 strong, while during a 20-mile march the men are forced to walk ten miles leading their animals. The remount department telegraphed to inquire the requirements of the cavalry. General French's reply was that he required 5,000 remounts – an eloquent testimony as to the state of the horses. The condition of the mounted infantry is no better.

A frontal attack against Botha's position on the Pienaar's Poort range was out of the question. The approaches which the Lorenzo Marques Railway followed crossed an almost flat plain, intersected with spruits, it is true, but affording no substantial cover right up to the frowning cliffs of the hills, many of which appeared almost perpendicular. The plain was also singularly deficient in artillery positions for the attack, except at very long range. Monday was spent by the Field-Marshal in feeling for an accessible opening against which a successful attack might be developed. From the first reconnaissance everything pointed to the left of the position being the most vulnerable. Consequently General Hamilton, advancing from Garsfontein, was able to work straight upon Donkershoek, the portion of the position which is crossed by the Pretoria wagon road. But Monday was an anxious day. As already pointed out, the halt of Broadwood's and Gordon's Brigades on Sunday placed them at a disadvantage on Monday – a disadvantage which the former was not able to shake off on the following day. In fact, the operations on Monday all along the line were not promising until the evening. French on the extreme left was checked, Broadwood heavily engaged, and Hamilton himself had found that the Heidelberg commando had evaded Gordon on the extreme right and was in a position to menace his own right rear or the Johannesburg communication, weakly held from Pretoria to Vereeniging by Smith-Dorrien's Brigade. So severe was the menace that Hamilton found it necessary to detach a battalion (the Derbyshire Regiment) and the section of a field battery to protect this flank. The little column, taking advantage of a country under mealie cultivation, were able to roll aside the Heidelberg attack and drive the latter back upon Gordon. But the enemy in front of General Hamilton were very tenacious, and they held the broken ground in the vicinity of Kleinfontein for the best part of the day. In fact, at one time it seemed that the infantry was making such little progress that the Field-Marshal sent a message to General Hamilton to ascertain if he found the position too strong for him. But then the 11th Division, where headquarters were, was about six miles distant, and the telescope did not represent the true state of affairs. The enemy clung on to the lower ridges with extreme tenacity, but when in the afternoon the heavy guns as well as the field guns began to search them out they broke and fled, and the infantry of General Hamilton were able to bivouack on the first position which they had held.

De Wet's importance to the continuing Boer resistance was quickly realized by the British, and he became the focus of a number of drives to either destroy or capture him and his commando.

MAFEKING, AUG. 31.

Lord Methuen arrived here on the 27th inst. in order to give his men a well-earned rest, and to rehorse and equip them before commencing operations in the northern districts. He has been practically always marching and fighting since he left Boshof on May 14, and he chased and cornered that very "slippery customer" De Wet, who at the last moment escaped, owing to the evacuation of Oliphant's Nek by General Baden-Powell. On August 5 Lord Methuen occupied Potchefstroom in order to watch Mooi River, so as to give information of De Wet's movements, should he attempt a westward movement after crossing the Vaal, but with orders not to oppose his crossing should he attempt to do so. On the 5th orders arrived from Lord Kitchener asking Lord Methuen to occupy Scandinavia Drift, and, if possible, to block Winkel Drift, on the Rhenoster River. He accordingly concentrated his forces there on the 6th, it being known that De Wet held a position at Schoeman's Drift. The Colonial Division, 1,500 men under General Knox, was on the Rhenoster, the infantry being to the east of it, the cavalry and mounted infantry brigades, under Generals Broadwood, Ridley, and Little, holding positions east and south-east of De Wet, leaving only the north side open. News was brought in that De Wet was crossing into the Transvaal by Schoeman's Drift; Lord Methuen at once started with mounted men and guns across country to effect a flanking movement, sending for four companies of infantry, two guns, and 15 squadrons to join him at once from Rockraal. As it was imperative that no unnecessary delay should give the enemy any additional chance of escape, as little baggage as possible was taken, the troops slept without blankets, and an advance was made at daybreak. The enemy were found to be holding some kopjes west of Tygerfontein, but were soon driven out, and Methuen thus gained possession of the road north from Schoeman's Drift. The enemy also held a stronger position to the east, and the Imperial Yeomanry were sent to outflank them. After two attempts the latter were forced to retire, owing to the impossibility of moving quickly over the rough, rocky ground, and at the same time being under a heavy rifle fire from the adjacent hills. This was the signal for a regular bombardment, and the infantry prepared to advance against the position. The Boers now brought up some guns, but removed them without firing a shot, as the Yeomanry opened a heavy rifle fire as soon as they made their appearance. So hasty was the enemy's retreat that they left one ammunition wagon behind, and it is believed that their guns were broken down, owing to the awful ground they had to get over. The position was eventually taken by the infantry, but the enemy offered a very determined resistance, and retired only at the last moment. The whole convoy and army were next seen retreating north-east on the north side of the Vaal, along a road not marked on the map. Lord Methuen decided to camp at Tygerfontein, as his men had had a hard day's fighting, losing six officers and nine men killed and wounded. The following day was spent at Tygerfontein, as news was brought in that De Wet contemplated doubling back to the Free State, and the general decided to rest his men and await developments. The same night Captain Cheyne arrived on foot, having come through the Boer lines in order to give Lord Methuen general dispositions of our other columns. An order also arrived from Lord Roberts saying that Potchefstroom was to be evacuated. Orders were therefore sent to the garrison to destroy all stores which they were unable to carry away, and to join the main body as soon as possible.

A start was made at 7 a.m. on the 9th inst., and the enemy were located in the Buffleshoek Mountains. Some guns and a large body of Yeomanry were at once ordered to advance, and before long the Boer convoy was seen in front, heading north-east. A heavy fire was opened on it, and stopped some of the wagons. The enemy then made a rush to the flanks to occupy kopjes and so protect their wagons, but, after having been well shelled by "Pom Poms", the 3rd Imperial Yeomanry bravely rushed the position, thus commanding the pass from the right, whilst the 5th Imperial Yeomanry took some small hills commanding it on the left, affording protection to our guns, which were exposed to a heavy rifle fire. Lord Chesham was on the extreme left with the 10th Imperial Yeomanry, to frustrate any outflanking movements the enemy might contemplate making in that quarter. The enemy, however, still held a kopje east of that taken by the 3rd Imperial Yeomanry, and were eventually shelled out of it, but not until they had wounded Colonel Younghusband and killed Lieutenant Knowles and some men. A further advance was then made, some dead and wounded Boers being found *en route*, and a few wagons were shelled, but most of the convoy had gone; some of the enemy were seen retiring across our front, but were not shelled, as some men were seen amongst them who looked like English prisoners. The enemy were followed up and shelled until late, when it was decided to occupy the newly-gained positions and camp for the night. Towards the close of the fight Lord Kitchener's guns were heard on the right, and signalling communication was established between the two columns. He had seen the Boer convoy trekking north-east, but it appears that De Wet had collected his scattered forces and marched in a north-westerly direction.

Early next morning a move was made due north, and a runner sent through to Smith-Dorrien, who held the railway, telling him to try and head De Wet on the Gatsrand; but his force was chiefly infantry, and therefore not equal to the task. A large cloud of dust was seen ascending the pass from Bufflesdorn, but too far to be reached, and next morning De Wet had once more disappeared. It was then decided to march on Fredrickstad, so as to keep to the left of De Wet, thus heading him off from the west, where he seemed anxious to go, Lord Kitchener being relied on to hem him in on the east, as the latter was marching on our right about eight miles distant. A cloud of dust in the distance looked like De Wet's rear guard, but turned out to be Smith-Dorrien's men, who were sent out under Colonel Spens to open the pass from his side. Fredrickstad was reached the same afternoon, and a few Boer patrols were seen moving northwards. Smith-Dorrien reported that De Wet had passed close to Welvidiend Station the night before, but his movements were so very rapid that it was impossible to locate him or to have the faintest idea as to when he would make his next appearance. Information came to hand that some of the Transvaal commandos were assembling at Cyferbult in order to join De Wet there or at Mooi River. Lord Methuen therefore arranged a joint attack with Lord Kitchener and left camp the following morning with 1,100 mounted men and ten guns, taking the Ventersdoorp road. The supply question was a serious one, the Colonial Division having neither rations nor forage and the remainder of the troops being very short of both; but everything was loaded on light wagons during the night, and Lord Methuen started off, as lightly equipped as possible, determined to have a really good attempt at capturing the wily Boer general. Beyond Cyferbult, where news of the convoy was heard, some Boer patrols were encountered. About 1 p.m. some of the advance guard opened on a fairly large body of the enemy, when suddenly the whole Boer convoy came into view crossing our front, distant about four miles and moving north-west. A position was selected as probably commanding the road, and some of the Yeomanry were sent to take it, but on their getting close it was found that the enemy had forestalled them. A very heavy fire was opened on the troops, who had to take shelter until the arrival of the guns. These, owing to the heavy ground, were a considerable time in coming into action, and a large portion of the convoy disappeared, but by a flank movement they managed to surprise the enemy and poured a heavy shell fire into them at about 1,500 yards range, scattering them in all directions, one shrapnel shell killing five of the gun horses. This gun, on being taken, turned out to be one lost by Gatacre at Stormberg. On went the column, 5th Imperial Yeomanry and 3rd Imperial Yeomanry on the left, with "Pom Poms" and 4th Battery R.A., 10th Imperial Yeomanry and Major Powell's Battery in the centre, whilst the Colonial Division brought up the right flank. The horses were dead beat, but the column still kept on, and after four miles had the satisfaction of catching up some wagons. Thereupon the Boers fired them and retreated, leaving behind the prisoners, who numbered about 60 men. The wagons chiefly contained ammunition, and the explosions continued far into the night; rifle and gun ammunition was also scattered all over the veldt. Five wagons were burnt, and two were abandoned a little further on; these, with nine others captured earlier in the day, made 16 wagons and one gun captured, 60 prisoners released, and about a dozen Boers taken, while the troops had done over 32 miles' marching.

It was thought that by keeping on De Wet's track we might further increase his demoralization, and, as the North Lancasters had been left with General Baden-Powell to occupy Oliphant's Nek, his capture was considered a certainty, should Lord Methuen be able to turn him in that direction. Oliphant's Nek is one of the most important strategical positions in the Transvaal, as there is no road over the Magaliesberg Mountains for 40 miles eastward, and was held by our troops; while the Magato Pass, 12 miles westward, was commanded by the troops at Rustenburg and had been fortified by Baden-Powell. At 3 a.m. on the 13th a move was made, the first object being to find water, which had been unobtainable the night before, and a short halt was made at Kranskop to water horses and fill water-bottles. Soon after starting again we came in touch with the rear guard, without, however, coming into action, as they beat a hasty retreat. Following hard on their tracks, we reached Rietfontein and saw the last of the Boers disappearing in the distance, taking the most easterly road leading to Oliphant's Nek.

News now came in from Lord Kitchener to say that General Baden-Powell had been ordered to leave Oliphant's Nek with all his troops, but he assured Lord Methuen that General Ian Hamilton was sure to be there before the 13th, so that we could reasonably look upon De Wet's capture as a certainty, as there was only one loophole of escape – namely, along the road leading west towards Zeerust. Lord Methuen, believing in making everything secure, left at 1.30 a.m. without baggage and with only half a day's rations, to cut off this point of egress. The road was very heavy and the night dark, so that progress was of necessity very slow, and at 5 a.m. he found that the road he intended to follow was occupied by Boers. It was then also that he heard that De Wet had made a movement to the west, apparently not liking to risk Oliphant's Nek. We therefore started at 8 a.m. to make a long detour in order to enclose him. Signalling communication was opened with General Broadwood, who was engaging the enemy's rear-guard and reported De Wet's convoy to be moving ahead and only a few miles west of Oliphant's Nek. We still kept on and soon saw dust away to the east, and came upon a few Boer patrols all heading in the same direction.

It seemed now as if nothing could save the Boer convoy, English generals being on all sides, and the only road of escape being held by General Baden-Powell. At 2.30 came the awful news. De Wet had found Oliphant's Nek open and was now marching out. No one can describe the feelings of both officers and men. Here we had been enduring forced marches, heavy days of fighting, privations of all sorts, including want of food and blankets, but of these we had thought nothing when we believed that at last we had our man. And then to find that the bird had flown! Never during the whole war have we encountered a man of such vital importance as De Wet is to-day and never has there been such a flagrant piece of mismanagement as the evacuation of this all-important position. Why is it that even to-day these mistakes are made? Another question suggests itself – viz., why was Potchefstroom evacuated? The infantry garrison were of no possible use to Lord Methuen for the class of work he had undertaken, and two train-loads of stores were burnt which would have been a great boon to the troops on their occupation of Fredrickstad. Moreover, the moral effect of having to pull down the British flag is always bad, and should never be incurred except in cases of the direct necessity. Every column in the district which knew of Lord Methuen's pursuit was loud in its praises of him. And it is not too much to say that nothing could have exceeded his zeal and generalship. He was untiring in his efforts. Shortness of food and forced marches both by night and by day were counted as nothing. No movement of De Wet's was left unchecked, and to Lord Methuen alone belongs the credit of having got the Boer army, a force far exceeding his own, into a corner from which, save through the mistake of others, there was no escape.

Lord Methuen speaks very highly of the behaviour of the Yeomanry, whose courage and determination have given them a place amongst the best and bravest. In all, Lord Methuen marched 84 miles in three days, besides fighting on the 12th, and having already marched and fought on the 7th, 9th, and 10th; in all 160 miles and four fights in eight days. General Douglas also did a fine infantry march, covering 68 miles in 76 hours, and joining Lord Methuen on the evening of the 15th.

The appointment of Lord Kitchener to succeed Lord Roberts as Commander-in-Chief in South Arica led to a reorganization of the British forces in the theatre of operations.

PRETORIA, JAN. 21.

Despite the fact that the greater portion of the British Army in the Transvaal and Orange River Colony had been for the past two months and more engaged in the uncongenial task of "sitting tight", much has been accomplished which in the immediate future may be expected to produce important results. Organization has prepared the way for the final swoop which will surely finish the war, and the end, which, to the superficial observer, possibly seems an indefinite distance away, is really so close at hand that those well-informed people scout the idea that the struggle will continue for a longer period than another three months at the most. When Lord Kitchener took over the command, he and those generals who were associated with him had to face a condition of affairs closely resembling that which met Lord Roberts on his arrival in South Africa 12 months ago. In the natural course of events a certain amount of disorganization had set in. Troops had become loosely distributed all over the two colonies. Brigades which should have been able to operate in conjunction had lost touch with each other. On our lines of communication there were points where bunches of horse, foot, and artillery had been collected, while other and equally important points were inadequately guarded and open to sudden attack at any moment. Positions which might prove of considerable strategic value were totally unoccupied, and entire battalions had become isolated in other positions in such a manner as to be rendered practically useless. Sections, and in some cases whole batteries, of artillery held places which there was not the faintest prospect of the Boers' ever visiting, and other places, which a few guns would have made perfectly safe, were exposed to almost certain attack and very possible capture. It must not be imagined that Lord Roberts was in any way to blame for this state of affairs. It was the inevitable outcome of a protracted campaign in a difficult country and over an enormous area and of the complete change in the character of the war on the part of the enemy from a war of defence to an offensive guerilla war. The war drama itself was over, but there remained the epilogue. This epilogue – very different as it was from the play proper – required that the stage should be reset and the properties rearranged. This task demanded both time and hard work. So the curtain was rung down, and the audience – that is, the public – had to wait while Stage Manager Lord Kitchener and his staff of generals and brigadiers prepared the stage for the last great scene of all. And now everything is ready. Each and every actor is in his place, eager to take up his cue at the right moment, and the curtain is about to rise upon the last and briefest but, in some respects, most dramatic scene of all.

At this point it may not be out of place to explain in some detail the work of reorganization which has filled up the long two months of waiting. When Lord Kitchener took over the command he found himself at the head of an army which on paper numbered 210,000 of all ranks. Of this force, fully 20,000, from illness and other causes, were for the time being non-combatants. Another 50,000 had to be detached for garrison duty and to preserve our lines of communication; so that the force available for active and offensive operations did not exceed 140,000

Lord Roberts (to left)
and Lord Kitchener
(white horse) reviewing
the troops entering
Kroonstad

officers and men. But reinforcements had been demanded, and were even then on their way, and by February 6 next, when the general movement will begin, the Commander-in-Chief will have at his disposal an army of perhaps 160,000 men, quite half of whom will consist of field artillery, cavalry, and mounted infantry. These will operate in brigades, and each group of brigades will be under the central command of a general of division. The old divisional commands are even now in process of being broken up. Some divisions – the 7th, for example – have already ceased to exist altogether. There are now altogether 38 brigades in the field, of which no fewer than 26 are commanded by officers who have been appointed to their commands with local and temporary rank.

These brigades will work in an exact and systematic manner. For the purposes of the new plan of campaign the whole area affected by guerilla warfare has been treated as a military chess board, and the squares will be covered by groups of brigades, to every unit of which a clearly defined area of operations has been allotted. Each brigade has its own ground to cover and will move in an arranged direction, clearing the ground as it goes until it reaches a point within the square belonging to the brigade of another group. If it is found advisable, the brigades will then retrace their steps, quartering the ground a second time, but the general movement will be inwards as well as forward, from north, south, east, and west simultaneously, so that, say, four groups of brigades could very easily be massed at any given point very quickly, if necessity arose for the concentration anywhere of an overwhelming force. It is apparent that the plan must, if carried out, as it will be, exactly on the rules laid down, work out with mathematical precision. Each brigade will be able to keep in touch, through its outlying scouts and patrols, with the brigades to its right and left, front and rear. Moving steadily in a known direction, they must inevitably come in contact with the enemy very quickly, and, if the Boers, with their well-known luck and cleverness, are able to slip through the brigades of one group, they will only do so to find themselves in the midst of another, while the group behind them will return and close in on the enemy from the rear.

The arrangements for ample and continuous food supplies are beautifully simple and complete. Depôts have been established at short distances apart and furnished with provisions and necessaries sufficient to maintain the army in the field for months. Actually, there will be no necessity for any brigade ever to be more than a couple of days' journey from a supply depôt, and if, as may possibly happen, the enemy successfully raid one collection of supplies, it will have practically no effect upon our troops, beyond, perhaps, compelling this or that brigade to put up with half rations for one, or at most, two days. Being always within easy reach of central depôts, our troops will be able to travel light, and the mounted men of each brigade will always have with them a sufficient number of spare horses to enable them to change animals pretty frequently. The field hospitals will be managed on a somewhat original plan especially adapted to the conditions under which the army will operate. Anything like a breakdown in the medical arrangements is now almost impossible. The plan of campaign has been carefully elaborated and every detail practically tested, and now works with beautiful precision and smoothness. In perfecting it the Commander-in-Chief and his staff have necessarily been compelled to refrain from attempting to strike any blow the premature nature of which might have disorganized the whole fabric of the complete scheme and rendered it, in part at least, ineffectual. They have been content to act on the defensive, pure and simple, for weeks and months on end. But the period of inactivity is over, and about February 6 the curtain will rise upon the epilogue of the great war in South Africa.

The Times' correspondent was sure that Kitchener's plan for the systematic scouring of the country would lead to the ultimate and relatively speedy defeat of those stubborn Boers still in the field. Unfortunately, De Wet and the other Boer leaders had other ideas, the first of which was a second invasion of Cape Colony.

CAMP KALK KRAAL, 50 MILES NORTH OF BRITSTOWN, FEB. 23.

When I arrived in Cape Town there were no less than 23 detached columns operating against the invaders. These columns were working upon three distinct lines. These lines corresponded to the direction the three invading commandos had taken. The eastern commando had been driven by Colonel D. Haig, 7th Hussars, into the Steynsburg hills, where it was comparatively inoffensive. Here it was reported to be dissolving. A force under General Brabant was collecting at King Williams Town with the object of meeting this invasion in case De Wet should choose to direct the reinforcements under his command on to this line. The midland invasion was less formidable. Finding no support in the Murraysburg district, it had crossed the line between Beaufort West and

Fraserburg Road Station in small parties and had joined the western and most dangerous body of invaders. This body was commanded by Hertzog, late Judge in the Orange Free State. He had with him Commandant George Brand, President Brand's son, Wessels of Harrismith, and Pretorius. Their duty was to prepare the way for the real invading column under De Wet and Froneman, to collect recruits, supplies, and horses. They invaded through the Hopetown and Prieska district, passed down through the Carnarvon, Fraserburg, Calvinia, Sutherland, and Clanwilliam districts, eventually arriving at Piequetberg, where it will be remembered that their advance guard was turned back from the Picquetberg Pass by the timely arrival of a handful of enthusiastic cyclists belonging to the Cape Town Town Guard. Perhaps the most notable result of this invasion was that the Boers for the first time during the campaign succeeded in reaching the seaboard. It was owing to their having arrived at the coast in Clanwilliam that H.M.S. Sybille was lost. But apart from the interesting fact that the Boers succeeded in doing in January last what they should have done early in the campaign, when we were powerless to prevent them, it was generally thought that the guerillas intended to open up communication with their European agents through Cape Colony, either for the purpose of replenishing their supply of war munitions or in order to secure a means by which the more implacable leaders might join the refugees in Europe. I myself do not believe that the much-prophesied attempt upon the British main base was ever intended. But the scare had a good effect. Including the Town Guard, over 12,000 civilians enlisted for service in Cape Town, and this large number of men under arms released a considerable number of more serviceable troops, who were able to operate directly against the enemy. Hertzog and Brand found that they were upon no bed of roses; they were constantly headed and buffeted by Colonel Bethune's and Colonel de Lisle's columns. They showed no desire to fight at all. As a matter of fact, none of the guerillas still carrying on the struggle south of the Vaal show any inclination to fight. They are just like quicksilver. They gather, and as soon as an armed body comes into contact with them they disperse to the four winds, to gather again at some distant centre. This is the whole secret of the prolonged hostilities. There is no enemy with sufficient cohesion or confidence to risk an engagement, and the whole of the Imperial resources are frittered away in the pursuit of phantom commandos ever dissolving like the mirage of the South African veld. These commandos will gather to overwhelm a small detached post or to capture a train. Then, having divided the spoil, they turn their prisoners adrift and scatter, to concentrate 50 miles away from the scene of their success. As long as the weather and the chance of raiding farms or small convoys enable the individual Boer and his pony to keep the field, so long will the present state of affairs continue. If the energy and efficacy of Lord Kitchener's measures, offensive and defensive, combined with the approaching winter, once succeed in making this task of maintaining himself too difficult for the ordinary burgher now in the field, the enemy's forces will automatically vanish without a single big blow being struck.

Although De Wet was quickly pushed out of Cape Colony, his incursion had the effect of highlighting the inability of the British forces to protect large areas of South Africa.

This impression was reinforced by the way he was apparently able to move about the country at will and evade capture.

AASVOGKL KOP, MARCH 8.

Another De Wet hunt is over, and the slim commandant is clear of the mobilization which, based from Naauwpoort, was intended to encircle him. He has slipped through the double ring which we attempted to lay round him, and has passed north on the road to Kroonstad, where fresh levies and fresh columns wait to take up the running. But it is an ill wind that blows no one any good, and, although the Free State leaders who attempted the dash upon the Colony have not been found prisoners' quarters at Green Point Camp, they have been so roughly handled from the first day of their invasion until they evaded Plumer and Bethune at Abram's Kraal that all fear of a repetition of the endeavour to raise the Dutch colonists may be dismissed. The meeting of Cape Dutch at Worcester, and the fact that supplies and horseflesh in the Orange River Colony were running low, induced the Free State leaders to make in earnest their long-promised invasion of Cape Colony. A preliminary invasion was made at the end of last year to prepare the way. This invasion was conducted in three columns. The two Hertzogs, Brand, and Wessels crossed the Orange River to the west and passed down to Calvinia and Clanwilliam, and would even have captured the Piquetberg passes if it had not been for the prompt action of a few sections of rapidly organized Cape Cyclist Volunteers; a second column under Kruitzinger made its way down to Murraysburg; while Scheeper with a third column, crossing in the vicinity of Aliwal North, pushed down to the Steynsburg hills. These were but advance guards; their orders were, while they avoided battle, to collect recruits, furnish convenient depôts, and procure remounts for the main advance under De Wet and Steyn in person. What success they had is already known. They created considerable anxiety in Cape Town, they collected a considerable amount of stock and horseflesh, for which they gave receipts in the name of the Orange Free State Government, but they failed to enlist many recruits. In fact, they only succeeded in securing an infinitesimal portion of the numbers anticipated, the majority of whom were irresponsible youths or indigent *bywoners*. The Dutchman, who is a past-master in the art of procrastination, preferred to remain sitting on the fence until the last moment. While extending every sympathy to the advance guard, the colonists said that they would not put on bandolier or saddle a horse until the Free State hero arrived in person to fulfil his promises. This was the spirit in which the original invasion was received, and it was in reliance upon this spirit that De Wet and Steyn made the attempt. In the meantime the advance guard had been considerably harassed by Brabant, Girouard, and Haig on the east, and De Lisle's and Bethune's columns on the west, so that, unless reinforced, there was no hope for them of a further success than the occupation of small isolated villages.

When De Wet finally made up his mind to carry into effect his scheme of invasion, his movements were made with his usual celerity. He was at the beginning of February in the Winburg district with the means of collecting a force of about 2,500 to 3,000 men. We held the Thaba Nehu-Bloemfontein line with a chain of posts which at the time were considered sufficient to prevent any considerable force from breaking through into the south-east districts of the Orange River Colony. But they proved as tissue paper to De Wet, and on the night of February 11, although General Bruce Hamilton with three flying columns was on his heels and constantly engaged the rearguard which the Boers threw out, the commando succeeded in making its way to the Orange River. From there it doubled back, crossed the railway in the vicinity of Jagersfontein Road, seizing a train of transport animals *en route*, and made Philippolis without trouble. The Philippolis and Fauresmith districts were more or less friendly districts, as, ever since Brand and Hertzog passed through them in December, the British magistrates had been superseded by landdrosts who held their position in the authority of ex-President Steyn. At Philippolis De Wet collected his strength for two days. As far as the British Intelligence Department could ascertain, the leaders whom De Wet and Steyn rallied round them here were Cronje, Brebner, Wessels (of Harrismith), De Vos, Haasbroeck, Steenekamp, Theron, Pretorius, Kolbe, Koetze, and Joubert, in all nearly 3,000 men, with two 15-pounders, one "Pom-Pom," and one Maxim. Piet Fourie, who is perhaps the best fighting leader that the guerillas now possess, refuses to do more than co-operate with De Wet. He openly states that the latter is demented and will not go into laager with him. He consequently, with a following of about 400 men, moved to the left flank, and since the invasion was made in earnest has conducted his own operations. At the time of writing Piet Fourie is in the vicinity of Dewetsdorp, having remained in Rouxville during the invasion.

On February 11 the Cape Colony was invaded by De Wet's commando. They crossed the Orange River by Sand Drift, 25 miles north-west of the Colesberg Wagon Drift. General Lyttelton, who had been specially sent by Lord Kitchener to the Colony, to deal with this invasion, at that time had his headquarters at Naauwpoort, where the various columns destined to meet the invasion had concentrated. It was anticipated that De Wet would take the western line, and, in view of such a contingency, preparations were made which were to allow him to go south – remove him as far as possible from his base – and then deal with him. The possession of the railway allowed of very rapid concentrations, and the scheme as it was set down was roughly as follows. As soon as De Wet was well south on his road to Calvinia the following columns were to echelon in his rear:– General Plumer in his direct rear; Colonels Crabbe and Henniker moving west at a convenient distance would make the next parallel, with De Aar-Britstown their base. The Cape Cavalry Brigade under Colonel Bethune made the next parallel, moving from Richmond Road, on the Britstown–Prieska line. The next echelon was formed by Colonel Haig at Fraserburg Road, while Thorneycroft was due to form a southern line from him. Generals Knox and Bruce Hamilton were held in leash to support Plumer if he brought De Wet to a standstill, while General Paget had orders for Victoria West. A column was ordered out of Kimberley to prevent a break back across the Orange River from the Britstown district, while De Lisle was at Carnarvon to receive the much-harassed enemy as soon as he arrived south. Colonel Gorringe was left to deal with Kruitzinger's advance-guard in the Murraysburg and to prevent the latter's junction with the main column. But the best ordered and soundest plans often fail in war. Plumer, who had entrained to

Colesberg with the Queensland M.I., the Imperial Bushmen, and two squadrons of the 1st King's Dragoon Guards under Colonel Owen, came in touch with the enemy at Philipstown on March 13, and on the same date the Orange River came down in flood. On the following day heavy rain set in, and so hampered De Wet that Plumer was able to maintain his touch and engage the enemy heavily. De Wet moved west, and Plumer followed him with such good effect that when De Wet crossed the railway in the vicinity of Hout Kraal he was nipped by two armoured trains and the small column commanded by Colonel Eyre Crabbe, and lost a gun, a Maxim, the whole of his ammunition, transport, and many prisoners. He succeeded in getting clear with his stripped force and two guns. The fighting was not desperate, as De Wet made no attempt to stand, but the history of the week's skirmishing between Philipstown and Houtkraal contained an unpleasant incident. A detachment of the King's Dragoon Guards, under Major S. B. Smith, fell into the enemy's hands. As is the custom of the Boers, their horses and arms were immediately taken from them and they were forced to follow the commando on foot. When the men were thoroughly weary Major Smith told the attendant guards that it would be impossible for his men to go on further on foot. The guard said he would call a commandant. Presently a burly Boer came up in a great rage and called for the officer who had complained. When Major Smith was pointed out the Boer rode up to him with an oath, and struck him with a sjambok. Major Smith immediately closed with the irate commandant, and commenced to pull him off his horse, when revolvers were produced by the Boers standing by, and under their menace the incident closed. It has been reported that this cowardly assault was made by De Wet in person. But there is some doubt on this point, as De Wet is not a big, burly man. It is more likely to have been the Harrismith Wessels.

After crossing Houtnek, the Boers headed north, and, as Brand and Hertzog were reported to be retiring north upon Prieska, the whole order of the operations changed, and every nerve was strained to pen De Wet in a loop of the now swollen Orange River. It is possible that the very dash and tenacity of Plumer's pursuit, superb as it was, may have led to the failure of the combined operations. As the last weeks of February proved, Plumer was not strong enough to capture the invading Boers himself, and by pressing them so hardly he prevented the co-operation of other columns. Single-handed Plumer was not strong enough to reduce De Wet's commandos; all he could hope to do was to pen him in a bend of the river. But as has been amply shown by the history of all wars, a swollen river is not an impossible barrier to mounted troops, providing they are content to abandon their *impedimenta*. It must be remembered that when in the Colony the Boers were bound to keep together, and that as long as they were invaders they presented a concrete objective to be operated against. But once they recrossed the Orange River they were back in their own country, and if pressed could fade away into small detachments to reunite at the next *rendezvous*. It would therefore perhaps have been better policy for the advance column to have waited on De Wet until sufficient troops were within reach to reduce him by a *coup de main*. Another fault was also made in the manoeuvring of the forces of the echelon, which were directed north as soon as it was evident that De Wet had given up his intention of pushing south-west. The Cape Cavalry Brigade under Colonel E. Bethune, 16th

Lord Kitchener

Lancers, consisting of the 1st King's Dragoon Guards, 3rd Dragoon Guards, Prince of Wales's Light Horse, "G" Battery R.H.A., and one "Pom-pom" section, had marched from Richmond Road on February 16. It reached Britstown in two days, concentrating there with General Bruce-Hamilton's column (Major Whyte's flying column – 16th Lancers, Denbigh Yeomanry, and "Pom-pom", and Manroe's flying column – Bethune's Mounted Infantry and two guns and Rimington's Guides). On the following day the combined force, under the command of General Bruce-Hamilton, moved out in the direction of Houwater – historic as the scene of the first engagement of the City Imperial Volunteers just about a year ago. It was reported that Brand's commando had spent the night at Houwater. This proved to be correct, for Rimington's Guides met the column moving forward to summon Britstown to surrender. There was a skirmish and Brand's commando faded away in the darkness of night. It was then Colonel Bethune's intention to take the Cape Cavalry Brigade directly north upon Strydenburg, with the object of taking up the running in co-operation with General Plumer. Subsequent events prove that three days would have brought him up in time to pick up the line from exhausted Plumer in the vicinity of Gelukspoort, after De Wet had recoiled from Mark's Drift. But a senior officer spoiled the plan, and the fine Cape Cavalry Brigade, fresh from the base and keen for service, was kept marching uselessly up and down dusty roads in rear of a senior officer pursuing a phantom enemy. Thus ten days were lost, and the only consolation that the officer commanding the Cape Cavalry Brigade had was that he had intended to make the right move and had obeyed orders. In the meantime, though General

Plumer had refitted, he was outpaced by De Wet, and the Boer commando, diminished, it is true, recrossed the railway in the vicinity of Panwpan Station and was heading back searching for an opening back into the Orange River Colony. The invasion had proved abortive, but De Wet was in a position to shake himself clear of the scrape which he was in.

Kitchener became more and more exasperated by his inability to put an end to Boer resistance. As the guerilla campaign dragged on and on, the British adopted ever more severe methods to deal with those Boers who refused to surrender. The derailment of trains was a favourite Boer tactic; the British responded by executing some of those they found engaged in train-wrecking.

DE AAR, MARCH 19.

The sentences of death which were passed on Jan Petrus Ninaber, Sarel Ninaber, and Jan Andries Neiuwoudt, who were convicted of treason and murder by the military Court last week in connexion with the wrecking of a train with a loss of five lives near Taaibosch siding, have been confirmed by Lord Kitchener and were carried out to-day. The men were shot at sunset. The garrison was paraded under General Settle, the firing parties being under command of Major Drummond-Hay. The proceedings were quiet. Death was instantaneous. The Minister of the Dutch Reformed Church at Hanover remained with the prisoners to the end. The men were also visited by their relatives. The other two men concerned in the affair – Hermanus Nieuwoudt and Frederick Neiuwoudt – have been sentenced to five years' penal servitude.

These methods were, however, insufficient to deter the Boers from continuing their guerilla activity. In August and September 1901 the Boers attempted to stage an invasion of Natal.

NEWCASTLE, OCT. 4.

The sudden recrudescence of Boer activity in the South-Eastern Transvaal forms a chapter by itself in the history of the disjointed operations now marking the last stages of the Boer war. For various reasons the attempted invasion of Natal by the force specially raised for this purpose by Louis Botha acquires importance, not least of all from the significance attached to the operations by the Boers themselves. Beyond having frustrated the enemy's plans, we, however, cannot lay claim to any signal advantage derived from these operations; but the fact that Louis Botha, abandoning the customary Boer tactics of moving merely to elude our troops, arranged, in conjunction with De Wet and Steyn, a big combined movement which resulted disastrously for the Boer arms should have a distinct influence on the closing scenes of the war. We may not be able to recognize this influence immediately, and possibly it will not take the form we should most desire. But, should the only result be that the war now assumes exclusively the guerilla type, an account of the last attempt on the part of the Boers to concentrate for a specific object will be of interest.

As far back as the second week in August it was known that the Boers were concentrating in the South-Eastern Transvaal. The reports, however, were vague; no information as to the enemy's numbers was forthcoming, nor was there any certainty at first that their objective would be Natal. Indeed, it was thought that the concentration, if in earnest, was merely Botha's method of replying to Lord Kitchener's proclamation, and, although it was undoubtedly intended to divert the attention of burghers from September 15, subsequent events proved that it was not wholly undertaken in a spirit of bluff. No action was taken in the matter, and for nearly a month little more was heard of the Boer concentration. On September 4 Lieutenant-General Lyttelton took over the command of the Natal District from Major-General Hildyard, who returned to England on leave. The situation at this time was similar to that in most other districts in the Transvaal and Orange River Colony. Boers were scattered about in groups of various sizes, and our columns, guided by local information, endeavoured to come into touch with them, clearing the country as far as possible along the line of march. It was in this work that the columns under Colonel Pulteney and Colonel Stewart, assisted by a small force under Colonel Blomfield, were engaged when General Lyttelton arrived at Newcastle. After securing fresh supplies at Vryheid, on September 1, they had proceeded in a south-easterly direction to a farm called Apologie. Information was received here of a mill about 15 miles to the east which the Boers were holding and turning to good use. With the object of destroying this mill the two columns marched together due east from Apologie on the 4th. They found the enemy in force on an intervening farm, and after considerable fighting drove the Boers from their position. But the columns were not strong enough to follow up their success, and fell back the same evening on their former camp. In view of the Boer numbers and the nature of the country, it was decided that without reinforcements it was impossible to follow the Boers eastwards, and the columns continued in their original direction to the Nqutu district of Zululand.

It had now become evident not only that a concentration of the Boers had already taken place under Louis Botha in the Ermelo-Amsterdam district, but that it had as its definite object the invasion of Natal. Although no estimate could yet be accurately formed of their numbers, and there was uncertainty as to which point on the Natal frontier would be their first object of attack, several precautionary measures were at once taken. Colonel Pulteney's column was brought into Dundee and entrained for Volksrust, while the garrison at Wakkerstroom, which was possibly destined to be the first objective of Louis Botha's force, was reinforced by 80 men of the 8th Hussars. Two extra columns under Colonels Garratt and Colville, which had been operating north and north-east of Standerton, were brought nearer the threatened area. At the same time the question of calling out the Natal Volunteers was considered, but it was deemed sufficient to order all the rifle associations to be ready to take the field at two days' notice. On September 13 Major Gough's Mounted Infantry, 580 strong, arrived at Dundee from Kroonstad, and proceeded two days later to De Jager's Drift, on the Buffalo River. On the same day (September 15) the first definite information of the Boer movements was received. Colonel Garratt, by this time at a farm 25 miles south-west of Amsterdam, learned that the enemy had left the north-eastern extremity of the

Slangapies Berg, south-west of Piet Retief, on the night of the 12th and had gone south. A prisoner captured by his column reported that Louis Botha had with him 1,500 men, one Creuzot, a Pom Pom, and a Maxim. The Boers being now located, all available troops were at once moved with the object of breaking up, if possible, Botha's force. Garratt followed the enemy from the north; Pulteney, who on the 15th had reached Wakkerstroom, headed for Utrecht; while Gough and Stewart were sent from Dundee towards Vryheid. Unfortunately the movements of our troops at this time were much impeded by rains and bad roads, and it was difficult to get into communication with the columns in the field. Pulteney was, in consequence of the weather, delayed in reaching Utrecht, and Garratt, who had been lost sight of since he had located the enemy, marched into Wakkerstroom intead of co-operating immediately with Pulteney. The result was that the Boers, instead of being confronted by converging columns, as had been intended, were left to deploy unopposed along the Elandsberg and the Schuereberg between Utrecht and Vryheid. From here a part of the force, estimated at from 400 to 500, took up a position about Scheeper's Nek, apparently for the purpose of attacking a returning convoy from Vryheid. As the latter town depended for its supplies entirely on road transport from De Jager's Drift, the free passage of the convoys was a matter of urgency at a time when it was meant to serve as an advance depôt for troops operating in this district. The columns under Colonel Stewart and Major Gough were accordingly ordered to clear the road and to bring the convoy on its way to De Jager's Drift. On the morning of the 17th Major Gough left De Jager's Drift for Rooikop, followed at an hour's interval by Colonel Stewart. Advancing from Rooikop, Gough sighted about 300 Boers leaving Scheeper's Nek, who shortly afterwards off-saddled at the entrance of Blood River Poort. Hoping to surprise the Boers by making a detour, Gough, after informing Stewart by a verbal message of his plan, galloped with three companies of his mounted infantry and two guns to a ridge on the western side of the Poort. No sooner had he approached this ridge than the company on the right flank found itself attacked by about 400 Boers. Charging in amongst our troops, the enemy immediately overwhelmed them, and then without any delay galloped round on to the rear, where the guns were. At the same moment a still larger body of Boers attacked Gough's force in front, and after a brief struggle the whole of the three companies were overcome. Two guns of the 67th Battery and one Colt gun were captured, but the gunners had succeeded in damaging first the sights and breech blocks of the field-guns. The Boers whom Gough had sighted on Scheeper's Nek were a part of the main body. Whether the capture of our troops was the outcome of a clever trap set by the Boers or was brought about by their cleverly seizing the opportunity afforded them by Gough's rash gallop is not known. The mishap was another of those regrettable incidents which have punctuated this long war, but in the present case it is difficult to stigmatize Gough's action by a harsher word than "rash." Certainly no blame attaches to General Lyttelton's intelligence; and, in view of the fact that the number of the enemy and their presence in the district were known, one can only lament that an able and energetic officer met with disaster in acting with the promptitude and dash which might well be practised more often at this stage of the campaign.

In the meantime Colonel Stewart, having seen Gough galloping towards the Poort, hurried up to support him. But almost immediately heavy fire was opened upon his column, and two large bodies of the enemy attempted to outflank him. In danger of being surrounded himself, and seeing that he was unable to render Gough any assistance, Stewart fell back, after losing 45 horses, but without other casualties, and retired on De Jager's Drift.

That same night Major Gough and Captain Craycroft, of the mounted infantry, escaped from the Boers and made their way to the Buffalo River. The rest of the prisoners were subsequently released and sent in to Vryheid.

The Boer concentration had assumed a dangerous aspect. Louis Botha's force was numerically stronger than any one of our columns, and if he had at once invaded Natal he would have been able to penetrate a considerable distance into the colony before our troops could have stopped him. The situation was further complicated by the activity of Boers on the Orange River Colony frontier. On the morning of the mishap to Gough's force 150 Boers of the Bethlehem commando, wearing yellow puggarees, had attacked the magistracy at Upper Tugela. They were driven off, and retired towards Olivier's Hoek Pass. Major Brown, 14th Hussars, commanding the post at Acton Homes, at once went in pursuit with some cavalry and one gun. The Boers, who had a large herd of cattle with them, turned south, and Major Brown came up with them as they crossed the Tugela. The cattle were recaptured and one Boer was killed. The rest escaped over Olivier's Hoek Pass, profiting by a mist to slip through General Rundle's troops, who were holding the Drakensberg and the neighbouring country in the Orange River Colony.

It was reported that De Wet subsequently ordered all burghers from the Frankfort, Reitz, Lindley, Heilbron, and Villiersdorp districts to assemble near Tafelkop and to march in the direction of Van Reenen's Pass for the purpose of invading Natal. Both Steyn and De Wet were at one time supposed to have been at the *rendezvous*, but beyond causing a more careful guard to be kept on the Drakensberg heights the threatened concentration of the Boers on this frontier led to nothing.

The immediate result of the mishap to Gough's force was the calling out of the Natal Volunteers, while the next week saw the troops under General Lyttelton's command increased to nearly 19,000 men. Already on the 18th Colonel Allenby's column had arrived at Dundee from Pretoria. There now followed in close succession General Spen's column, General Gilbert Hamilton's column, General Walter Kitchener's and Colonel Campbell's columns. On September 22 General Bruce Hamilton arrived at Newcastle and assumed command of Colonel Pulteney's and Colonel Garratt's columns.

In the meantime the Boers under Louis Botha had made an incursion into the Nqutu district of Zululand, threatening Vant's Drift and Rorke's Drift. A patrol of the Natal Volunteer Composite Regiment engaged the enemy's advanced patrols and drove them back about two miles, wounding two. The attempt to force a passage through Nqutu, however, was soon abandoned by the Boers, probably by reason of the Buffalo being unfordable, and the main body retired across the border.

The next few days were spent by the various columns in taking up their respective positions for the combined movement. When the Boers moved south from Blood River Poort a slight alteration had to be made in the original plan, which had for its object an attack on the main body at the Poort. There was at present no indication of the real intentions of the Boers, and the only conclusion to be drawn from their apparent indecision seemed to be that a serious invasion of Natal was not really contemplated. It was deemed advisable, however, to strengthen our forces in Zululand, and General Dartnell was sent from the Orange River Colony to Natal to take command of the local forces, while additional troops were despatched to Greytown and Eshowe. On the 23rd two officers and 60 men of the 5th Division of Mounted Infantry from Fort Prospect reinforced the post at Itala, while an officer and 48 men of the Durham Militia Artillery left Melmoth for Fort Prospect. Louis Botha had now made up his mind to enter Zululand, and made an attempt to conciliate a Zulu chief of the Nqutu district. Over 900 head of cattle that the Boers had raided the previous days were sent back with a letter asking why the Zulus were fighting against the Boers, and adding that if the Zulus refrained from molesting the Boers on their passage through Zululand no harm would be done to the natives. The Zulu chief replied that he would be loyal to his King, and returned the cattle.

Owing to the weather and the heavy state of the roads, it had been found impossible to begin the combined movement on the day arranged, and the Boers remained unmolested on the Nqutu border. On the 25th they moved south, and on the following day the memorable attacks on the two posts just within the Zululand border took place. The details of these engagements will be familiar to every one – the midnight attack at Itala on the advanced post one mile from the main body by 600 men under Commandant Potgieter, the rushing of this post followed by the general attack on the main camp from the west by about 800 men under Chris. Botha and Scholtz, from the south-east by Oppermann and 500 men; the whole operations being conducted by Louis Botha from the top of Babanango Hill by means of a heliograph and mounted orderlies. The question of the casualties on the Boer side has given rise to much discussion, and, in view of the non-inclusion of any numbers in Lord Kitchener's weekly total, it may be as well to refer to this matter. Major Chapman, who was in command of the Itala post, estimated that the Boers lost 128 killed and 270 wounded. The figures are arrived at after careful calculation and sifting of evidence. A party of men, including a sergeant, taken prisoners state that they actually assisted in laying-out 61 Boers for burial, 75 others they saw carried away wounded. These were quite distinct from the Boers who fell and were buried in the vicinity of our trenches. The Boer attack was made with great determination in the early morning; a mist partly prevented the separate forces of the Boers from learning what was happening to the other attacking parties. Moreover, a Natal rebel with the Boers owned to some of our prisoners that they had had 350 casualties. The fact that the Boers retired in tacit acknowledgement of their defeat tends to prove that the reverse was a serious one. The credit for the signal success of our arms rests with the members of the garrison collectively. The post was not well chosen, nor was it strongly enough fortified in view of the time it had been occupied, but these drawbacks were overcome by the

In the Orange River
trenches holding back the
Boers

gallantry of the men and officers and by the careful manner in which the
expenditure of ammunition during a 19 hours' engagement was regulated.

Fort Prospect was similarly assailed throughout the day, but here the excellent
intrenchments diminished the danger and the loss of the small garrison. The fight,
though on a smaller scale, was as stubborn as that around Itala, and there is no
reason to restrict the honours of the day to the larger post.

On the same day as the fights at Itala and Fort Prospect a party of Boers, about
150 strong, invaded Natal from the Orange River Colony. They attacked a post in
the vicinity of Normandien's Pass, but were repulsed, and on the arrival of
reinforcements from Newcastle withdrew over the pass with a few casualties. The
Boers in the Orange River Colony continued to display signs of intending activity,
but beyond threatening one or two of the numerous passes over the Drakensberg
accomplished nothing.

The attempted invasion of Natal was over. A large number of Boers were still in
Zululand, and on the 28th they captured a convoy of 31 wagons destined for Itala.
But they were already retiring northwards. As soon as the news of the attack on
Itala reached General Lyttelton, General Bruce Hamilton moved towards that post
with the columns commanded by General Spens and Colonels Allenby and
Pulteney. The Boers, however, were in no humour to try conclusions with this
force, and continued to retreat the way they had come.

Kitchener's answer to the continued intransigence of the Boers was to launch a twofold
campaign. First, in order to curb the Boer's biggest advantage, that of mobility,

Kitchener decided to divide the country by building a series of lines with fortified posts at strategic points. Once this was done drives would be staged between these lines, with the objective of pinning the Boers against the defensive lines. At the same time Kitchener launched a scorched earth policy against the Boer civilians living in areas affected by guerilla activity; this was done to deprive the Boer guerillas of supplies and safe havens. This policy resulted in large numbers of Boer civilians, men, women and children being confined in what came to be known as concentration camps. The building of Kitchener's block-house system called for a massive expenditure of time and money. But Kitchener's idea proved to be the right one; gradually the Boers were forced into smaller groups and their areas of activity were slowly eroded. Even men like De Wet were unable to break the iron lines of Kitchener's system.

PRETORIA, FEB. 10.

A detailed account of the big combined movement just carried out in the Orange River Colony will have reached you from official sources. Although the drive failed of its main object, the capture of De Wet, the number of prisoners and horses taken constitutes no small, if inadequate, success. The whole movement, from the first feint eastwards, which tempted De Wet, according to expectations, to break west, was a brilliant piece of strategy on the part of the Commander-in-Chief, while the manner of its execution left nothing to be desired, a thing which cannot be said of all operations undertaken by a limited number of troops acting over an enormous area.

The sides of the triangle, Heilbron–Wolvehoek–Kroonstad, into which the Boers were to be finally driven, are 30 and 66 miles long respectively, and the base is 55 miles; consequently it is no matter for surprise that the Boers, with their intimate knowledge of the country – for all belonged to local commandos – were able to avail themselves of the slight gaps in our line of troops. As it was, the Boers in breaking back through the columns adopted the only means of escape open to them, for to try conclusions with the railway would have been to court heavy losses, if not complete disaster.

Owing to Lord Kitchener's close attention to the details of this big move the railway was rendered such a formidable obstacle for 96 miles that even the Boers, hard pressed as they were, shrank from attempting a crossing. The Heilbron line on Friday afternoon presented throughout its whole length the appearance of a field-day. Between the blockhouses the infantry, who had been dropped at intervals on the veld by train earlier in the day, were busy intrenching, while three columns were distributing themselves over 30 miles. At nightfall two armoured trains deposited more men, and then took up their work of patrolling the line. Once or twice the searchlight revealed a Boer, who was evidently anxious to test the strength of the line. The fusillade that greeted his appearance must have settled any doubts in his mind, for no real attempts were made to cross. At Heilbron, however, a determined attack was made on the defences. This was probably in order to cover the passage of a large body of the enemy through the columns.

The main line of railway, while not so closely guarded for its whole 66 miles as the Heilbron line, proved sufficiently formidable. Four armoured trains plied up and down, while three stationary searchlights supplemented those on the trains.

Three Boer generations in the war, 1900. Left to right: P.J. Lemmer (65), J.D.L. Botha (15), G.J. Pretorius (43)

The spectacular effect, as seen from the armoured trains, was striking. By the side of the railway were the dark forms of men lying in the trenches or standing on sentry duty beyond. The gloom of the moonless night was relieved from time to time by the sweep of the indefatigable searchlights. Rifle fire resounded continually, while now and then a Pom-Pom or a heavier gun announced that the columns near Heilbron were engaged.

At daybreak the last stage of the drive commenced. The columns on the Heilbron–Kroonstad road swept into the main railway, but it was soon apparent that the Boers had escaped our meshes. In the afternoon the Commander-in-Chief's special train arrived at Koppies Station. In the drive over 283 Boers were accounted for. It is a pity De Wet was not of the number, but the result of the few days' work was good, and who can say that next time we may not be more successful?

Also as time passed the British methods of searching for the Boers became more and more sophisticated. No longer content to pursue the Boers only during the daylight hours, some British commanders mounted ambitious night marches against their mobile enemy.

ERMELO, JAN. 16.

For too long a time in the closing stages of the war our troops had been content to adopt a stereotyped form of operations, from which a deviation was hardly ever made – the regulation day-march of from 13 to 20 miles, in the expectation that the combined movements of several columns would corner the Boers in that district and effect their capture. Times without number it was found that the Boers merely kept a safe distance in front of the columns and when too hard pressed slipped through them at night. Night marches, it is true, had frequently been undertaken, although, I fancy, the majority of column leaders viewed them with distrust as being likely to lead to disaster, apart from the strain they entailed on the troops. But until recently no regular attempt had been made to carry out a continuous system of night marches for the purpose of surprising, at the first streaks of dawn, a party of the enemy located at a definite spot. The credit for proving that these night surprises could be undertaken with conspicuous success, in fact that they were the only way now for dealing with the Boers, rests with Lieutenant-Colonel Wools-Sampson, in whose hands the Field Intelligence of the Eastern Transvaal has been since the beginning of 1901. An opportunity of introducing night surprises as a more or less regular system, however, was not given him until September. He was lent by General Blood as Intelligence Officer to Colonel Benson. In the latter Colonel Wools-Sampson found a column leader as keen as himself to try any scheme, to endure any hardships, provided only the cause of our arms could thereby be promoted. The history of the short period during which these two were associated together will still be fresh in everybody's memory. In two months' time the column had so distinguished itself as to become the special object of a Boer concentration under Louis Botha. After a fine ride of over 50 miles the Boers fell upon the rear of the column as it was marching into camp. Benson was shot in the leg almost immediately. As he lay on the ground during the engagement he raised himself on his arm to give a message to an officer who had crawled near him and received two more wounds. One proved fatal, and Colonel Benson died a few hours after being brought into camp. The Boers had so far achieved their object as to be rid of the column leader, but Wools-Sampson escaped unhurt. Shortly after the death of Colonel Benson he joined General Bruce Hamilton. There was a brief respite in night marches, and *ipso facto* in Boer captures. But with Wools-Sampson's former successes as a precedent, and with his own energy to prompt him, General Bruce Hamilton was not long in following in the footsteps of Benson's column, and Wools-Sampson was once more given a free hand. As a result, during the month of December the columns operating under Bruce Hamilton accounted for 508 Boers.

In view of the successes attending these night marches, it may well be asked why they are not more generally adopted. The answer is two-fold. First, a system of intelligence such as that organized by Wools-Sampson does not exist elsewhere in the Transvaal and Orange River Colony; and, secondly, at this period of the war, unfortunately, many column leaders are apt to allow the hardships attendant on frequent night marches to weaken their confidence in the information as to the enemy's whereabouts; their intelligence is characterized as vague, and nothing is done. One or two attempts are, no doubt, conscientiously made, but if unsuccessful the practice is dropped altogether. The secret of the confidence which column leaders place in Wools-Sampson is indubitably the fact that his information will only be at fault once every nine or ten times that it leads to successful captures. Night marching entails hardships. It is not altogether a light matter to be all night and the greater part of the next day in the saddle, with only a few short rests snatched while the columns are collecting their scattered portions, or a brief halt is called; and the satisfaction of capturing Boers at daybreak is required to make up for the physical strain.

On Christmas Day the three columns under Colonels Rawlinson, Wing, and Williams had returned with General Bruce Hamilton to Ermelo after a tiring expedition of five days, the success of which had been marred by heavy rain and dense mist. After remaining there four days to rest his men and to procure provisions and a few horses, General Bruce Hamilton moved out again in an easterly direction on the night of December 29 with the same three columns and with Colonel Sampson's in addition, in all some 2,500 mounted men.

Darkness had just fallen when the columns left Ermelo. A cool clear night came as a relief after the heat and glare of the day, and the first few hours passed pleasantly enough and without incident. Shortly before 1 a.m. the Vaal was reached. It was found to be even higher than when, five days previously, it had delayed the troops on their return to Ermelo. Materials for a pontoon bridge were being carried by one of the columns, but the river was too wide to be bridged at the ordinary drift. Search was made for a suitable place for throwing the bridge across, and after a short time one was found about half a mile higher up. While the bridge was being built I tried to snatch a brief rest in the long, damp grass that bordered the river, but midges and mosquitos rendered any such indulgence impossible. By 2.30 a.m. the bridge was complete as far as it would reach, and the work of passing some 2,000 men and horses over it in single file began. It was 7 a.m. before the four columns had crossed. The transport had not left Ermelo until two hours after the mounted men. The bridge that served for the latter, leaving part of the river to a depth of 3ft. and the marshy ground beyond to be waded by the horses, would not do for wagons, and the pontoons had to be conveyed yet higher up the Vaal. The difficulties in the way of getting a convoy carrying provisions for 3,000 men for 12 days across the river may be judged from the fact that some of the wagons did not reach camp, a distance of 26 miles, until midday, December 31. Meantime, as soon as two of the columns had made their way across and had formed up on the high ground beyond, a start was made. It was already daylight, and any chance of surprising Boers seemed to have been lost. But the troops pressed on and on nearing the farm where the Boers had been located the previous day had the satisfaction of learning from the native scouts that horses were still grazing near the house. A slight rise hid the farm from view; behind this the troops lined up, and when all were ready the order to gallop was given. The ground was uneven and broken, while a sufficiently formidable donga had to be crossed; but the horses scrambled across it somehow, and with no vestige of the regular line of horsemen that had marked the commencement of the gallop the troops bore down on the farm. Seven men had been sleeping in the house, and these were too surprised at the appearance of our troops to do more than regard us with open-mouthed astonishment. Knowing the Vaal was unfordable they had considered themselves in safety for at least some days, and nothing could have been more unexpected than our arrival at such an hour of the morning. Not many minutes were occupied in securing the prisoners and, in the hope of finding more Boers on the next farm, the column galloped on as best they could, down and up the steep sides of a valley, now wading through a broad marsh, now clattering over rocky ground. But the quest was not successful; the Boers, a party of 50 under Barend Smit, must have sighted us or received notice of our coming and had put several miles between themselves and our force. In the distance we had just time to see the last of their cattle disappearing over a ridge. A brief halt was called, for, owing to the nature of the ground, the greater part of the force was little more than a long straggling line. A mile and a half further on we were to camp, and presently made our way across the intervening valley, while parties were detailed off to round up some cattle that had been abandoned by the Boers and were within our reach. A climb to the top of Bankkop, the long flat ridge on the slopes of which we were camping, brought us within sight of the Swaziland border. Twenty-five miles behind lay Tafelkop, a prominent hill a mile out of Ermelo and a conspicuous signalling station for this district; in front, the wide valley of Amsterdam; away to the south, the bold outline of the Slangapies range. It was a grand panorama, but the view is soon forgotten as field glasses are levelled and the country stretching away at one's feet is closely scanned for Boers or cattle. Both are soon descried, and, as they have also discovered us, they are seen making off with all haste. Meantime, some of the men have worked round Bankkop and, giving chase, succeed in cutting off two Boers, a wagon, and some cattle. When complete stock has been taken of the country and the last Boer has disappeared out of sight a movement is made to the camping ground.

It is nearing midday; the summer sun is unpleasantly hot and there is no trace of shade anywhere. A dismantled building provides some sheets of corrugated iron roofing for a few of the first arrivals – for the rest shelter has to be improvised out of the blanket each man carries on his horse. Officer and men are taking a well-earned rest while waiting for the transport. Presently the field telegraph arrives, and communication is opened with Ermelo. But the first news is from the convoy. The Vaal has proved a serious obstacle to the wagons; many have stuck fast in the marshy grounds, and there is no chance of their reaching camp that night. It is sad news. The more so as the sky has in the meantime with characteristic suddenness become overcast, and at 5 p.m. a terrific storm bursts. The lightning and thunder are incessant, the rain comes down in torrents. For three hours the storm lasts and then gives place to steady rain for the greater part of the night. A thick mist envelopes everything. One and all are huddled up in macintosh or its substitute, trying to outwit the elements. Now and then a hapless Tommy who has been on an observation post gropes his way past, drenched to the skin, endeavouring to find his own particular camp.

During the night and until 2 o'clock the following afternoon the transport struggled in. There had been another bad drift to pass and the roads had been rendered terribly heavy by the prolonged rain. The next evening, the last day of the old year, the columns were due to move on at 7, but owing to the darkness and dense mist it was decided not to make a start until midnight when the moon would have risen. The mist continued and hampered the movements of the columns which were camped at some distance apart from one another, and it was past 2 a.m. before a regular start was made. Rain fell steadily in the early hours of the morning and intermittently during the day, but one could always console oneself with the thought that the worse the weather the less likely would the Boers be to expect us; and so it turned out. Under cover of the mist, the Burgher Corps, 70 strong, attached to one of the columns, was sent off to round up a farm lying at some distance from the road. They returned with 7 Boers, 5 wagons, and some cattle. We were now well within striking distance of several small groups of Boers, and the force was split up to follow in pursuit of them. Colonel Williams' column forging ahead crossed the Usutu River twice before the fresh Boer spoor was found. Following this we soon sighted the enemy with some wagons driving away a few herds of cattle with all possible speed. They were some distance off, and all we could hope to do was to overtake the cattle. A long chase ensued, and six wagons and some 300 head of cattle fell into our hands. Meantime the troops left behind had surprised another party of Boers hiding in a kloof, and when camp was reached at 5 o'clock it was found that the total captures on New Year's Day amounted to 22 Boers, 16 wagons, and about 500 cattle.

That night and the following day saw the columns resting, while information as to the Boers' whereabouts was being collected by Colonel Wools-Sampson. We had not long to wait. Previous operations in this part of the Transvaal had been confined to flying visits from the various columns. The Boers had learned from former experience that they had only to hide a day or two and then would find that our troops had been withdrawn. They had one favourite place of concealment, a long winding valley south-west of Amsterdam, and it had never been found out by us. But this time they had reckoned without Wools-Sampson, for during the day information came in that the remnant of the Pretoria commando were to make this very valley their resting place for the night. Accordingly the columns moved off shortly after 6 p.m. It was a clear starlit night. On the horizon the lightning played behind a heavy bank of clouds, flash darting after flash in ceaseless succession; on either side the bull-frog croaked and the cicala ground its monotonous accompaniment to the dull tramp of the horses' hoofs. Here and there a nightbird gave warning to its kind of our approach, or another bird would rise from its nest on the ground uttering indignant protest at this disturbance of its rest. It was an ideal night for marching.

The column was being led by a Boer guide, and, riding by his side, one had ample opportunity for reflecting on the advantages the Boers have in this war over our troops from their knowledge of the country. We have left every semblance of a road and are striking straight across country, picking up a footpath here, now passing alongside a Kaffir kraal, now skirting a massive outcrop of rock, yet we never once swerve from the right direction. A Boer force of our strength, where each man would be his own guide, would perform the distance in a third of the time.

With us there must be continual halts to allow the column to close up, and much time is inevitably lost. But in spite of all drawbacks we press on, and near our destination. All the information obtained during the night from Kaffirs went to show that the Boers were in Amsterdam, and it seemed as if we ought to act upon it. But just before dawn the enemy's spoor was found leading from Amsterdam towards the valley; there was no time to be lost. Following up the spoor a short distance, General Bruce Hamilton divided up his force. One part was sent to the nearest entrance to the valley; the remainder with General Bruce Hamilton and Colonel Wools-Sampson rode on for another hour, reaching the other end of the valley just as the first light of day appeared. The ground was rough and broken, and before all egress from the valley could be stopped a few Boers managed to effect their escape. In a very short time, however, our men had gained the necessary positions, and we could advance into the valley to see what it contained. Immediately two men appeared with a white flag and stated that Commandant Erasmus was prepared to surrender. Hurrying down the steep slope we came upon Erasmus and the remnant of his Pretoria commando, 30 men in all, with natives and cattle. They were all in the saddle and had been ready to make off; but they saw escape was impossible. Working down the valley to the end blocked by the other part of the force the troops found a few more Boers and cattle, and by the time the two parts of the force had reunited the total captures amounted to 47 Boers and 300 cattle. A brief halt was called, and from the high ground we now occupied the surrounding country was closely scanned. Three or four miles off some Boers and cattle were sighted, and it was seen that they would have to come some way towards us in order to cross a certain drift. A party was despatched to cut them off, and a long chase ensued. The Boers, one of whom was in a cart, while two others were on horseback, driving cattle and horses, had a good start; but soon cattle and cart were abandoned, and the three Boers were riding away at full gallop. Gradually our men gained upon them; now they were within rifle range, and while some continued the chase others fired a few shots. One of the Boers' horses was shot, its rider was taken prisoner, and eventually one of the other two Boers as well. Our prisoners now numbered 49, with 332 cattle; the night march had been eminently successful. A halt was called from 9 till 12, and towards 6 p.m. the troops regained camp after an absence of 24 hours. In addition to the Boers in the Kolwani Valley Colonel Wools-Sampson had located a smaller group within a few miles of our camp, and the work of surprising these was entrusted to Colonel Wing. It proved a very easy matter. The column left camp shortly before 7 p.m., found the Boers exactly on the spot indicated, and returned to camp with 20 prisoners before 11 o'clock.

Another night march was undertaken to the actual borders of Swaziland, but with indifferent success. The Boers had evidently received warning from the natives of our coming and managed to elude us. Instead of the number we had expected to find, only six Boers were captured, one mortally wounded. By this time the Boers in this district had become so thoroughly scared that they had been careful to put themselves beyond our striking distance. Provisions were running short, and the columns moved back to Ermelo. The expedition had resulted in the capture of 105 Boers and some thousand cattle.

The credit for these captures undoubtedly rests with Colonel Wools-Sampson, whose system of intelligence is both as accurate and comprehensive as the colonel himself is indefatigable. But it must be remembered that it is not enough merely to locate the Boers. The columns must be prepared to act upon the information at once and with all energy. And it is in this respect that Colonel Wools-Sampson is fortunate in being associated with General Bruce Hamilton. Other intelligence officers report the whereabouts of the Boers, but, unhappily, not every column leader is prepared to place implicit trust in his intelligence officer and to act upon his information. Too often one hears the excuse made that "the information is too vague," "it is too far off to take the men for what is not a certainty," and the like. This is not the spirit in which to bring the war to an end. The time has come for us to put forth all our energy without any hesitation. The men are by no means averse to these long night marches; as a matter of fact, they find the monotonous trekking day after day without catching sight of a Boer far more irksome. As one man in these columns put it, "It's the best sport we've had during the war." That final galloping down of the Boers in the early morning soon throws the tediousness of the march, the rain, and the mist into oblivion. Nor is it enough in these night marches to tramp along listlessly, leaving everything to the guide or the intelligence officer. Officers and men alike must be on the *qui vive*, and the column has to be kept together the whole time, so that when the Boers are sighted the order to gallop may be given at once. On these occasions there can be no question of scouting, save what is done without any delay by natives; it is known roughly how many Boers are in front, and if the column charge down at once in full force there will be no resistance. It is partly the mutual confidence between himself and his intelligence officer that has enabled General Bruce Hamilton to score his successes.

With grim determination the British noose gradually tightened around the isolated Boer commandos. Kitchener realized that his system of block-houses was breaking up the Boer commandos, and that the scorched earth policy was forcing them to spend more and more time searching for supplies. So the British leader constantly refined and improved his system, and the resulting stranglehold placed on the country led to the surrender of the Boers in May 1902.

PRETORIA, JAN. 24.

In *The Times* of December 25 there appeared a brief account of the various blockhouse lines and a short sketch of the usual spheres of activity of the various Boer leaders and commandos. In this article an attempt will be made to bring such information up to date and to place on record the districts to which civil administration has been extended in the newly acquired territories.

On the accompanying map lines of blockhouses and South African Constabulary posts are marked with small crosses. It is not necessary to make any distinction on the map between the two, but where reference is made in the text to constabulary posts they will be so designated. The main difference between these posts and blockhouses is that, while the latter are purely lines of defence, the former are provided to a varying extent with a striking arm. No hard and fast rule or type is adhered to in either case, but, generally speaking, constabulary posts are established at intervals of five or six miles with occasional blockhouses between them. The perimeter of each post is marked by four or more blockhouses, and within these is the intrenched position for the garrison and horses.

The blockhouses have spider-web, barbed-wire entanglement, the four being connected with a barbed-wire fence. The strength of the posts varies between 50 and 100 men. The blockhouses in between are manned by a corporal and six men.

A blockhouse line, on the other hand, may consist merely of a number of blockhouses manned by from seven to 16 men, and set at intervals varying from 700 yards to 2,000 yards. All railway lines are "blockhoused" in this way, and where possible the blockhouses are connected with barbed-wire fencing, set sometimes with spring guns or electric alarms, while a trench has been dug on one or both sides of the railway. It will be understood that the whole of the 2,300 miles of railway blockhoused have not been connected with fencing, while the additional strengthening has been confined to the more threatened portions of the line. In the case of cross-country lines of blockhouses the smaller intervals are generally employed; but here again the nature of the country, questions of transport, and military exigencies, play a considerable *rôle*. The custom is to entrust to a column the task of running out blockhouse lines. A start is made from the railway, and at first the blockhouses are erected with wonderful rapidity, the builders being, as a rule, the infantry regiment that is to garrison the line, assisted by a few sappers and natives. But as the "blockhouse head" recedes from the railway the rate of progress decreases. Material has to be laboriously brought out by ox-convoy, and the supply of neither wagons nor oxen is unlimited. If there is urgent need for the completion of the line (and where is there not?) the work will be hurried on by putting up the blockhouses at wider intervals, leaving the spaces to be filled in and the fencing to be completed later. The blockhouse must now be so familiar an object to the British public that a description of it here would be superfluous. Once installed in their corrugated iron home, the small garrison set about strengthening their defences. Earth bags and barbed wire are the customary material, while trenches are assiduously cut all round. If the fencing between their blockhouse and those on either side is not complete, the garrison will help to construct it, and that finished, a trench from blockhouse to blockhouse will be begun, each man digging a certain length every day. To a regiment that has been marching continuously for many months blockhouse duty comes as a welcome relief, and the life, though naturally tending to be monotonous after a while, is by no means unpopular with the men. Tommy rarely fails to exercise his ingenuity in his new home, and often the regulation dummy sentry, the modest kitchen garden, and the whole enclosure within the barbed wire are models of neatness.

At stated intervals in a long line of blockhouses there will be posts resembling the constabulary posts described above, with the difference that the garrison, not being mounted, is still meant for defensive purposes only. These posts are responsible for the blockhouses in their sections; rations and water will be distributed from them, and every blockhouse will be visited during the day by an officer. Convoys passing along the blockhouse line, if not accompanied by a sufficient escort to be independent, spend the nights at one or other of these posts.

Let me enumerate the various lines of blockhouses and constabulary posts actually or practically complete at the present moment. All railways are blockhoused. In the Eastern Transvaal the South African Constabulary hold a line stretching from Groot Oliphant's River Station on the Delagoa Railway to Val Station on the Natal line. A formidable blockhouse line runs from Standerton to Ermelo, and is now being continued to Carolina to connect with the line already built from there to Wonderfontein. Blockhouses also connect Volksrust, Wakkerstroom, and a point on the Swaziland border 15 miles north of Piet Retief. Between De Jager's Drift and Vryheid there are a few posts, but no blockhouses.

In the Western Transvaal the Magaliesberg Range, which at one time it seemed impossible to clear, is held by numerous blockhouses. The Pretoria–Rustenburg road (65 miles), which crosses the Magaliesberg 25 miles west of Pretoria and then runs north of the range, was until recently occupied by the constabulary. In the present unhealthy season it has been found necessary to remove the posts to the high ground south of the Magaliesberg. There is a blockhouse line from Klerksdorp through Ventersdorp to Tafelkop, which will eventually be continued until it meets the line of posts running through Rustenburg at a point yet to be fixed upon. In the meantime the country included in the polygon Tafelkop, Klerksdorp, Johannesburg, Pretoria, Rustenburg is occupied by the constabulary, who are continually pushing out their posts westward. Other garrisons remain between these and the Pretoria–Johannesburg Railway, the main depôt being near the junction of the Crocodile River and the Six Mile Spruit. The Vaal from Klerksdorp to Standerton is lightly blockhoused, the country between it and the Klerksdorp–Johannesburg–Standerton Railway being patrolled by the constabulary.

With such a network of blockhouses and posts it would seem as if large tracts of country ought to be effectively cleared of the enemy. But, unfortunately, such is not the case. Under cover of night the Boer, if sufficiently determined, seems able to pass through nearly any fencing. His presence is noted, though generally too late, while rifle fire at night is notoriously inaccurate. As a result, therefore, and in view of the fact that five Boers can make a district of 1,500 square miles "unsafe", what are familiarly known as picnic areas are still restricted. Anywhere beyond 20 or 30 miles east and west of the Pretoria–Johannesburg Railway an individual horseman would run the risk of meeting a few Boers who had succeeded in eluding our columns and the constabulary. Several parties of Boers have recently crossed the Groot Oliphant's River-Val line of South African Constabulary posts from east to west. They have been immediately pursued by our troops and invariably lose cattle or men before escaping east again; but others seem always ready to follow their example. East of this same line, as is well known, the Boers under numerous leaders can probably still concentrate a thousand men, and consequently none but large bodies of troops can move in this district, except along the lines of posts and blockhouses. These latter are absolutely safe highways, and while columns are operating in the district display a continuous stream of traffic. West of the main railway the country between the Krugersdorp line and the Vaal has been pronounced clear of the enemy, but north, or, rather, north-west, of Krugersdorp small isolated groups of Boers are still sighted from time to time.

At first sight this may seem a discouraging report, but it must be remembered that a year ago Louis Botha was able to threaten Johannesburg with several thousand men. It is on looking back several months that one realizes that steady progress is being made. It is a common taunt that we hold the railways while the Boers hold the country. But that is not the whole truth. In certain districts the Boer has profited by the temporary absence of our troops to plough or to harvest; but for every acre where he has enjoyed this tranquillity there are thousands of square miles where he has to sleep with his horse saddled and bridled, and is kept on the move half the night and half the day. The enemy's so-called hold on the country resembles that of a brigand chief who terrorizes neighbouring villages and exercises brief and restricted sway until hunted down. Save in his own vast country, the Boer would have been run to earth long ere this. As things are, in spite of our Army of 200,000 men, there are not sufficient troops to deal at one and the same time with the whole of the country that lies open to a fugitive enemy. North of the Delagoa Bay line Lord Kitchener has been obliged to leave the enemy in comparative security for some time. Columns under Colonels Urmston and Park are operating in this district, but they are not strong enough to make much headway against the enemy in such difficult country. The National Scouts this week made a raid on Jan Visagee's laager, at the junction of the Oliphant's and Wilje Rivers, but found that the Boers had left the farm on which they had been located. General Ben Viljoen has been taken prisoner and it is not improbable that his capture will contribute to an earlier surrender on the part of many burghers in this district. But for the moment the Boers are practically in undisputed possession of the country north of the Delagoa line. Schalk Burger and the so-called Government remains in the neighbourhood of Roos Senekal, while a commando under Commandant Stephanus Trichardt acts as its bodyguard, with posts on the Tantesberg, the Bothasberg, and at Blinkwater (north of Middelburg) watching the several roads by which our troops can approach. Muller remains inactive at Pilgrim's Rest or Sabie Drift (north-east of Lydenburg). The country further north, the Ohrigstad Valley (north of Lydenburg), is exceedingly fertile, and the Boers have been able to secure the full benefit of this year's crops. The grain has been milled first at Pilgrim's Rest, until the mill was pluckily blown up by one of our Intelligence agents, and subsequently at Sabie Drift, where there is a large women's laager. From there it has been freely distributed about the country, and, unless we can discover where it has been hidden, will materially assist the Boers to hold out through the coming winter. The Roos Senekal–Lydenburg district is mountainous and well suited to Boer tactics, but as soon as a sufficient number of troops can begin to operate here, the Boer security will be short-lived. North of the present Boer position are various native tribes, who will not readily submit to an invasion of their country by the Boers.

The only town we occupy north of the Delagoa line is Lydenburg. It is strongly garrisoned and will serve as a base for future operations.

To the south of the Eastern railway, Carolina, Bethel, Ermelo, and Piet Retief are occupied by our troops as purely military posts. Wakkerstroom, Utrecht, and Vryheid are garrison towns where civil administration is represented by a resident magistrate and schools have been opened. There is a school at Nigel (south-east of Springs), which, though not on the railway, is well within a "safe" area. In the Western Transvaal, Zeerust, Lichtenburg, and Rustenburg are garrison towns with acting-resident magistrates. Schools are open at the first two and will be started shortly at Rustenburg. Jacobsdal, Ventersdorp, and Christiana are also held by our troops. Ottoshoop has no permanent garrison, but is occupied from time to time.

From Christiana to Klerksdorp there are no regular posts along the Vaal, but, as already stated, the river between Klerksdorp and Standerton is guarded by blockhouses. In the country between the Mafeking railway and the Vaal, Delarey's sphere of activity, the Boers enjoy considerable freedom. Lord Methuen, Colonel Kekewich, and various columns have continually swept this district, but the country west of the railway forms an excellent source of supplies, and parties of the enemy are continually crossing the line for the purpose of replenishing their stock of cattle. Ammunition must also have reached Delarey's commandos by this route from the coast, for quite recently a Cape cart carrying a considerable quantity was cut off and captured by an armoured train. Ploughing and harvesting have been carried on spasmodically by the Boers, Wolmaranstad being one of the favourite neighbourhoods.

There are a few Boers west of the Kimberley line, among them Van der Merwe, who is near Kuruman, and was recently joined by the rebel Kruger and 70 men, and Celliers, with from 50 to 100 men of the Lichtenburg and Marico commandos.

In the Orange River Colony three main lines of blockhouses traverse the country east of the railway. (1) Heilbron–Frankfort–Vrede–Botha's Pass, and thence along the Drakensberg to Ikatane (near Volksrust), the portion between Vrede and Botha's Pass being not yet complete. (2) Kroonstad–Lindley–Bethlehem–Harrismith; a small gap between Lindley and Bethlehem has yet to be completed. (3) Bloemfontein–Thaba Nehu–Ladybrand and the Basuto border. A fourth line runs from Fouriesberg *via* Retief's Nek to Bethlehem. On the west there are two lines – (1) Kroonstad–Klerksdorp; (2) Vet River–Bloemhof, on the Vaal above Warrenton. Apart from the towns traversed by these lines of blockhouses, we hold Ficksburg, Wepener, Smithfield, Rouxville east of the line, Boshof, Jacobsdal, Bultfontein, Koffyfontein, Fauresmith, Jagersfontein to the west.

As in the Transvaal, blockhouse lines are a means to an end, and not the end itself. They have been and are being run out in various directions to facilitate the clearing of the country, but none of the districts which they enclose are yet clear. The main body of the enemy under De Wet is between the Frankfort and Bethlehem lines of blockhouses; one or two commandos still remain between the Frankfort line and the Vaal, but with the completion and final strengthening of these two northern lines they should be dealt with without much trouble. The Brandwater basin, north-east of Ficksburg, which, resembling the Magaliesberg in the Transvaal as a natural stronghold, was for a long time the favourite haunt of the Boers, has at last been cleared and is being held by us. There are few Boers left in the south-eastern corner of the colony, but, as has already been stated, it requires a very small number of the enemy to render a very large extent of country unsafe. Here and to the west of the railway the South African Constabulary are always extending their posts, and are gradually redeeming the country. The Bloemhof–Vet River line represents the present limit of their extension to the north. Between that line and the Klerksdorp–Kroonstad line two or three small commandos roam about, while about 200 Boers are still to be found in the Klerksdorp–Kroonstad–Vereeniging triangle. There is a wide area round Bloemfontein that has for long been free from any incursion of the enemy, but at the moment of writing I have no record of the actual extent. The line of towns held by us in the west without blockhouse connexion – Jacobsdal, Koffyfontein, Fauresmith, Jagersfontein – tends to show that the enemy in this part of the country are in no great strength. There are several commandos, but none show much activity, and they will retire as soon as a force can be sent out against them. At Boshof, Jacobsdal, and Koffyfontein there are resident magistrates; schools are also open at the latter two places. In the southern half of the colony, on both sides of the line, our hold of the country established after the occupation of Bloemfontein was subsequently relaxed, and the work of civil administration interrupted by the withdrawal of our troops has only been able to be restarted gradually. There remains the Cape Colony, where there is but one cross-country line of blockhouses, recently begun, which will eventually stretch from Victoria West Road through Williston, Calvinia, and Clanwilliam to Lambert's Bay. The majority of the invaders have passed into the country lying between this line and German South-West Africa, and the purpose of the blockhouses will be to prevent them from penetrating south. In their present situation they can do little harm and they can be dealt with at an opportune moment. There has been a fresh raid into the midlands from the north-eastern district, where Fouché, Myburg, and Wessels have for a long time evaded all our efforts to capture them, the latter having crossed the Port Elizabeth line to the west. General French has, however, been able to clear this district once of these peripatetic marauders, and Wessels will, doubtless, receive the close attention which led to such satisfactory results in the case of Lotter and Scheepers.

CONCLUSION

The Times' coverage of the Second Boer War can be said to have failed in a number of ways. As we have seen *The Times*, faced with a potentially boring and unpatriotic situation when the Boers were in the ascendancy in the early stages of the war, chose to adopt a cynically patriotic approach to its war reports. This approach in particular was responsible for the promulgation of the Victorian myths of Ladysmith, Kimberley and Mafeking. The reports from Kimberley and Mafeking represent a gross misrepresentation of the events. In the coverage of the siege of Kimberley, *The Times* allowed itself to become part of Cecil Rhodes' publicity machine, and in doing so enabled him to escape the censure he so richly deserved for his appalling conduct during the siege; instead he became the hero of Kimberley, replacing men such as Colonel Kekewich, who had a much greater claim on that title.

The reporting from Mafeking was if anything worse than that from Kimberley. The siege was blown up out of all proportion to create in Baden-Powell the archetypal Victorian hero. So as not to tarnish the image of this perfect Victorian knight-errant, *The Times* conveniently forgot to report the way in which Baden-Powell systematically starved to death the African population of Mafeking in order that he might feed the Europeans of the town, and thus keep the siege going, a siege which was by this stage of the war of no real strategic value whatever.

These failings are quite serious lapses in journalistic ethics, but they pale into insignificance when placed against *The Times'* coverage of the concentration camp issue. As mentioned above, Kitchener, driven to distraction by the Boer guerilla tactics, pursued a scorched earth policy against a large section of the Boer population. This resulted in the gathering together of large numbers of Boer refugees in camps run by the British authorities. The conditions in these camps were uniformly appalling. The camps lacked even the most basic of sanitary and medical amenities. To make matters worse, the food supplies for the camps were kept at a deliberately low level. In the camps a two-tier ration system was in operation: those refugees who had relatives still fighting were placed on a lower level of rations than those whose families had surrendered.

In these circumstances, with thousands of poorly fed and clothed individuals crowded together in insanitary conditions, it was only a matter of time before disease began to take a toll on the inhabitants of the camps. As this happened people such as Lloyd George began to ask questions of the Government. It was at this point that *The Times* began a campaign to reassure the British public that the distressing reports of the mass deaths of women and children in the camps were a distortion of the truth.

BLOEMFONTEIN, JULY 25.

The total number of white refugees in the Orange River Colony camps on July 20 was 35,831, an increase of 4,137 since the end of June. The average deaths in June per thousand were 109.1, against 116.76 in May. The rate is still very high, but shows a tendency to diminish, though epidemics continue prevalent in some camps. The camp at Bloemfontein, which has the highest death-rate, is steadily improving. In the first 25 days of July there have been 84 deaths, against a total of 137 in June. The population of the camp this morning was 5,108. The cost of the refugee camps in Orange River Colony during June was just under £44,000; the cost for the four months from March to June was £102,271.

In view of the interest taken in the condition of the refugees I spent some time during the last two days in the Bloemfontein camp, and can honestly say that everything possible in the circumstances is done for the unfortunate people. The hospitals, for which the Boers are slowly overcoming their dislike, are in perfect order. The doctors have a free hand to prescribe everything necessary for both in-patients and out-patients. The chief drawback is the scarcity of fuel, which is exceedingly hard to procure. Over £300 were spent on wood and 100 tons of coal were supplied last month, but the refugees steadily increase in number and the authorities are hampered by lack of transport and the single line of railway.

The advisability of closing the schools during the epidemic of measles has been under discussion. It is hoped that the measure will not be found necessary. The children seem to take readily to the schooling, and it gives an excellent opportunity to a large number to learn English. The children will in any case be in contact with one another in the camp. Moreover, if the medical officer makes a daily inspection he will discover the children who are ailing. Frequent intervals during schooltime are allowed, so that there should be no harm in keeping the schools open.

The committee sent to inspect the camps will, it is hoped, finally set the public mind in England at rest, but I would suggest that if the members of the committee were to do a month's trekking with the columns among the Boer farms which are still occupied it would greatly aid them in forming an unbiased judgment. It is the right of British subjects to be tried by their peers, and it is not fair that people who have never seen a tent except with strawberries and cream inside should judge Boer refugee camps by an English drawing-room standard. From my own experience I know that Boer women occasionally do butchers' work, while the men in one family which was peculiarly dirty owned a prosperous farm well provisioned with forage, mealies, and live stock, and with abundance of water near the house. I do not mention these cases by way of apology for the refugee camps, for I am convinced that none is required, but for the enlightenment of privileged tourists who may be hysterically inclined and of other critics who have never seen a veld Boer or a *bywoner* home.

Reports were available from people such as Miss Emily Hobhouse, who had actually visited the camps: 'The shelter was totally insufficient. When the 8, 10, or 12 persons who occupied a bell-tent were all packed into it, either to escape from the fierceness of the sun or dust or rain storms, there was no room to move, and the atmosphere was indescribable, even with duly lifted flaps. There was no soap provided. The water provided would not go round. No kartels [bedsteads] or mattresses were to be had. Those, and they were the majority, who could not buy these things must go without.

Fuel was scanty . . . The ration [the punitive double scale was still in operation] was sufficiently small, but when . . . the actual amount did not come up to the scale, it became a starvation rate.'[1] Faced with this evidence *The Times* dragged up the testimony of any backwoods imperialist who could be relied upon to cast doubt on the reports of people who questioned the Government's policy over the camps.

THE CONCENTRATION CAMPS

We have received the following statement from Mrs. Sarah Heckford, who has just returned to England after a residence of many years in the Transvaal. Mrs. Heckford is not unknown in philanthropic circles in this country, and some readers may yet remember the description given nearly 35 years ago by Charles Dickens of his visit to the children's hospital which Dr. and Mrs. Heckford had just brought into existence, and where they lived, in the neighbourhood of Shadwell. Mrs. Heckford settled in the South African Republic more than 20 years ago, and has passed through both the Transvaal wars. Having lived as a farmer among farmers, she has naturally acquired a peculiarly intimate knowledge of the Boer character and way of life. Mrs. Heckford says:-

Miss Hobhouse, in the letter to Mr. Brodrick which *The Times* published a few days ago, asserts that she is well qualified to give an opinion on the state of the concentration camps. Pray allow me the opportunity of asserting publicly that she is not. Her report reveals this to any one who has lived for many years amongst the Boers, and has, besides, passed through more than one war. I wish to say most emphatically that to any such person that report is rather a vindication than an indictment of the Government. In a country distracted by war no camp can be otherwise than unhygienic. It appears from the report that the Government had exerted itself to make the concentration camps visited by Miss Hobhouse as little unhygienic as possible, and, when possible, has acted on any reasonable suggestion aiming at improvement. It is inevitable that children and feeble adults should suffer when war is sweeping through a country, inevitable that the death-rate amongst such should rise lamentably. All hearts may well bleed when realizing the cost of war. When, however, Miss Hobhouse harrows her own feelings and endeavours to harrow the feelings of others by describing what she imagines to be hardships to Boer women and children in the concentration camps she provokes a smile from those who know the habits of the Boers. Over-crowding is habitual among them to a shocking extent; so is indifference to what would strike Miss Hobhouse as the elements of comfort, and even decency, amongst rich as well as poor Boers. Her description of the tents (paragraph 2, p. 4) reminds me of many I have sat in when visiting well-to-do Boer families who were in the "Bush veld" with their cattle, on what constitutes to large numbers of these people a sort of annual pic-nic.

When Miss Hobhouse laments over the removal of families into concentration camps she is ignorant of the fact that the Boers under arms hailed their removal as a special boon. They said justly that their women and children would be far better off than if left at their homes, and that the knowledge that they were being protected by us from the severest evils which inevitably accompany war would enable them to fight us with a better heart. Nor is this approval confined to the men still in the field. I will cite one instance as an example. A nephew of Paul Kruger, a man named Caspar Kruger, whom I know well, surrendered about a year ago and has been for months anxious to have his family brought from their home to a concentration camp. At his urgent request I more than once brought his very natural desire to the notice of the authorities in Pretoria, but it was only when I was leaving, about the middle of June, that military exigencies allowed of an attempt being made to do so. He left Pretoria with a column of our troops about the same time that I left for England.

Miss Hobhouse is, I conclude, unaware of how well the Boer women have served, and are still serving, the commandos as intelligence officers, spies, and even as decoys. If she knew this she would hardly consider their being kept under some supervision a hardship, or wish them to be left at liberty. They cannot appeal to sympathy on the plea of harmless womanhood, for they have proved themselves to be very dangerous enemies. We may admire their courage, but they have forfeited the right to be considered non-belligerents.

There is one point in Miss Hobhouse's attitude which appears unaccountable. Why is she not touched by the sufferings of those persons who are, and always have been, loyal subjects of the Empire, who were driven from their homes by the Boers, and who are still enduring as much as or more than the worst cases adduced by her amongst the Boer refugees? Why does she not plead their cause? One fact is, however, evident. If we deliberately postpone the interests of our loyal subjects to the interests of the Boers the latter will regard our beneficence as savouring of weak conciliation rather than of sympathy.

I would not, however, neglect conciliation when it can be practised in accord with Imperial interests. There is an olive branch which I know that the Boers in the Transvaal, and I conclude those in the Orange River Colony, will accept. Education for adults, as well as for children, offered under conditions which would facilitate its acceptance, would do more to render the Boers loyal to the Empire and do more to strengthen the loyalty of the already loyal English Afrikander than all else. It is but little known to those who have not dwelt for years amongst the farming population of the Transvaal that learning is the one thing a Transvaal Boer reverences. I have no accurate knowledge except of the Transvaal, therefore I speak of it alone; but the South African problem is concentrated in the Transvaal.

The question of adult education is one of political emergency rather than of education in the ordinary acceptation of the term. If we do not occupy the waste fields of adult ignorance and not only sow good seed therein, but guard them from the crafty sowing of bad seed by our enemies, these will not be slow in taking advantage of our want of promptitude. They will frustrate our efforts to conquer the country in its schools, and we shall see what has been lost when it is too late to retrieve it. The question of how to deal with adult ignorance in the Transvaal is of vital importance to the Empire. The farmer class are keenly alive to the fact that they are ignorant. They are hungry for knowledge, but the conditions of their life are such that it is difficult to offer it to them in a palatable as well as wholesome form. It is worth taking much thought to do this, for on it depends the solving of the South African problem as far as the white population is concerned. That population is now to a great extent massed in concentration camps or in the towns of Pretoria and Johannesburg. Do not let us lose this opportunity, which will cease when the farmers return to their homes. Let us use these camps as the seedling beds of a plantation.

I have in my possession a letter from a friend in the Transvaal dated June 30, 1901. He is a farmer and an ex-burgher, having been one of those who in 1881 were retroceded against their wish. He is now a refugee and employed by a Government contractor, who supplies concentration camps with clothing, &c. Being an English Afrikander he is better educated than most Boers, and, when the commissioner of a camp where he was stationed started a night school for adults at his own expense, he volunteered to take a class. He has now been sent by the contractor to another camp, much to his regret, "for," to quote his words, "I was much interested in the night school. I had a class of middle-aged men, and you would be surprised how quickly they learn – two men especially. I taught them their alphabet, and in a week they could read quite fluently words of three letters. Don't you think that good for people who, as they say, scarcely ever mixed with English? But they seem very eager to learn; you can see them (I mean the scholars) walking about with their books trying to read. At first they did not take to it, saying it was no use, they would never learn as they were too old; but finding that one pupil picked it up quickly they simply made a rush for the night school. You can often see them trying to converse with each other in English, a good sign, don't you think? So you can quite imagine that I did not care about leaving."

Let us learn a lesson from the enthusiastic officer and his enthusiastic assistant who, thrown together by the chances of war, have been showing their loyalty to the Empire and their sympathy for their fellow creatures by spending their money and time more profitably than in bewailing inevitable suffering and endeavouring to redress imaginary wrongs.

On one or two occasions, apologists for *The Times* and other newspapers have attempted to blame the military censor for the inaccuracy of reports concerning the concentration camps, but this report from *The Times*' own correspondent disproves this assertion.

PRETORIA, AUG. 6.

Newspapers containing accounts of the agitation at home with regard to the censorship and the alleged suppression of news arrived by this mail. As my position brings me in direct contact with the Commander-in-Chief, I consider that the occasion calls for the following statement:–

Until June the representatives of newspapers were allowed every freedom, and were given support from headquarters. I can quote my own experience, for two appeals against decisions lodged by me received prompt redress from headquarters. Then arrived a period when the home authorities saw fit to suggest that the censors should be held responsible for the truth of messages. This resulted in the present state of affairs. If the Chief is held responsible for the truth, chapter and verse, of messages, delay and suppression must follow, as the interpretation of events by the local commanders who report them rarely tallies with the impressions of independent chroniclers. The Chief is naturally guided by official evidence.

With regard to the alleged suppression of news, there is no suppression as to the state of affairs. All English correspondents are permitted to send mail letters without censorship. The peculiar nature of the position is evidently not appreciated. There are now 61 columns operating in three colonies. These columns have few engagements other than affairs of outposts and patrols. Boers are caught or killed by ones and twos. It would be absurd, if it were practicable, to send officially a daily diary of these operations. Any one who has accompanied these columns knows that they camp for days together without an event worthy of mention. Further, local correspondents from base towns are given to exaggerate small affairs out of their due perspective. Evidence is collected from private soldiers and wounded, which lends greater colour to the affair than the occasion warrants.

Consequently, since the home authorities require the censors to be responsible for the truth, such serious statements as those relating to Boer atrocities have been held in abeyance until the truth can be proved. This I can certify – that I have heard of no success or disaster of any magnitude during the last six months which has not been officially reported.

At one point during the latter part of the war the death rate in the camps was running at approximately 35 per cent for white inmates of all ages, while the figures for children were much higher (58 to 62 per cent). As was usual, the death rate for the black population who found themselves caught in the white man's war was much higher all round. Although conditions did improve in the camps, this was more the result of the work of concerned individuals rather than of the Government. In stark contrast to *The Times*' reporting of the scandal of medical care in the Crimean War, this time *The Times* was instrumental in the covering up of scandal.

INDEX

Passim indicates separate mentions on successive pages. Illustrations are in *italics*.